THE MATHEMATICS OF THE
SCIENCE OF REINCARNATION

THE MATHEMATICS OF THE SCIENCE OF REINCARNATION

Book 2
The Matrix of Consciousness Series

By Bob Good
With co-authors
Dean Radin, Stephan A. Schwartz,
Titus Rivas and Cathie Hill

IASOR
PRESS

Boynton Beach Fl

The Matrix of Consciousness Series
Book 1 The Science of Reincarnation

The Matrix of Consciousness Series
Book 1 The Science of Reincarnation
Book 2 The Mathematics of the Science of Reincarnation
Book 3 The Applications of the Science of Reincarnation
Book 4 The Science of Reincarnation 101 College Level Textbooks

© copyright 2020 by Bob Good

IASOR Press
67 Cambridge Lane
Boynton Beach, Florida 33436

Library of Congress Cataloging-in-Publication Data has been applied for.

ISBN: 978-1-7351185-2-9 paperback edition
ISBN: 978-1-7351185-1-2 epub edition

This book was typeset in Baskerville and formatted by Elite Authors

Cover image commissioned from Tom Egan © copyright 2020 by Bob Good

To send correspondence: info@iasor.org

For Harper and Dylan

I wouldn't change my grandchildren for the world
But I would like to change the world for my grandchildren

The Mathematics of the Science of Reincarnation

The Matrix of Consciousness

The matrix of consciousness is a scientific look at consciousness in all its manifestations. In many of its manifestations it transcends the 3 spatial dimensions and one temporal dimension that define our everyday reality. This book is about how new discoveries are changing how we view ourselves and our impending deaths, which by the math we are seeing in our evolving view of ourselves and our reality most likely means being born into a different state of cognition. That state is collectively described by people who have been there in some form, whether as a near death experiencer, a child who remembers a prior life, or though past life regression which is one of the many manifestations of psi, which we all have. This book is about the structure of your own mind, and what we have to do to study it.

This is part of consciousness science, but consciousness science is foundational for Artificial Intelligence. We are developing Artificial Intelligence (AI) along the lines of our own awareness and are seeing fractal alignment between the two in the upload and download of information either to the cloud or your particular version of heaven. This common matrix of consciousness then introduces a new real science, the science of reincarnation which is incorporated into this emerging matrix of consciousness as part of the information and spatial topology.

The Matrix of Consciousness Series
Book 2
The Mathematics of the Science of Reincarnation

The Matrix of Consciousness Series
Book 1 The Science of Reincarnation
Book 2 The Mathematics of the Science of
Reincarnation
Book 3 The Applications of the Science of
Reincarnation
Book 4 The Science of Reincarnation 101 College
Level Textbooks

A Note to the Reader

A note to the reader about The Mathematics of the Science of Reincarnation and how to read it.

If you are reading this to read the 450-million-dollar Consciousness Science Moon-Shot Research Program Proposal go right to Chapter 17 and start there. Academics in consciousness research should start there.

If you are interested in the political ramifications to this science and its dangers start at chapter 16. Politicians should start there.

If you are the CIA, the FSB, the Mossad or any intelligence organization start with Chapter 14.

If you want to read the science and its math, chapters 1-9 are for you. However, if you just want to know about the results of the science and the changes it predicts then just start at chapter 9.

And finally, if you are a billionaire, then Chapters 10-13 make the case for how you can stay a billionaire and become a multi billionaire given the changes that are coming at us quickly.

Or you can just read it from chapter 1.

The math treats us all the same, it's a new global condition like corona virus, we all have to deal with it. Good luck, stay safe.

Bob Good

Table of Contents

Abstract

This book makes the mathematical case that the electrical charge measured by an electrocardiogram (EKG) is actually you.

That electrical charge wears and sheds bodies. You don't have the same body you did when you were six. There is statistical proof that the electrical charge comes back to other lives in other bodies similarly to how we upload and download files on our computers to the cloud.

This brief description of the process of birth, death, and rebirth is more scientifically correct than any other description of what happens after we die and what it means to be dead.

Consciousness science and reincarnation science mean that you have lived before and will again. Our religious beliefs are not wrong and not right, and we have to incorporate this new science into them.

The Matrix of Consciousness incorporates our observations and our experiments to come up with a model of consciousness that reflects and includes our scientific models of reality and our observations.

What this science demands is that we dissect that electrical charge. We know it is conscious because it is us. This study is called consciousness science.

Breaking down that electrical charge is a new area of science. It is more than just bioelectrical; it helps us understand and dissect the electrical polarity of personality and consciousness. It treats that electrical charge as life itself and recognizes that same charge when it manifests itself again. We have to be open-minded enough to accept this new reality in order to study it. Refusal to see it clearly will leave us in a self-induced blindness.

The derivatives of such science change the nature of our decision-making processes both individually and as a group. Religious, political, military, family, and personal decisions all change based on this new information. This new information treats us all the same. It matters not if you are black, yellow, white, or red. It matters not if you are smart or dumb, Christian, Hindu, Muslim, or Jew.

This book offers the mathematical structure for a scientific proof of reincarnation and what we need to do to make that scientific proof complete. To get to that complete proof, we need to address what the math is saying and it seems to be saying that reincarnation is mathematically probable if not a certainty already.

No other analytic system or narrative provides a mathematical proof about what happens after we die whose components are verifiable, repeatable, and examinable.

Many in the science community disagree with this, and among those who agree there is disagreement about how to approach this complex problem with sensitivities on all sides. The answer is to let the mathematics speak.

Foreword

I want to provide a guide to this book so you can anticipate and understand more easily what I am about to show you. It is a complex presentation based in mathematics. Don't be intimidated if you don't do math; it will be easily understandable. Those who wish to advance counterarguments to confuse the weak-minded will have to defeat the math.

Goal

The goal of this book is to use predatory logic. In setting out to write this math book, I wanted the truth. If I looked at all the manifestations that reincarnation shows itself in that seem so unrelated, and if I charted and measured the landscape, what would I see? Would it be like camouflage art, where a picture within a picture emerges the longer you study it? The right tool here is predatory logic, relying strictly on facts rather than beliefs but taking beliefs into account because they are there. What numbers would reveal themselves if we looked at nothing else? The goal of this book is to use a fact-based, logic-driven analysis of reincarnation using normal accounting methods.

Every science is made of disciplines that tell us where the science is and where it is going. Each discipline is like an account in a chart of accounts in accounting. To "prove" a set of books, you have to crossfoot all the accounts into matching totals at the bottom of the page. We bring that measure to this endeavor and then challenge any alternative system to prove better than the one presented here.

Purpose

The purpose of this book is different from the goal. The purpose of this book is to increase money spent on research in the consciousness sciences by a factor of ten. A moon-shot proposal is defined as increasing by a factor of ten an industry or a science. The Defense Advanced Research Projects Agency (DARPA) did this when it created the router, which was the technical side of creating the internet. Another example is when we went to the moon. The last three chapters of this book describe a moon-shot proposal to protect and save humanity from itself and the coming threats to us individually and collectively by redefining our reality based on our current scientific understanding. This cannot be done without a clear sales and branding plan to advance these goals.

Heuristic

In this book we will discuss and analyze readers' belief systems and incorporate them into the overall analysis.

You have to be prepared for something unexpected if you are to look logically at the facts because these facts change the game politically, socially, sexually, and personally. If you believe in Jesus, Mohammed, or Moses, do you see what you believe? Do you believe what you see, namely scientific data analyzed and vetted through repeated double-blind experiments? How do you choose what is real? How do you choose what you think is correct? How you choose what you choose is your heuristic.

Quantum probability and order

We have a lot of data that doesn't make sense under our current understanding of science. Either the data is wrong, or our understanding is wrong. According to an emerging scientific model, we live in a holofractal, a multidimensional reality. We are aware in four dimensions, and our reality is generated from an enfolded dimension.[1]

Quantum mechanics is tough to understand, but how this affects you can be easily explained. Your flesh and blood are based on chemistry, biology, and now quantum biology because your quantum energy is as ordered as your biology. If you are alive, you have this structured quantum system, and if you die and shed your body, this quantum energy retains coherence, and you are still you. That electrically aware you is aware after your death, and it is still you, and you are part of what is called a matrix of consciousness.

Strategy

How do we plan if this is the true model of our reality? Do we keep fighting each other based on false suppositions? Do we continue to have prejudices that force one group down at the expense of the other?

We have to change our collective cognition so we can cohesively face our reality that we all will be alive after we die. We need to map that environment that we exist in after we die. We have firsthand accounts of that environment, and we have a new understanding of that space; it is a fourth spatial dimension, an enfolded dimension predicted by quantum mechanics.

In that new model, we have seven senses, but in our current reality, we are limited to five. It seems intuition and nonlocal access are very weak in this reality, as is gravity, but in that enfolded fourth spatial dimension, it is stronger. We need to map the cognitive space. But before we do that, we have to acknowledge it.

Ramifications

The ramifications of the science of reincarnation being included in the consciousness sciences and being funded, taught, and studied can change the world. The business, military, and social consequences of not just information acquisition but its subsequent manipulation through processes like CRISPR (clustered regularly interspaced short palindromic repeats) will be far reaching and give those who get there first unlimited power within the paradigm. Can we edit genes to enhance nonlocal consciousness? Can that be supplemented with artificial intelligence (AI) since, if we do the needed experiments, we can quantify that wavelength? It will be accessed with AI, and the timeline is short. The oceans of the universe will become a nonlocal pond, and the profits generated will be beyond huge. But the research needs to be funded.

* * *

I want to thank the scientists who contributed their time and interest as well as their criticisms to evaluate what I propose regarding the consciousness sciences. They were my teachers. First is Dean Radin. In 2009 I wrote a book called *The Science of Reincarnation,* and as a first-time author, I did not realize I had stepped all over copyright laws, specifically the Chicago Manual of Style's standards on copyright law. That meant my editor told me I had to get permission from the original researchers and authors to use their material or I needed to rewrite the book. Many had no interest in responding, and some said, "Go ahead but don't use too much." Dean said, "Send me what you wrote." He reviewed it, updated it, improved it, and said "Go ahead; good luck." More responses came in, and Stephan Schwartz followed with the same kind of support. I can't thank these two men enough. What I learned about science through this process is that it is uneven, part of it is intellectual property, and it can be manipulated and slanted against logic and facts. I also want to thank Titus Rivas and Cathie Hill, who contributed essential parts in ways much better than I could.

Note

[1]   https://futurism.com/the-byte/reality-hologram-quantum-physics.

Chapter 1

The Matrix of Consciousness

Designing Artificial Intelligence and Beyond

Truth: not the words of the teacher
—James Madison's personal seal at his home in Virginia

The goal of this book is to present the most probable mathematical model for what occurs to us after death. At the same time, this book will present the other models pertinent to the evidence based on probability, fractal geometry, information and spatial topology, and scientific and mathematical protocols.

What you choose to believe after I present the best scientific information is solely based on your ability to evaluate the material and the mathematics.

My job is to present the information and evaluate it. That means I have to judge how I make the decision about what is most probable. I have to judge my decision-making process. You have to do the same if you are going to come to your own best conclusion. You have to do the same if you don't let your prejudices or cognitive biases interfere with your search for the truth. You have to be aware of your own personal heuristic, or how you judge the information presented.

A heuristic technique is any approach to problem-solving, learning, or discovery that employs a practical method not guaranteed to be optimal or perfect but sufficient for the immediate goals. Where finding an optimal solution is impossible or impractical, heuristic methods can be used to speed up the process of finding a satisfactory solution.

In psychology, heuristics are simple, efficient rules learned or hard-coded by evolutionary processes that have been proposed to explain how people typically make decisions, come to judgments, and solve problems when facing complex problems or incomplete information.

Interfering with the heuristic method are our cognitive biases. One example is the halo effect, a type of immediate judgment discrepancy, or cognitive bias, where a person making an initial assessment of another person, place, or thing will assume ambiguous information based upon concrete information. A simplified example of the halo effect is when an individual who notices that a person in a photograph is attractive, well-groomed, and properly attired also assumes, using a mental heuristic, that the person in the photograph is a good person.

Another example is believing something a respected teacher taught you. Because you respect this individual so much, what he says must of course be true. Yet with your decision to believe what this person says, you suspend your own analytical judgement.

The assumption of ambiguous information happens any time you choose belief over facts. Sometimes you have to dig out the facts, sometimes they are misrepresented, and sometimes it is in our best interest to find out what they are.

That is what you and I are going to try to do here. We may come to different conclusions at the end of the book because our heuristic methods are different, but we will look at the same evidence, evaluate it, evaluate our own heuristics, and come to our own individual conclusions.

We are going to look at the probability of reincarnation using the scientific method, observations, double-blind experiments and hypotheses to achieve the most fact-based and logic-driven probabilities.

We have to break the larger math problem down to its component parts and assign probabilities to every subset. You cannot average percentages, but they are important indices collectively.

What constitutes mathematical proof? The numbers have to crossfoot. In accounting systems, the numbers "prove" if they all add up. Crossfooting is a method that accountants use to verify that all the numbers add up. In accounting lingo, summing a column of numbers is called footing. To crossfoot is to ensure that the sum of column totals equals the grand total.

That means the numbers say the same thing in each direction and that the numbers prove.

There is no room for beliefs in our results, but we will look at belief systems to try to understand why they may or may not accept reincarnation and what factual basis they may use to support their acceptance. No data is off-limits. We may one day be able to program reincarnation and take our consciousness across the threshold of death and back to a living and completely new body.

While that may seem an outrageous assumption today, DARPA is working on a neural link that could enable the uploading of information directly into the human brain. Elon Musk's organization is doing the same with its development of a neural net. In 2016 we were already able to link a camera to the optic nerve so the blind can see. We are now working on linking a processor directly to the brain. This book will explain where we are with that development, how that process works, and how the upload and download of information mirrors the process of reincarnation itself.

Regarding the development of AI, by 2020 IBM is promising us a brain in a box. The difference between human and artificial intelligence is that on the human side we measure synaptic operations per second (SOPS) while on the AI side these transactions are measured as floating point operations per second (FLOPS). That means to create a brain in a box we will have artificially created something that is two liters in size, has one kilowatt of power, and can do ten million transactions per second, the same wattage and processing power of a human brain. By 2035 artificial intelligence will be smarter than humans. When AI is smarter than humans, what will it believe? How can we design a belief system for AI without analyzing our own belief system? Will it choose to be a Muslim? A Hindu? A Christian? When AI is smarter than us, will it have a religious belief system at all? Will this emerging scientific model be it?

I can take people who have had a near-death experience into a lab as I can children who remember prior lives, but I can't take Jesus or Mohammed into a lab for a quantitative analysis. When AI is smarter than us, will AI look at this evidence as objectively as we are trying to? Or will it do that analysis better?

By 2050 we will be able to upload to the cloud and download to a new computer more information than exists in the human mind. But by looking at the observations and experiments that we have before us right now, we can make the case that this is already happening to us. We are in a sense being uploaded to heaven and downloaded to earth. While our bodies may change, we are electrical information. That electrical information transfer that is us is a fractal of the process we use to upload and download information to the cloud.

By mirroring human intelligence in the development of artificial intelligence, we are seeing the systems operate similarly. The uploading and downloading of information that we use every time we use a computer mirrors what we believe but haven't formally proven: reincarnation itself.

The fact that the two examples of upload and download are iterations of information transfer, that they are self-similar, and that they exhibit similar patterns at different orders of magnitude creates a basis for them being fractals. Our own belief systems make it difficult to look at this model objectively. Yet many of us believe in this model already.

Let us look at what people believe regarding reincarnation and an afterlife.

According to data released by the Pew Forum, not only do 25 percent of Americans believe in reincarnation but 24 percent of American Christians believe in reincarnation.[1]

In the UK, 53 percent of people believe in life after death, and 70 percent believe in a human soul.

Why?

There are many beliefs, but what is reality? What reality would a scientific examination of all aspects and facts produce? This is the science of reincarnation. If we apply the scientific method to the study of reincarnation, we have observations, experiments, and theories. What does that objective model look like? How do we measure it?

World Population	7.5 Billion	
Christians	2.18 Billion	33%
Muslims	1.6 Billion	21%
Nonreligious	1.2 Billion	16%
Hindus*	1.1 Billion	14%
Primal-Indigenous	450 Million	6%

World Population	7.5 Billion	
Chinese Traditional	450 Million	6%
Buddhists*	500 Million	6%
Jews*	16 Million	0.002%
Sikhs	20 Million	0.0036

* These religions support reincarnation.

Let's define the parameters of what reincarnation is and how we search for the criteria. Our search for reincarnation begins with our death and ends several years after our rebirth. Our consciousness would need to remain discrete after our death, meaning that you continue to be *you*, conscious and aware, after your death. In our study, we need to find out if our consciousness has the ability to leave our bodies in a measurable and repeatable way for scientific validation. We would then need to correlate all the related data points to have a complete model. We would need, for instance, to correlate the data of near-death experiences (NDEs), children who remember prior lives, and the nature of psychic phenomena (psi) itself. This model would need to be consistent with the other sciences as well.

If we are to prove that reincarnation is as natural as birth, the soul, or disembodied consciousness, would need to be discrete after the body dies.

We would need to be able to do the following:

- Look at the human body to see where the soul or mind might be housed. We now have quantum biology as an emerging field that might provide some answers. We now know that the human body completely replaces itself every two to seven years down to every atom. Memory is the only constant. This is an example of body replacement. The replacement of cells in all living organisms, not just the human body, is not controversial; it is basic biology. Cells reproduce, divide, and replace the old cells that die. White blood cells last about one day, and all the cells in our stomach lining are replaced after three days. Skeletal cells can take up to seven years to be replaced. In a way, this is reincarnation, as your mind has shed its body entirely and does so repeatedly over the course of your life. Yet our belief about reincarnation does not factor in how our bodies operate.

- Prove that the mind can reach outside the body. In fact, clairvoyance was proven using DNA evidence that would stand up in a court of law.[2]

- We have cases we can measure mathematically, using odds-against-chance probabilities, of people claiming to be aware after death. There are in fact millions of people who have died and been resuscitated.[3]

- Examine children who remember a prior life. There are children who remember a prior lifetime verifiable by written history, but more compellingly these children are believed by the people who knew them in a prior lifetime. What are the odds against chance of that happening repeatedly?

- Understand why people can be regressed, a form of hypnotism that allows access to memories of a prior life.
- Compare those narratives and then do an odds-against-chance meta-analysis of all the data.
- Evaluate the impact this information will have on the development of AI and how using a math-based model will support the design and the development of AI.
- Show how this information can help us reimagine how we should govern ourselves.

Once we see fractal patterns emerge, we will know our reality. This can be considered a mathematical proof of reincarnation.

What would leading mathematicians and scientists say about this data? What would a bookmaker say if he were giving odds about the right answer? Would he handicap one religion as opposed to another?

What happens to religion if this data is true?

Any religion that preaches an afterlife is immediately validated by the science model. Mellen-Thomas Benedict, who had one of the longest near-death experiences reported that all religions were present in the afterlife and could be visited.[4] Other people who have had NDEs corroborate his account. But does that prove life after death?

Not yet, but the numbers we are going to present in this book are beginning to add up.

Finally, in light of this new information, how should we govern ourselves?

If we accept the data presented here, the most likely scenario after death will be our return through the process of reincarnation. How should we prepare ourselves and the world we will return to?

The math that supports the science of reincarnation is the math that supports life. Uploading a file to the cloud and downloading it to another computer is the same type of iteration and self-similarity that we are observing in children who remember prior lives and people who have NDEs. It is also the math that supports the religious belief in an afterlife.

Once AI is smarter than us, it could control the nukes in Korea, America, or anywhere else, and that is a threat to us all. We need the collective intelligence and courage to know the truth.

You cannot speak truth to power if power has no use for truth. But you also cannot speak truth to power if you do not know the truth.

Notes

[1]   Pew Forum on Religion and Public Life (2009 survey).
[2]   Stephan Schwartz, *The Secret Vaults of Time: Psychic Archaeology and the Quest for Man's Beginnings* (New-

buryport, MA: Hampton Roads Publishing Company, 1978).

[3] Stephan Schwartz, *Six Protocols, Neuroscience, and Near Death: An Emerging Paradigm Incorporating Nonlocal Consciousness Stephan Schwartz (EXPLORE The Journal of Science and Healing 2015).*

[4] http://www.mellen-thomas.com/.

Chapter 2

Our Bodies

In 1850, French farmers came to French scientists in Paris and said, "Do you see these rocks? They fell from the sky."[1] The French scientists knew the farmers were lying. After all, they could look at the sky and see there were no rocks. It would be another hundred years before we understood the science of meteorites.

Rocks falling out of the sky were a scientific anomaly at the time, something science could not explain. The scientific paradigm of an individual science explains the science and predicts where the science is headed. The scientific paradigm of astronomy at that time could not incorporate this information into its explanation of what we saw and regarded as reality, and therefore the scientists regarded the information as false and the farmers as liars.

Anomalies are things that don't fit into our understanding of reality. Sometimes things happen that force the anomalies into the paradigm, which forces the paradigm to change to incorporate the new information. What happened in the case of meteorites was the invention of more powerful telescopes.

The metaparadigm is the paradigm that incorporates all the scientific paradigms into one overriding explanation.

The first metaparadigm was the Genesis metaparadigm. Science was based on God having created the heavens and the earth. The Genesis metaparadigm died in 1859 with the publication of *On the Origin of Species* by Charles Darwin. The theory of evolution defeated the perception that the earth had been made in six days. We saw the truth in the emerging sciences like geology and archeology.

The second metaparadigm is the grand material metaparadigm. By 1905, "The Grand Material world view now held unquestioned sovereignty. Its premises...are (1) the mind is the result of physiological processes; (2) each consciousness is a discrete entity; (3) organic evolution has no specific goal; (4) there is only one space time continuum, providing for only one reality. Its rules concerning the separation of the researcher and the experiment and the Covenant of Replicability (The Covenant of Replicability means obtaining consistent results across studies aimed at answering the same scientific question using new data or other new computational methods) became the only acceptable basis for science. All else was at best un-science and at worst mysticism and quackery."[2]

As science has advanced, new anomalies are weighing on the grand material metaparadigm. Near-death experiences suggest death may not be our end. Children who remember prior lives are now being catalogued, and their narratives are compared. Experiments in nonlocal consciousness are becoming better at providing interesting proof on parts of our larger reincarnation math problem.

The growing weight of these current anomalies is shaping something called the grand unified metaparadigm. In *The Field: The Quest for the Secret Force of the Universe*, Lynne McTaggart writes, "The communication of the world did not occur in the visible realm of Newton, but in the subatomic world of Werner Heisenberg. Cells and DNA communicated through frequencies. The brain perceived and made its own record of the world in pulsating waves. A substructure underpins the universe that is essentially a recording mechanism of everything, providing a means for everything to communicate with everything else. People are indivisible from their environment. Living consciousness is not an isolated entity. It increases order in the rest of the world. The consciousness of human beings has incredible powers, to heal ourselves, to heal the world—in a sense, to make it as we wish it to be."[3]

This scientific revolution of changing the metaparadigm impacts religion significantly as well as our view of ourselves.

McTaggart notes that science was not refuting god "science for the first time was proving his existence—by demonstrating that a higher collective consciousness was out there. There need no longer be two truths, the truth of science and the truth of religion. There could be one unified vision of the world."[4]

Change like this does not occur in isolation. The changing of the scientific metaparadigm forces change throughout the individual scientific paradigms, including but not limited to politics, medicine, and societal structures.

If we accept what the current scientific model is showing us, then laws within some religious dogma prohibiting apostasy and blasphemy should be immediately ended. This scientific model also means Catholic health-care organizations should not impose their beliefs upon those who come to their facilities. They should offer birth control, perform abortions when the mother's life is threatened, and offer full health care even when it contravenes their canonical beliefs. This now is a scientific argument, not an argument of belief.

So before we get too far ahead of ourselves, we must look at and understand what our increasing knowledge base is doing to our collective worldview. We are back to anomalies.

Sometimes in science we see an effect before we understand the cause, like in the meteorite example. These effects that we don't understand and can't explain with our current understanding of science are called anomalies. Understanding anomalies changes our understanding of our environment and ourselves. We have to let go of our old understanding and integrate the new information into our worldview. Once we do that, new sciences unthought of in the preceding generation begin to emerge.

The science of reincarnation is a science made up of parts called disciplines. Each discipline examines a different part of the science. All the disciplines together make up the paradigm of the science. The science is made whole when each discipline interacts with the other. A scientific paradigm explains the science based on the total of the disciplines and posits where the science is headed. To make our math case, we need to go through all the disciplines and calculate odds against chance or explain why an experiment is proof.

There are two types of disciplines, anecdotal and technical. Anecdotal disciplines use field reports and observations, and technical disciplines use experiments. Let's start with the anecdotal disciplines.

Observations are examinations of things in the real world. Sometimes we cannot explain what we are seeing, which makes these things scientific anomalies.

1. **Near-death experiences.** NDEs are becoming more and more common as the quality of medical care increases. NDEs are events where someone dies, is clinically dead for a period of time, and then is resuscitated. It is estimated that over 4 percent of people have had an NDE,[5] which is more than 13 million Americans or 300 million people

globally. People who have had NDEs describe a common process. They have an out-of-body experience (OBE) where they look down upon their own body.

2. **Children who remember prior lives**. These include children between the ages of two and five who claim to have lived a prior life. Studies began more than fifty years ago at the University of Virginia to investigate children who made these claims. These children could describe a prior life they had lived, locate the pace they lived, and find people who remembered them from a prior life. These people in many of these cases accepted the child as the individual they had known prior to the individual's death. Additionally, some of these children also had memories from before they were born and could describe their prebirth environment. The University of Virginia is coding 2,500 cases with 400 variables and hoping to find trends.[6]

3. **Past-life regression.** A past-life regression is when someone is regressed, through hypnosis or meditation, and can access information from a prior life. Our science cannot explain these events. They are anomalies. However, taken as a group, when these individual anomalies describe the environment after death, they describe a common landscape. The odds against chance that this would occur is improbably high, suggesting a root cause.

These three disciplines describe reincarnation from three different viewpoints: prebirth, postdeath, and prior lives.

One can actually meet and talk to people who experienced one of these phenomena, and there are hundreds of millions of them. They can include your next-door neighbor. To meet them you can simply go to their conventions. Near-death experience researchers and experiencers go to the annual IANDS (International Association for Near-Death Studies) convention. For remote viewing there is the IRVA (International Remote Viewing Association) convention, and for past-life regression you can go to a Weiss or Newton event. The largest organization is The Near-Death Experience Research Foundation (www.nderf.org).

The body we currently occupy is really a human biome. That means 50 percent of your cells are other organisms such as bacteria in your intestines. Of the remaining cells that are "you," all the matter in the cells changes completely every two to seven years. Your stomach lining changes every day, your skin cells change every two weeks, and even the enamel in your teeth and the calcium in your bones change completely every two years.

Your consciousness, not your body, is permanent until death. So where is your consciousness located? Does the fact that you replaced all the matter in your body in the last two years mean your consciousness has moved to a new body? Do you still have the same body you had when you were six?

You are primarily water (60 percent) and other chemicals (40 percent). Most of the 40 percent includes binders that hold the sack of water together. You have already reincarnated if you have moved on to a replacement body.

Almost 99 percent of the mass of the human body is made up of six elements: oxygen, carbon, hydrogen, nitrogen, calcium, and phosphorus. Only about 0.85 percent is composed of another five elements: potassium, sulfur, sodium, chlorine, and magnesium. All eleven are necessary for life. All of these elements are replaced completely every seven years.

But does the fact that your mind will move from body to body through your lifetime indicate that once you die it will migrate to a new body?

Much work is being done to locate consciousness and memory. It has been found that memory has been stored as a waveform throughout your body.[7]

An example of waveform memory is transplant memories. As our medical technology has developed, we are now able to transplant body parts from a donor body. An example of transplant memories can be seen in Clare Sylvia's case,[8] where she received organs from a recently deceased teenager who had died in an auto accident. She then reported having memories from his life as well as developing new tastes, in this instance for Chicken McNuggets and beer.

In Lynne McTaggart's book *The Field,* she talks about an experiment scientists in France did. They used a state-of-the art surgical technique for heart transplants and kept the heart of a male Hartley guinea pig alive on a purpose-built scaffolding. They then applied acetylcholine and histamine, two known vasodilators, then atropine and mepyramine, both antagonists to the others, and measured coronary flow and such mechanical changes as beat rate. They knew that these pharmacological chemicals would induce specific, measurable changes such as increasing or decreasing heart rate.

This is important if we can get these results with not just using chemicals but also with energy as described below. This is important for two reasons. First, it shows that we are doing work in quantum biology, that we are treating the body using physics, not just chemistry. In short, we are treating the body with electromagnetics the stuff the mind is made from. Second, this coupled with CRISPR shows that we can design a body.

Lynn McTaggart writes, "The only unusual aspect of the experiment was that the agents of change weren't actually pharmacological chemicals, but low frequency waves of the electromagnetic signals recorded using a purpose designed transducer and a computer equipped with a soundcard."[9]

A sound card is an expansion card for producing sound on a computer that can be heard through speakers or headphones.

They broke down the pharmacological chemicals into the component elements—hydrogen, oxygen, and so forth—digitized the signal, and shot the electromagnetic signature at the guinea pig hearts. The guinea pigs' hearts read the electromagnetic signals as though they were chemicals.

In short, the researchers digitized a chemical like atropine and sent their electromagnetic signals "which take the form of electromagnetic radiation of less than 20 kilohertz, which were applied to the Guinea pig heart, and were responsible for speeding it up, just as the chemicals themselves would."[10]

If chemicals can be digitized, can you? They retain "discreteness" and are simply the waveform of the particulate. In short, these chemicals retain the same identity whether they are a chemical or an electromagnetic wave; they are just different manifestations of the same information. Are you able to do the same thing? To look at this quantitatively, the chemicals have a particulate presence and a wave presence each compatible with the other. Can we break consciousness into similar component parts? In short, can we dissect the energy or the electrical charge that is you?

If these cells are made up of energy, where and how is our memory stored? Especially since the cells change all the time. So there are two questions, really. Where are "you" stored? And how are you stored there?

There is much evidence to say that what is regarded as

"you" as your body changes is not stored in cells but in energy and that that energy is manifested in those cells as it was in the hearts of the Hartley guinea pigs when wave energy was directed at their hearts. If we can change a guinea pig's heart with chemicals and change the guinea pig's heart with just the energy of the chemical, the energy that is us does the same thing by a greater order of magnitude.

Dr. Dean Radin, chief scientist at the Institute of Noetic Sciences and a distinguished professor at the California Institute of Integral Studies, offered the following thoughts to me in a correspondence:

Hi Bob,

"Proof" only makes sense in mathematics, logic, and alcohol. In the scientific world, in field studies, and in case reports, there is no proof. There is only evidence, and evidence is always in the eye of the beholder. That's why controversies persist— the same body of evidence might be highly persuasive to some but not to others.

For example, "Our bodies are 50% other organisms, and they are completely replaced down to every last atom every two years. That would seem scientific proof that our mind is able to migrate to a completely new body..."

Not really. Just because the material in our bodies is dynamically recycled, the *informational patterns* that constitute our physical structure can (and does) remain highly stable throughout our lifetime. If memory and personality are encoded in us physically (which most neurobiologists believe), then just because every couple of years we have a new set of atoms provides no evidence that the mind is separate from the body.

It's tempting to use suggestions deriving from the many different lines of evidence to make an airtight case for survival or reincarnation. But a devil's advocate could easily poke holes in each line of evidence, and in so doing they can take what seems like a strong overall argument and make it collapse like a house of cards. Indeed, this is the rhetorical approach that most skeptics specialize in. In some cases their counterarguments are probably sound; in others they are almost certainly wrong.

Some controversies are just ahead of their time; they clash too strongly with the status quo, and as such they're relegated to the fringe. But science marches on. Someday the mainstream will catch up. Meanwhile, efforts like what you're proposing, presented conservatively, can help sustain serious interest in reincarnation research long enough so that when the future scientific worldview becomes more compatible with the existing evidence, *then* it will be perceived as obvious.

Best wishes,

Dean

Now before we move on, Dean Radin is correct. Before we leave this chapter and begin our analysis, there are a couple of cogent points to carry forward. Proof is quantitative. There are times in life, however, when the absolute cannot be known but new information allows us to discard old thoughts. This science of reincarnation is driving that process.

You have to choose your heuristic structure. This will be a theme throughout this book. The questions will be posed in several ways. Do you have a grand material metaparadigm mindset or a grand unified metaparadigm mindset? That will decide how you evaluate this information.

What is your heuristic?

A heuristic is a technique or an approach to problem solving, learning, or discovery by using a practical method. These practical methods are not guaranteed to be perfect but sufficient for the immediate goals of the learner. Where finding an optimal solution is impossible or impractical, heuristic methods can be used to speed up the process of finding a satisfactory solution. Heuristics can be mental shortcuts that ease the cognitive load of making a decision. Examples of this method include using a rule of thumb, an educated guess, an intuitive judgment, a guesstimate, a stereotype, a profile, or common sense.

There is much scientific information to say you cannot change your heuristic once it's set. "You can't teach an old dog new tricks." "An entire generation of scientists have to die off for a science to advance." "Once people believe something, they only listen to what supports that belief."

There are situations where belief does not change just because new conditions scientifically support that belief, but mankind would be mistaken not to acknowledge that new conditions do exist. The world is no longer flat. The new condition is that consciousness science is beginning to support the religious contention of an afterlife, but the science is redefining the afterlife to be a different state of awareness with just our electrical being.

That is the science of reincarnation. In order to find the truth, we must be objective. That requires more than deducing the result. It requires avoiding cognitive biases to deduce the truth. A science must encompass everyone's truth to be real. Only then can you be on the fact-based, logic-driven path to knowing what the truth is, what is real, and what is not.

A mental monkey wrench has been thrown into the works, and that is AI with its own heuristic. You don't want your computer to have a cognitive bias because then you will get a wrong result. You could say the algorithm is wrong, or you could say, "Shit in, shit out." It's the same thing.

We need to do a comparative probabilities analysis against the competing theories and see which is most likely correct. While this is not proof, it takes us in the most probable direction to find that proof. To do that we must make our beliefs stand up to the truth. In a comparative probability analysis, the questions become: Do you believe what you see? Do you see what you believe?

Notes

[1] Stephan Schwartz, *The Secret Vaults of Time: Psychic Archaeology and the Quest for Man's Beginnings* (Newburyport, MA: Hampton Roads Publishing Company, 1978).

[2] Stephan Schwartz, *The Secret Vaults of Time: Psychic Archaeology and the Quest for Man's Beginnings* (Newburyport, MA: Hampton Roads Publishing Company, 1978), p. 270-1.

[3] Lynne McTaggart, *The Field: The Quest for the Secret Force of the Universe* (New York: HarperCollins Publishers, 2001), p. 223.

[4] Lynne McTaggart, *The Field: The Quest for the Secret Force of the Universe* (New York: HarperCollins Publishers, 2001), p. 226.

[5] Stephan Schwartz, *Six Protocols, Neuroscience, and Near Death: An Emerging Paradigm Incorporating Nonlocal Consciousness.*

[6] https://med.virginia.edu/perceptual-studies/our-research/children-who-report-memories-of-previous-lives/.

[7] https://www.sciencealert.com/your-brain-uses-a-clever-pattern-of-wavelengths-to-store-memories.

8   https://www.independent.co.uk/life-style/my-heart-belongs-to-tim-1257635.html.

9   Lynne McTaggart, *The Field: The Quest for the Secret Force of the Universe* (New York: HarperCollins Publishers, 2001), p. 59.

10 Lynne McTaggart, *The Field: The Quest for the Secret Force of the Universe* (New York: HarperCollins Publishers, 2001).

Chapter 3

The Anomaly of Near-Death Experiences

It would seem more improbable living once than living twice. By living once, you proved you could do it.

A near-death experience occurs when someone who is clinically dead is brought back to life. The people who have them typically report a similar experience. Since the information they give is anecdotal, it is difficult to apply hard science to what is occurring. Dr. Raymond Moody's book *Life after Life* in 1975 describes the near-death experience. Dr. Moody was a cardiologist.

He aggregated anecdotal information from people who had near-death experiences or went through clinical death and were later revived. What is striking about his research is the remarkable similarities in the stories of these people. I will provide excerpts from his book to give you an overview of these experiences and to show the common denominator that Dr. Moody found in his case studies. I will show later that this same common denominator appears in other events. Dr. Moody separates these death and near-death cases by the way in which the people arrived at them.

The experiences which I have studied fall into three distinct categories:

1. The experiences of persons who were resuscitated after having been thought, adjudged, or pronounced clinically dead by their doctors.
2. The experiences of persons who, in the course of accidents or severe injury or illness, came very close to physical death.
3. The experiences of persons who, as they died, told them to other people who were present. Later, these other people reported the content of the death experience to me."[1]

Dr. Moody then indicates the many similarities between these varying accounts.

Despite the wide variation in the circumstances surrounding close calls with death and in the types of persons undergoing them, it remains true that there is a striking similarity among the accounts of the experiences themselves. In fact, the similarities among various reports are so great that one can easily pick out about fifteen separate elements which recur again and again in the mass of narratives that I have collected. On the basis of these points of likeness, let me now construct a brief, theoretically "ideal" or "complete" experience which embodies all of the common elements, in the order in which it is typical for them to occur.

A man is dying and, as he reaches the point of greatest physical distress, he hears himself pronounced dead by his doctor. He begins to hear an uncomfortable noise, a loud ringing or buzzing, and at the same time feels himself moving very rapidly through a long dark tunnel. After this, he suddenly finds himself outside of his own physical body but still in the immediate physical environment, and he sees his own body from a distance as though he is a spectator. He watches the resuscitation attempt from this unusual vantage point and is in a state of emotional upheaval.

After a while, he collects himself and becomes more accustomed to his odd condition. He notices that he still has a "body," but one of a very different nature and with very different powers from the physical body he has left behind. Soon other things begin to happen. Others come to meet and to help him. He glimpses the spirits of relatives and friends who have already died, and a loving, warm spirit of a kind he has never encountered before—a being of light—appears before him. This being asks him a question, nonverbally, to make him evaluate his life and helps him along by showing him a panoramic, instantaneous playback of the major events of his life. At some point he finds himself approaching some sort of barrier or border, apparently representing the limit between earthly life and the next life. Yet, he finds that he must go back to the earth, that the time for his death has not yet come. At this point he resists, for by now he is taken up with his experiences in the afterlife and does not want to return. He is overwhelmed by intense feelings of joy, love, and peace. Despite his attitude, though, he somehow reunites with his physical body and lives.

Later he tries to tell others, but he has trouble doing so. In the first place, he can find no human words adequate to describe these unearthly episodes. He also finds that others scoff, so he stops telling other people. Still, the experience affects his life profoundly, especially his views about death and its relationship to life.[2]

There are even cases in which these people encounter someone (or something) while in their transitional state.

On individuals "meeting others," Moody writes, "Quite a few have told me that at some point while they were dying—sometimes early in the experiences, sometimes only after their events had taken place—they became aware of the presence of other spiritual beings in their vicinity, beings who apparently were there to ease them through their transition into death, or, in two cases, to tell them that their time to die had not yet come and that they must return to their physical bodies."[3]

Remember the old cliché of "going into the light?" Apparently, that light is an actual being, or at least one that's real enough to be commonly seen by an overwhelmingly high percentage of Dr. Moody's patients. To all these patients, its existence and its benevolence are undeniable.

Moody goes on to describe this "being of light," and he finds that what the most "incredible common element in the accounts [he has] studied, and is certainly the element which has the most profound effect upon the individual, is the encounter with a very bright light. Despite the light's unusual manifestation, however, not one person has expressed any doubt whatsoever that it was a being, a being of light. Not only that, it is a personal being. It has a very definite personality. The love and the warmth which emanate from this being to the dying person are utterly beyond words, and he feels completely surrounded by it and taken up in it, completely at ease and accepted in the presence of this being."[4]

If the question hasn't occurred to you by now, here it is in the words of Dr. Moody himself: "The most obvious is the difficulty of explaining the similarity of so many of the accounts. How is it that many people just happen to have come up with the same lie to tell me over a period of eight years?"[5]

Don't you think that there are only a handful of answers to this question? Could any of those answers exclude the possibility of something beyond the cessation of physical life? Below, I will provide Dr. Moody's ideas about the data he collected. See if you agree with his analysis. But first I have another question. Is it possible that people from the three anecdotal disciplines all came up with the same lie over not just eight years but two thousand years?

Moody hypothesizes "that death is a separation of the mind from the body, and that the mind does pass into other realms of existence at this point. It would follow that there exists some mechanism whereby the soul or mind is released upon death. One has no basis upon which to assume, though, that this mechanism works exactly in accordance with what we have in our own era somewhat arbitrarily taken to be the point of no return. Nor do we have to assume that it works perfectly in every instance, any more than we have to assume that any bodily system always works perfectly."[6]

According to Dr. Moody, there exist realms outside the one in which we live, and the mind will enter these realms upon death. This establishes that the mind—the individual consciousness (the soul)—is likely a separate entity from the body; therefore, a physical death does not mean a permanent one. What we can gain from this compelling theory is that if the death of the body does not mean the death of a person's consciousness, then a person's mind can potentially manifest itself in a different body down the road. If death isn't permanent, then reincarnation is possible.

The reports collected from people who have had near-death and clinical-death experiences contain a significant number of common elements. The majority of these people report an out-of-body experience and an encounter with a being of light that, usually, talks to them. The uniformity of the collected experiences, despite the large variance of their respective sources' circumstances, suggests that the experiences are not merely fictitious or dreamlike hallucinations but reports of an experience in an actual realm separate from our own, inaccessible to the clinically alive, and indicates that death is not permanent because the mind is able to travel independently of the body.

The NDE is a global phenomenon common to every culture. It is an example of a scientific anomaly, something we can observe, something that repeats itself, and something that is becoming more and more common as our health care improves. Kevin Williams is the creator of one of the leading website portals on near-death experience science. In his paper "Near Death Experiences and Hinduism," Kevin Williams says the following about how near-death experiences express themselves in another culture.

1. In 45 Hindu near-death accounts, Pasrich and Stevenson found no evidence of a tunnel experience which is frequently found in western accounts of the near-death experience. However, another

near-death researcher, Susan Blackmore, reported accounts of tunnel experience in her research of eight Hindu near-death experiencers.

2. Only one account contained an out of body experience, which is another aspect that is frequently found in western accounts. Osis and Haraldsson did find several accounts of out of body experience in the Indian near-death experiences they researched.

3. Consistent with western accounts, some Hindu near-death accounts include a life review. However, whereas in western accounts the life review often consists of seeing a panoramic view of a person's entire life, Hindu accounts consist of having someone read the record of a person's entire life called the "Akashic record." In Christian circles, this is equivalent to reading from the "Book of Life" as known from the Christian doctrine of resurrection. In Hindu circles, it is a traditional belief that the reading of a person's Akashic record occurs immediately after death. This concept is widely believed by Hindus all over India. However, the panoramic life review, which is commonly mentioned in western accounts, does not appear in accounts from India.

4. As in western accounts, Hindu near-death accounts sometimes describe the meeting of religious deities and deceased loved ones.[7]

Now that we have an overview, what follows is one of the best individual NDE commentaries. Mellen-Thomas Benedict was dead long enough before he was revived to have a deeper experience than most. He reports that he visited a variety of heavens or afterlives.

His commentary corroborates the others. Additionally, it is a comprehensive view rather than an individual view; he saw Jesus, but what he saw was reflected through his own feedback loop.

In 1982, Mellen-Thomas Benedict suffered from terminal brain cancer and died but miraculously lived to tell about it. While showing no vital signs for 90 minutes, Benedict had perhaps the most transcendental NDE ever documented. While on the "other side," Benedict journeyed through various afterlife realms. He was given access to universal intelligence and allowed to absorb a tremendous amount of spiritual and scientific knowledge, including the nature of reincarnation. Benedict's enthusiastic curiosity during his NDE took him far into the remote depths of existence—and even beyond—into the energetic void of nothingness behind the big bang. He was shown in holographic detail the evolution of both Mother Earth ("Gaia") and humanity, and he experienced the cosmology of our souls' connection with Gaia.[8]

As I began to move toward the Light, I knew intuitively that if I went to the Light, I would be dead. So as I was moving toward the Light I said, "Please wait a minute, just hold on a second here. I want to think about this; I would like to talk to you before I go." To my surprise, the entire experience halted at that point. You are indeed in control of your near-death experience. You are not on a roller coaster ride.

So my request was honored and I had some conversations with the Light. The Light kept changing into different figures, like Jesus, Buddha, Krishna, mandalas, archetypal images and signs. I asked the Light, "What is going on here? Please, Light, clarify yourself for me. I really want to know the reality of the situation." I cannot really say the exact words, because it was sort of telepathy.[9]

The Light responded. The information transferred to me was that your beliefs shape the kind of feedback you are getting before the Light. If you were a Buddhist or Catholic or Fundamentalist, you get a feedback loop of your own stuff. You have a chance to look at it and examine it, but most people do not. As the Light revealed itself to me, I became aware that what I was really seeing was our Higher Self matrix.

We all have a higher Self, or an oversoul part of our being. It revealed itself to me in its truest energy form. The only way I can really describe it is that the being of the higher Self is more like a conduit.

It did not look like that, but it is a direct connection to the Source that each and every one of us has. We are directly connected to the Source. So the Light was showing me the higher Self matrix. I was not committed to one particular religion. So that is what was being fed back to me during my life after death experience. As I asked the Light to keep clearing for me, to keep explaining, I understood what the higher Self matrix is. We have a grid around the planet where all the higher Selves are connected. This is like a great company, a next subtle level of energy around us, the spirit level, you might say.

[...]

I asked God: "What is the best religion on the planet? Which one is right?" And Godhead said, with great love: "I don't care." That was incredible grace.

They come and they go, they change. Buddhism has not been here forever, Catholicism has not been here forever, and they are all about to become more enlightened. More light is coming into all systems now. There is going to be a reformation in spirituality that is going to be just as dramatic as the Protestant Reformation. There will be lots of people fighting about it, one religion against the next, believing that only they are right.

Everyone thinks they own God, the religions and philosophies, especially the religions, because they form big organizations around their philosophy. When Godhead said, "I don't care," I immediately understood that it is for us to care about. It is important, because we are the caring beings. It matters to us and that is where it is important. What you have is the energy equation in spirituality. Ultimate Godhead does not care if you are Protestant, Buddhist, or whatever. It is all a blooming facet of the whole. I wish that all religions would realize it and let each other be. It is not the end of each religion, but we are talking about the same God. Live and let live. Each has a different view. And it all adds up to the Big Picture; it is all important.

[...]

The mystery of life has very little to do with intelligence. The universe is not an intellectual process at all. The intellect is helpful; it is brilliant, but right now that is all we process with, instead of our hearts and the wiser part of ourselves. The center of the Earth is this great transmuter of energy, just as you see in pictures of our Earth's magnetic field. That's our cycle, pulling reincarnated souls back in and through it again. A sign that you are reaching human level is that you are beginning to evolve an individual consciousness. The animals have a group soul, and they reincarnate in group souls. A deer is pretty much going to be a deer forever. But just being born a human, whether deformed or genius, shows that you are on the path to developing an individual consciousness. That is in itself part of the group consciousness called humanity.

I saw that races are personality clusters. Nations like France, Germany and China each have their own personality. Cities have personalities, their local group souls that attract certain people. Families have group souls. Individual identity is evolving like branches of a fractal; the group soul explores in our individuality. The different questions that each of us has are very, very important. This is how Godhead is exploring God's Self—through you. So, ask your questions, do your searching. You will find your Self and you will find God in that Self, because it is only the Self.[10]

All the individual NDEs tell a common tale. How do you connect the dots? Why do NDEs and children who remember prior lives and past-life regression *all tell a common story?*

In the paper "Six Protocols, Neuroscience, and Near Death: An Emerging Paradigm Incorporating Nonlocal Consciousness," Stephan Schwartz writes, "Recent well conducted studies reveal that about 4.2% of the American public has reported a near death experience. The population in the United States is a bit more than 315 million. So over 13 million people have reported having an NDE. To give that context, it is equivalent to all the Jewish people, all the Mormons, and Muslims as well, and most of the Buddhists. And that is but a fraction of it. The near-death experiencer population is almost certainly much larger than 13 million because research has also revealed that many people do not immediately report experiences. Often they do not speak of it at all until years or decades later, which is a problem for researchers, and why prospective studies, such as that of Dutch cardiologist Pim van Lommel in the Lancet 2001 are so important. Experiencers initially often keep quiet for fear of being ridiculed or embarrassed. As one experiencer noted, 'I couldn't talk about it, or I would've been committed to an institution.'"[11]

Schwartz's "Six Protocols" notes that Cherie Sutherland, "a visiting research fellow in the School of Sociology at the University of New South Wales, a near death experiencer herself, did a study, which showed that, when people tried to discuss the NDE, 50% of the relatives and 25% of friends rejected the NDE, and 30% of the nursing staff, 85% of the doctors, and 50% of psychiatrist's reacted negatively."[12]

The largest NDE research site in the world is The Near Death Experience Research Foundation (http://www.nderf.org/).

A rate of 4.2 percent extrapolated on a global scale suggests a potential 290 million near-death experiences. That is a large enough sample to meet our mathematical standard about whether or not we should believe something. This event happens, and almost everyone says the same thing, but this is not proof. If we add the children who remember prior lives and those who experience past-life regression, the probability is great that we have a cohesive picture of wave-state consciousness.

Critics say that near-death experiences are caused by neurochemicals and electrical events in our minds as we die. Yet these same impressions exist in children. They remember things verified by people who were living at the time, and we have thousands of such cases.

Children who remember prior lives and people who undergo past-life regression also describe a similar landscape. Aside from some concurrent data points, there is no conclusive proof connecting some of these disciplines, but others are connected.

Some believe that education is about making informed choices when not all the facts are available. That honestly describes where the science of reincarnation is today. More research needs to be done, and this type of research should move to the very top of our to-do list because it is research into the very core of who and what we are.

Science is about calculating probabilities when we don't have certainty so we can gauge the probable truth. What is new about the science of reincarnation is that it connects in a formal, teachable way the aggregate probabilities of all the events we are seeing. What is our most probable reality, and when do odds against chance matter? What does the math tell us?

Notes

[1] Raymond Moody, *Life After Life* (New York: Harper-Collins Publishers, 1975) p. 8.

[2] Raymond Moody, *Life After Life* (New York: Harper-Collins Publishers, 1975) p. 10-12.

[3] Raymond Moody, *Life After Life* (New York: Harper-Collins Publishers, 1975) p. 45.

[4] Raymond Moody, *Life After Life* (New York: Harper-Collins Publishers, 1975) p. 49.

[5] Raymond Moody, *Life After Life* (New York: Harper-Collins Publishers, 1975) p. 126.

[6] Raymond Moody, *Life After Life* (New York: Harper-Collins Publishers, 1975) p. 138.

[7] Kevin R. Williams, "Near death experiences and Hinduism," https://www.near-death.com/religion/hinduism.html

[8] Kevin R. Williams, "Near death experiences and Hinduism," https://www.near-death.com/reincarnation/experiences/mellen-thomas-benedict.html

[9] Kevin R. Williams, "Near death experiences and Hinduism," https://www.near-death.com/reincarnation/experiences/mellen-thomas-benedict.html

[10] Kevin R. Williams, "Near death experiences and Hinduism," https://www.near-death.com/reincarnation/

experiences/mellen-thomas-benedict.html (sections of Benedict's account have been reorganized-AU)

11 Stephan Schwartz, *Six Protocols, Neuroscience, and Near Death: An Emerging Paradigm Incorporating Nonlocal Consciousness.*

12 Stephan Schwartz, *Six Protocols, Neuroscience, and Near Death: An Emerging Paradigm Incorporating Nonlocal Consciousness.*

Chapter 4

The Anomaly of Children Who Remember Prior Lives

Why do we believe in an afterlife at all?

In order to explain the math, I must introduce fractal geometry. We cannot and must not use one form of math for our proof. It would be disingenuous and unscientific. Our most probable model has to fit seamlessly with our emerging understanding of physics and quantum biology to a degree of mathematical certainty.

The defining source for fractal geometry in nature is entitled *The Fractal Geometry of Nature* by Benoit Mandelbrot. Nature expresses itself in fractals. The best way to visualize this is to look at leaves on a tree. Each is similar to the others, and each is an iteration of the same thing.

When Mandelbrot looked deeper into fractals, he saw that the branching patterns of a tree were the same as the branching patterns of veins and the branching patterns of lungs. In fact, everything in nature is measured in fractals. Your heartbeat has a fractal pattern. When you look at something, your eyes use a fractal pattern to perceive the object and to observe its detail. Looking at somebody up and down is actually a fractal pattern your eyes follow. Fractals exhibit similar patterns at different orders of magnitude.

This can more easily be explained by imagining Russian nesting dolls. Each is a fractal, each is similar to the others, and each operates at a different order of magnitude because of its size difference.

While we are going to continue looking at the odds-against-chance probability of something occurring, we also need to see if a fractal pattern emerges. This fractal pattern will be mathematical proof of our reality.

Do our observations and experiments fractally line up with what we see in nature? Are the events similar iterations of each other? All the children's stories we will examine in this chapter have components that are similar to the others. They describe a landscape that is similar to all stories in the anomalies we are looking at.

Children who remember prior lives fall into several subcategories. The first is children who remember prior lives and also remember their own deaths. These deaths are unique in that the death wounds on the body of the prior life match birthmarks on the new body. The second category are children who remember a prior life and have an unquenchable desire to return to their prior family. When they do, they are able to recognize people from their prior lives. Those events defy calculating a reasonable answer using odds-against-chance probability in each individual case because the calculation would imply certainty. That is why some hesitate to say this calculation has meaning. They contend there is no corroborating proof. That is why we are crossfooting all the math columns. When taken as a whole, this math proves. The fact there will be readers who cannot process this is not the problem of the mathematician or the math.

Taken collectively, these stories point to a much more solid result. I will look at these cases and let you do your own calculations. If you disagree with my conclusions, you can propose your own alternative reality, but be sure your proposal is not slanted by your cognitive biases.

The first case is the story of "Kevin" from Jim Tucker's book *Return to Life.*

For more than fifty years, the University of Virginia has been studying cases of children who remember prior lives. Ian Stevenson first began the studies, and Jim Tucker has continued the work. One case they worked on together was Jim's first. In the following example, "we" refers to "Stevenson and Tucker."

Patrick, who was nearly eight, grew up in a compact house in a small Midwestern suburb. His mother became convinced her son was his deceased half-brother, Kevin, returned to life. Born nearly twenty years prior, Kevin had lived with his mother after his parents split. They were doing well despite the breakup until Lisa, his mother, noticed the sixteen-month-old limping. Multiple hospital visits finally revealed that Kevin had metastatic neuroblastoma.

X-rays soon discovered a mass at the top of Kevin's left kidney, and a skeletal survey "found various lesions and an opaque area over his bulging left eye."[1] After half a week in the hospital, doctors decided to operate, so a biopsy of the nodule above his right ear was taken. Doctors then "inserted a central line, a large IV, in the right side of his neck."[2]

Six months after his first admission, Kevin began "bleeding from his gums." His cancer had intruded into his bone marrow, and bruising around his right eye formed in addition to faded bruising around his left. The bone marrow could not create new platelets. By this point, his mother knew Kevin was blind in his left eye. Kevin's disease "was considered end stage by then, meaning the little boy would die soon, but along with a platelet transfusion, he did receive one day of chemotherapy and one day of radiation to his right eye socket. He was discharged and died two days later."[3]

As time passed after Kevin's death, Lisa remarried and gave birth to a daughter. The couple divorced after four years, and Lisa married again. She had a second son, and then twelve years after Kevin died, Lisa gave birth to Patrick.

Lisa noticed "a white opacity covering Patrick's left eye. The doctors diagnosed it as a corneal leukoma. Patrick was seen by an ophthalmologist and examined periodically. The opacity shrunk after several weeks but did not completely disappear. While his vision was hard to assess with any precision when he was very young, he was essentially blind in his left eye just as Kevin had been blind in that eye at the end of his life."

Lisa then discovered a tangible lump on Patrick's head. The lump was located above his right ear, the same location where Kevin's tumor had been biopsied. Stevenson and Tucker write that when they examined Patrick, they "felt the nodule above his ear. It had migrated slightly behind his ear by the time he was five, but Lisa had said it was directly above the ear when he was born. It was hard, elevated, and more or less round."[4]

As Stevenson and Tucker continued to examine Patrick, they also noticed that he was "born with an unusual mark on his neck. A dark slanted line that was about 4 millimeters long when we met him, it looked like a small cut. It was on the front of his neck on the right. This was the area where Kevin's central line had been inserted…it was on the right side of his neck, where Patrick's birthmark was."[5]

Amazingly, Stevenson and Tucker concluded further that one of "the most inexplicable features of the case was that Patrick limped once he got old enough to walk. He had an unusual gait in which he would swing out his left leg. This matched the way Kevin had walked, since he had to wear a brace after breaking his leg."[6]

By the time Patrick was four years old, he began referencing Kevin's life. One of the first comments he made was that "he wanted to go to the other house. Patrick talked about it for a while and seemed desperate at times to go there. Lisa asked him why he needed to return...he answered, don't you remember I left you there."

Later, Patrick became excited at the sight of a picture of Kevin. Lisa didn't keep pictures of Kevin displayed in the house, so Patrick had never seen Kevin's image before that moment. With trembling hands, Patrick said, "Here is my picture. I've been looking for that." The boy was definitive. "That's me."[7]

When Stevenson and Tucker left the house and returned to their lab, they wanted "to calculate the likelihood that Patrick's defects matched Kevin's just by coincidence. Not even taking the limp into account, how likely was it that a child would be born with three lesions that match ones on a sibling?"

Stevenson already determined the birthmark odds. He had calculated that "two birthmarks matching wounds on another body by chance were about one and 25,000. He began with the surface area of the skin of the average adult male being 1.6 meters. He then imagined that if this area were square laid on a flat surface it would be approximately 127 centimeters by 127 centimeters. Since he considered a correspondence between a birthmark and a wound to be satisfactory if they were both within an area of 10 square centimeters at the same location, he calculated how many 10 centimeter squares would fit into this body surface area and found that 160 would."[8] So with those calculations taken into account, they determined that the "probability that a single birth-mark would correspond to a wound was therefore 1/160. The probability that two birthmarks would correspond to two wounds was (1/160) squared or 1 in 25,600."

Stevenson acknowledges that critics challenged that figure. He decided to get some help with Patrick's case, so he met with two statisticians. After Stevenson explained the situation to the two medical school statisticians, he finally heard back from one of them who, despite initial interest, declined to report an estimate by saying that "any calculations would oversimplify a complex system. He added, 'Phrases like "highly improbable" and "extremely rare" come to mind as descriptive of the situation.'"[9]

For years, Stevenson had been interested in birth-mark cases as they drew on his interest in the interaction between mind and body that dated back to his earlier days in psychosomatic medicine. Even before he met Patrick, "he published *Reincarnation and Biology*, a 2,000-page work, many years in the making, that covered over two hundred cases of children born with birthmarks or birth defects that matched wounds, usually fatal ones, on the body of a previous person."[10]

The two University of Virginia statisticians' calculation about odds against chance in this case are both right and wrong. The calculations Ian Stevenson did here are correct. The statisticians are also correct because one case, regardless of the calculations of odds against chance, cannot make the case that this proves anything. They did not calculate that three matching wounds and birth-marks add to the odds against chance. If they had, the odds against chance of this happening would be 1 in 160 to the third power, or 1 in 4,096,000.

This still doesn't tell the mathematical story because the math stands alone on one single case. It does not take into account the other 2,500 cases that are self-similar, which are fractal iterations. So it was not the odds against chance that were calculated wrong; it was that the math problem itself had only used one type of math and was incomplete. If we add only one matching wound or instance from the other 2,500 cases, the odds against chance of finding 2,500 cases would be 1 in 4,096,000 to the 250th power. The odds against chance of Stevenson finding Kevin with three lesions and another 2,500 cases would exceed 1 in 1 billion, which is the six-sigma level.

Six sigma is a disciplined, statistical-based, data-driven approach for eliminating defects in a product, process, or service. In science we can never be certain, but we can get close enough using statistical methods. Simply put the six-sigma level is a statistical measurement that means the odds against chance of us being wrong in this instance are a billion to one. It is the science that says this is our level of certainty while still allowing for that one in a billion instance.

But one mathematical proof is not enough. First, this proof must meet the covenant of replicability. The gold standard of science says this has to be replicable. Second, our observations have to be founded in our understanding of physics. We will get there, but for the moment, the math clearly says this is our reality.

The University of Virginia has studied over 2,500 such cases of reincarnation. So how do we calculate the odds against chance, and how compelling are these narratives? Even more importantly, what happens to our calculations when we see the narratives from these children match the narratives of each other?

I believe the numbers should be allowed to speak. The numbers should be allowed to make their case. For the numbers to speak, they have to tell us what the odds-against-chance probability is based on what we are seeing. The way you calculate odds against chance with a coin is to flip it. It will either come up heads or tails, so there is a 50/50 possibility that it will be heads and a 50/50 possibility it will be tails, or a one in two chance. There is a higher probability against heads or tails coming up twice in a row. There is an even higher probability for three times in a row or four times in a row. When we get to 1,000 percent odds against chance, we can be fairly certain that that's our reality.

In the cases of children who remember prior lives, a child of two or three will begin talking about their prior family virtually as soon as they can talk. They will claim, for instance, that the parents who bore them are not their real parents. How much they know cannot be explained by our current scientific metaparadigm, nor can we incorporate this anomaly into our understanding of consciousness.

I need to pause the narrative here to talk about trees, forests, and fractals. Kevin's case examined by Jim Tucker is an iteration of a fractal. Kevin is one of 2,500 cases the University of Virginia has studied. It is like one tree in the forest. A single tree is an iteration, and the forest itself is many fractals or iterations of trees.

Mathematically using fractal geometry, we know that if we cut one large tree down and measure its branching patterns, we can infer from the ratios the number of large trees, medium trees, and small trees in the forest. This is how fractals work whether we're determining coastlines or the architecture of our bodies. Trees, like a head of broccoli, are natural fractals. They are pattern that repeat smaller and smaller copies of themselves to create the biodiversity of the forest.

What makes this significant is that the numbers are crossfooting. The math we use to calculate truth is exposing the structure of the science. Because the odds against chance are so high and contradict our conventional understanding of life, we don't know what to make of this. But when we look at this from the point of view of fractals, we see the iterations in the other disciplines, and our observations begin to have meaning.

Jim Tucker has felled one tree called Kevin, and he is measuring it. If we were scientists and had done this in the forest, we would measure the tree and begin to extrapolate the number of trees and distributions of sizes of trees within that forest, and we would know our results to be accurate. This presupposes that the forest has not been altered by an outside force, such as man, or a natural event, such as a forest fire.

Since a tree is a fractal of the forest and we can count the number of trees in a given area, we can extrapolate the number of trees in the forest by using the branching patters of larger branches to smaller branches.

A fractal is a pattern that the laws of nature repeat at different scales or different orders of magnitude. Trees are natural fractals, patterns that repeat smaller and smaller copies of themselves to create the biodiversity of a forest. The tree itself is an iteration of the forest, so when we measure the branching pattern of a tree, bigger branches to smaller branches to even smaller branches, we are measuring the distribution of the sizes of the trees in the entire forest. The individual tree itself is an iteration of the entire forest.

The tree will do more than just give us measurements that truly and accurately portray the forest; Jim's "tree" Kevin accurately portrays the landscape of consciousness. It produces exceptionally high odds-against-chance numbers, but we dispute them if we don't connect them to anything. In order to properly evaluate the numbers, we need to step back and see the entire forest.

There is one other concept I need to introduce at

this point. We are hunting in this forest. I, the author, and you, my reader, are hunting the truth. But we are hunting ourselves, our consciousness and what happens to it. Zen Buddhism describes it as looking for the bull while riding the bull. You can search forever, but you will never find the bull if you are unaware it is under you. Jim has measured one instance correctly, but for the case to be made that this is our reality, the math must extend across the anecdotal disciplines and match our experiments.

Suzanne Ghanem was able to identify fifteen separate relatives and their relation to her prior incarnation. The odds against chance of this happening are exceptionally high, the equivalent of 15 heads coming up in a row in coin flips. James Leininger, whom we will look at shortly, knew 200 or more things that he shouldn't have been able to know. That's 200 heads coming up in a row on coin flips. The higher the odds against chance, the more probable it is reality, even if it is unaccepted within the structure of our current metaparadigm.

The following story is from a now-defunct website dedicated to Hanan Monsour. That website no longer exists and is redirected here: https://reincarnationresearch. com/. The new website does not include the story that follows, but references to the story and quotes from it can be found elsewhere on the internet. Because the internet is a fluid medium to use for sourcing, I am leaving the link to the original website in the endnote following this story and will let the reader navigate the sourcing from there.

Planning Lifetimes: Hanan Predicts She Will Die & Be Reborn with Memories of her Past Life

Hanan was born in Lebanon in the mid-1930s. When she was twenty, she married Farouk Monsour, a member of a well-to-do Lebanese family. The couple had two daughters, Leila and Galareh. Hanan had a brother, Nabih, who became prominent in Lebanese society but died as a young man in a plane crash.

After having her second daughter, Hanan developed a heart problem, and her doctors advised her not to have any more children. Not heeding the warning, she had a third child, a son, in 1962. In 1963, shortly after the death of her brother Nabih, Hanan's health started to deteriorate. She then started to talk about dying. Farouk, Hanan's husband, said that Hanan told him that "she was going to be reincarnated and have lots to say about her previous life." This was two years before her death.

Before her Death, Hanan Tries to Telephone Leila.

At the age of thirty-six, Hanan traveled to Richmond, Virginia, to have heart surgery. She tried to telephone her daughter Leila before the operation but couldn't get through. Hanan died of complications the day after surgery.

Spirit Communication: An Announcing Dream from the Spirit Realm

Ten days after Hanan died, Suzanne Ghanem was born. Suzanne's mother told Ian Stevenson that shortly before Suzanne's birth, "I dreamed I was going to have a baby girl. I met a woman and I kissed and hugged her. She said, 'I am going to come to you.' The woman was about forty. Later, when I saw Hanan's picture, I thought it looked like the woman in my dream."

Hanan is Reborn as Suzanne Monsour & Tries to Telephone Leila

At 16 months of age, Suzanne pulled the phone off the hook as if she was trying to talk into it and said, over and over, "Hello, Leila?" The family didn't know who Leila was. When she got older, Suzanne explained that Leila was one of her children and that she was not Suzanne, but Hanan. The family asked, "Hanan what?" Suzanne replied, "My head is still small. Wait until it is bigger, and I might tell you."

Past Life Memories: Suzanne Identifies & Names 13 Past Life Family Members

By the time she was two, she had mentioned the

names of her other children, her husband, Farouk, and the names of her parents and her brothers from the previous lifetime—thirteen names in all.

In trying to locate Suzanne's past life family, acquaintances of the Ghanems made inquiries in the town where the Monsours lived. When they heard about the case, the Monsours visited Suzanne. The Monsours were initially skeptical about the girl's claims. They became believers when Suzanne identified all of Hanan's relatives, picking them out and naming them accurately. Suzanne also knew that Hanan had given her jewels to her brother Hercule in Virginia, prior to her heart surgery, and that Hanan instructed her brother to divide the jewelry among her daughters. No one outside of the Monsour family knew about the jewels.

Before she could read or write, Suzanne scribbled a phone number on a piece of paper. Later, when the family went to the Monsour's home, they found that the phone number matched the Monsour's number, except that the last two digits were transposed. As a child, Suzanne could recite the oration spoken at the funeral of Hanan's brother, Nabih. Suzanne's family taped the recitation, though the tape was subsequently lost.

Suzanne Still Loves Farouk, her Past Life Husband

At five years of age, Suzanne would call Farouk

three times a day. When Suzanne visited Farouk, she would sit on his lap and rest her head against his chest. At 25 years of age, Suzanne would still telephone Farouk.

Suzanne Identifies Past Life Friends from Photos

Farouk, a career policeman, has accepted Suzanne as the reincarnation of his deceased wife, Hanan. To support this conclusion, Farouk points out that from photographs, Suzanne accurately picked out scores of people they had been acquainted with and knew other information that only Hanan would have known.

Physical Resemblance from One Lifetime to Another

Suzanne Ghamen has the same facial features as Hanan Monsour, her past life personality. It is significant to note that Ian Stevenson first studied Suzanne in Lebanon when she was only a small child in the late 1960s. He revisited Suzanne in 1998 when he traveled to Lebanon with Tom Schroder, a journalist with the Washington Post who was writing a book on Stevenson. In 1998, Suzanne was now 35 years old and it was only at this point that Stevenson realized that Suzanne had the same facial features as Hanan Monsour. The point is that we are continuing to accumulate new evidence involving cases that have been evolving over decades.

Spirit Being Involvement

Hanan announced her upcoming birth to her future mother in a dream. In addition, Hanan's soul appears to have known that Hanan would die prematurely and be reborn with memories of her past lifetime, as Hanan predicted this turn of events to her husband, Farouk.

Relationships Renewed through Reincarnation

As Suzanne, Hanan was reunited with the Monsours, her past life family, and demonstrated love and affection for Farouk, her past life husband.

Split Incarnation

Suzanne was born only 10 days after Hanan died. If it is assumed that the soul is involved in the development of the fetus, then the soul of Hanan was animating Suzanne's fetus while Hanan was still alive. This overlap of lifetimes occurred for almost the entire duration of Suzanne's gestation.

The author of this story, Ian Stevenson, was a professor of psychiatry at the University of Virginia. He originally wrote this story in a very academic style as his target audience was fellow scientists. On the IISIS website, his past-life cases were presented as reincarnation stories to make his academic work easier to understand. For those interested in appreciating the scientific rigor of his research, such as his use of multiple witnesses to establish corroborated testimony, please refer to the original reports written by Dr. Ian Stevenson.[11]

One cannot count the odds against chance as fifteen to one for Hanan. Look at it from the members of her family who came to accept her. For them to accept her as Hanan, Suzanne had to not just identify them but communicate little known facts about her prior life. The heuristic method that each of those fifteen family members used had to come to a six-sigma level before they could accept Suzanne as the reincarnation of Hanan.

* * *

The following story is from the online *Psi Encyclopedia*.

James Leininger is the subject of a well-known American child reincarnation case. In early childhood, he had frequent nightmares about being trapped in a burning plane that was crashing. In further statements to his parents he said he'd been shot down in a plane near Iwo Jima, had been based on a ship named "Natoma," and had a friend named Jack Larsen. These and other details were found to match closely with the life of James Huston, Jr., an American pilot killed in action in March 1945. James's parents wrote a best-selling book about their investigation, and the case received widespread media attention.

Overview

James Madison Leininger was born on April 10, 1998 in San Francisco, to Bruce Leininger, a human resources executive, and Andrea Leininger, a resume-writer, homemaker and former professional dancer. The family moved shortly thereafter to Dallas, Texas and then to Lafayette, Louisiana. James's expressions of past-life memory manifested mostly between the ages of two and five, following the move to Lafayette. The combination of his detailed memories and the ability of the parents to verify them through painstaking research makes this a particularly interesting case, and it is one of the best-known of its kind in the Western world.

Memories and Behaviors

When James was 22 months old, as reported by the parents, his father took him to the James Cavanaugh Flight Museum in Dallas. There he was transfixed by the sight of the WWII planes, and at the end of the visit had to be forced to leave.

Passing a toy shop when James was just shy of two years, his mother noticed a display bin filled with plastic toys and boats: she pulled out a little propeller plane and handed it to James, adding,

"Look there's even a bomb underneath it." He said, "That's not a bomb, Mummy. That's a *dwop* tank." Talking about this with her husband later she learned that a drop tank is an extra fuel tank fitted to an aircraft to extend its range.[12]

Shortly after turning two, James began having night-mares, as often as five times a week, in which he would scream and kick his legs in the air, crying "Airplane crash! Plane on fire! Little man can't get out!"

At 28 months, in response to questions, he told his parents the little man was himself and that his plane had been shot by the Japanese. About two weeks later, he added more details: his name had been James; he'd flown a Corsair; and he'd flown from a "boat," whose name he gave as "Natoma"—which de-spite sounding Japanese he insisted was American. Over the next three months, James added that he'd had a friend, a fellow pilot named Jack Larsen, and that he'd been shot down near Iwo Jima.[13]

In play, James crashed his toy planes into furni-ture, breaking off the propellers. He also began ex-pressing his memories in art, obsessively drawing naval-aerial battles between Americans and Japanese, in which planes were burning and crashing, bul-lets and bombs exploding all around. These were always WWII scenes, with propeller-driven aircraft, not jets or missiles. He named the American aircraft as Wildcats and Corsairs and referred to Japanese planes as "Zekes" and "Bettys," explaining that the boy's name referred to fighter planes and the girl's name to bombers. This was correct.

He sometimes signed the drawings "James 3," and when asked why, said he was "the third James," possibly a reference to him following James Huston Jr.

When buckling himself into the back of the car he would often mime putting on headgear, a movement that his mother recognized during a visit to a local airshow, when he mounted the cockpit of a Piper Cub and put on the pilot's headgear.[14]

In this case there are over 200 consecutive hits as James not only identified the 80-year-old men he met correctly but also produced a body of information about their alleged common experience. The 80-year-old men he met who he claimed to have served with 60 years before accepted him as the person he claimed to be because he knew at four years old the intimate details of that life. He shared a common memory with them.

A six-minute video can be found on the website www. iasor.org.

* * *

There is one more case that I want to add to this chapter. That is the case of Luke, a white boy, who remembered a previous life as a black woman. He lived in Cincinnati, and as a child he was very concerned about safety. He also began referring to himself as Pam. He used to say, "When I was a girl, I had black hair," or "I had earrings like that when I was a girl." His frustrated mother said to him, "Who is Pam?" He said, "I was." He said, "I died and went to heaven and met God, and he pushed me back down, and I became a baby again, and you named me Luke."

So his mother went ahead and asked him how he had died. He said, "I died in a fire," and he made a motion with this hand as though he were jumping off a building. "Where was this?" she asked. He told her, "Chicago." His mother asked what color Pam's skin was. He told her she was black.

His mother searched the internet and came across the fire at the Paxton Hotel. The Paxton Hotel was located in a predominantly black area of Chicago. In March 1993, a fire raced through the property, trapping most residents on the upper floors, and nineteen people died, including a woman named Pamela Robinson. Pamela died by jumping out of a window.

While working with the documentary show *Ghost Inside My Child* on the Lifetime Movies network, Luke's mom and dad decided to put Luke to the test, and while the cameras were rolling, Luke identified a picture of Pamela Robinson and said, "Here I am. I remember when that picture was taken." A five-minute video about this case can be seen on YouTube.[15]

The reason I am presenting this particular case is because it typifies the sex-change cases in the particular anomaly where children remember prior lives. In a later chapter we will dig deeper into its significance.

As I was writing this book and seeking to make a mathematical case, Dean Radin said this:

Bob,

It's not only difficult to develop a probability for case studies, whether one case or many, but even if a rigorous calculation could be performed that resulted in odds against chance of gazillion to one, that wouldn't persuade skeptics. The assumptions used in the calculation, which are unavoidable, could always be questioned. Meanwhile, believers don't need statistics to be persuaded. So, I'm not convinced that such an effort would be worth it.

The same issue comes up often with synchronicities. Extremely odd coincidences do happen (someone, somewhere, is going to win the lottery even with odds of one hundred million to one), and to the person experiencing the synchronicity, it can seem wildly improbable. But when it comes to any type of uncontrolled, real-time event, it's nearly impossible to know what is and what isn't due to chance. That's why we try to take these phenomena into the lab, where we do know how to discriminate between chance and no chance. So far, we

don't know how to take reincarnation into the lab. So this type of evidence remains nonquantitative.
Best Wishes,
Dean

Jim Tucker from the University of Virginia also shared his thoughts on this:

Hi Bob,
I share Dean's concerns. Though I believe our cases offer compelling evidence for past lives, much of it is really not quantifiable. Even if it were, skeptics still wouldn't believe it, as Dean says.
  Your goals are laudable, and we'll all continue to fight the good fight.
All the best,
Jim

People with entrenched beliefs are not the target audience of cutting-edge science. We have an obligation to inform our descendants what our best scientists think the most likely reality is. That common, most probable reality will force many to do something very uncomfortable: change. So on this scientific precipice, I stand nearly alone and am willing to watch the social and geopolitical dominoes fall.

This speaks directly to the development of artificial intelligence. How do you wish to design AI? If you want the best answers from your artificial intelligence based on facts and logic, then you want this structural paradigm for making those decisions. We can choose that and reverse engineer some of our social-decision making, or we can design an artificial intelligence dysfunctional in making evaluations.

We are harmonizing two different fractals in the same structural standard, our own intelligence and the artificial intelligence that we are developing, each a fractal of the other. If math supports and describes our reality, then a fractal design is scientific and mathematical proof.

To identify the fractals of information movement, let's look at this problem this way. Let's say you believe that when a man dies, his soul is uploaded to heaven. And you take content from your computer and upload it to the cloud. Then you download that information to a new computer. When you download information to a new body, that's called reincarnation. Each is a fractal, and each is an example of information topology.

Our observations from all three anecdotal disciplines indicate that you are downloaded to a new body, and the three disciplines corroborate and duplicate each other's narrative to a six-sigma level.

Detractors say this explanation is not a proof with just two fractals, but in fact, as we make the case for the most probable reality, fractals will emanate outward, perhaps into a holofractal design.

Hedy Lamarr was one of the three names on the patent

for frequency hopping, a way to inform a torpedo of its target using radio waves after it was fired that could not be blocked by radio jamming. That frequency hopping design is apparent in the uncertainty principle. We can only assign a probability about where a particle might be. We don't know where it really is. It could exist in ranges outside the ones we currently understand. In short, we don't have the whole map of frequencies. We are, after all, only seeing the reality we perceive through a sack of water that changes every two years.

The beliefs of the current generation may not be changed, but providing the next generation with the most accurate description of reality we can is a scientific obligation. With it will come funding, and that is an imperative for the military application of what we're discovering with this new science.

It's not the absolute model, but it is the most probable model for what occurs after death. We have billions of people across the globe believing in a model with no apparent foundation. It doesn't matter whether you are Christian, Muslim, Hindu, Jewish, or any other religion; there is no foundation of facts to support those beliefs except the science here, which supports those beliefs.

Titus Rivas, the Dutch psychologist, philosopher, and author of *The Self Does Not Die: Verified Paranormal Phenomena from Near-Death Experiences,* sent me a letter. Titus and I were discussing strengthening the case made here by mathematically connecting two disparate anomalies into one linked database. This is called coherence in data. I appreciated Titus doing a better job with this than I could.

Hi, Bob.
Here is the paper I wrote for you.
There is coherence in data of survival-and-reincarnation research.
"It is very remarkable that these messages from children correspond with messages from persons who had near-death Experiences and were clinically dead."—Joanne Klink

Introduction
Physicalist (pseudo) skeptics—also known as debunkers, proponents of a super-psi explanation of the findings of parapsychological or psychical research into survival after death and reincarnation, as well as agnostics concerning the right explanation of findings—may sometimes stress the apparent divergence of these data. In their view, some results, taken at face value, suggest that we only survive death in an impersonal way and lose our personal identity while merging with a transpersonal consciousness or divine soul. Other data, they claim, would point to the reality of personal survival in a spirit realm and of after-death communication. Finally, the findings of reincarnation

research would suggest that only fragments of someone's mind or personality survive and get attached to a new body. All this is clearly incoherent, and it would demonstrate that there simply is no unequivocal evidence for personal survival or reincarnation and that phenomena in these fields are therefore probably nothing more than an expression of various belief systems that shed no light on our personal fate after physical death.

Now, this is a very misleading presentation of the facts because apart from some relatively minor differences within the data available, there are also important commonalities between these categories of experiences that give us a very good reason to believe they offer a coherent picture of postmortem existence. It may be important to note that some critics seem to be unaware of memories of a discarnate existence before the present life and therefore sincerely believe that data from research into NDEs are inherently incompatible with data from other subfields, such as reincarnation research.

In what follows, I'll give a concise summary of some relevant issues.

Concentrating on evidence with anomalous aspects
Before we proceed, I think it is important to limit ourselves to data occurring in an anomalistic context, i.e., against the background of phenomena

that cannot be explained within mainstream, orthodox physicalist theorizing, according to which all mental phenomena are products of the physical brain. If there is nothing (objectively or intersubjectively) anomalous about experiences, these could—at least in principle—be explained away in orthodox physicalist terms, which would automatically imply that they are not connected to a real, more-than-fictitious afterlife.

The kind of anomalous aspects I have in mind concern informational, psychogenic, and psychological features of experiences that cannot be reconciled with the physicalist production theory about the brain-mind relationship. For instance, extrasensory perception in a near-death experience during cardiac arrest, the psychokinetic production of birthmarks corresponding with specific lethal wounds in cases of children who remember previous lives, and the strong, anomalous identification with a total stranger.

Debunkers typically hold that such paranormal aspects of the evidence simply do not exist and therefore overlook their theoretical importance. So they will probably find the rest of this paper irrelevant. More open-minded readers will understand why it is crucial to focus on types of evidence that contain anomalous aspects.

This has consequences for the status of most

so-called channeled texts, which are not in any way connected to paranormal phenomena (other than the purportedly anomalous channeling itself); they can't be given much weight from a parapsychological point of view. It is remarkable if the contents of specific channeling texts (with no paranormal aspects) converge with other data, but there is really nothing more to it than that. In this sense, doctrines in channeled treatises are about as relevant for survival-and-reincarnation research as passages in the Bible or any other holy book.

Convergent findings from case studies
Parapsychology in the original sense of psychical research uses several different methods, two of which are important here, namely naturalistic case studies and experimental or semiexperimental studies.

Case studies concern phenomena such as memories of an intermediate state between two incarnations among children who recall a past life, near-death experiences, spontaneous memories of a spiritual preexistence outside the context of reincarnation memories, and apparitions of the dead.

Several authors such as Ian Stevenson (1987), Joanne Klink (1994), Neil and Elizabeth Carman (2013), Kirti Swaroop Rawat, and the present author (Rawat & Rivas, 2005; Rivas et al., 2015, 2016) have repeatedly pointed at the remarkable commonalities between individual cases of near-death experiences, intermission memories, and prebirth memories. These commonalities suggest that memories of an intermediate state between lives constitute a continuation of near-death experiences, and in their final phase, also match prebirth memories without memories of a previous life.

This makes it important to concentrate on the phenomenology of intermission memories as has been done by, among others, Poonam Sharma and Jim Tucker (Sharma & Tucker, 2004), James G. Matlock and Iris Giesler-Petersen (Matlock & Giesler-Petersen, 2016), Ohkado Masayuki (Ohkado & Ikegawa, 2014; Ohkado, 2015), and Dieter Hassler (2015).

As we can read in an overview written by James Matlock (2017) for the online *Psi Encyclopedia*, we may distinguish five stages of the intermission experience. The first is a transitional stage following death, generally lasting until the body is buried, cremated, or disposed of in some fashion. The second is more stable and often passes in a fixed location. The third involves choosing parents for the new life. Drawing on surveys of prebirth as well as past-life memories in Japan, Masayuki Ohkado identified a fourth stage, life in the womb, and a fifth stage, birth and its immediate aftermath.

Only the first three stages are part of a model originally presented by Sharma and Tucker (2004) because these concern stages of discarnate existence between death and reincarnation. However, the additional two stages identified by Okhado form a bridge between intermission memories in the strict sense and very early memories of the present life, reaching far beyond normal childhood memories.

Sharma and Tucker point out that intermission memories indicate unusually strong memory because subjects "not only claim to have memories of the intermission between the deaths of the previous personality and their own births, but they also demonstrate more ability to recall a variety of memories from the past life." This means that the absence of intermission memories does not imply an absence of intermission experiences, just like the absence of an NDE does not imply that a patient has not undergone any near-death experience.

In more than one stage, veridical perception of events on earth of the kind that we find in near-death experiences (Rivas, Dirven, & Smit, 2016; Rivas, et al., 2016) may occur.

Other examples of convergence concern the out-of-body experience during the first stage of the intermission experience and an interest in observing the condition of the physical body or responses of relatives or friends to the subject's clinical or irreversible death.

The first stage often ends when the subject is directed by an "elder or an old man dressed in white" to a place where he or she then stays for the bulk of the intermission experience. Similar experiences are also a well-known feature of many NDEs. Though relatively rare, there are intermission memories that include other typical elements of NDEs, such as seeing a transcendent light, as in the well-known case of Shanti Devi (Riawat & Rivas, 2005), and passing through a tunnel.

Concerning the second stage, which may once again involve further veridical perceptions of earthly reality, subjects may also recall having dwelled at physical locations such as a tree, a pagoda, or somewhere near the place of death, and of having seen discarnate entities or interacted with them.

Such features are also well-known from reports about NDEs.

During the third stage, subjects report having had veridical perceptions of the future parents of the next incarnation. Election of these parents may be based on free choice or assisted by spiritual beings. This may be compared to some NDEs in which the patient is shown various outcomes of choices to be made, including that of returning to the physical body or staying in the discarnate realm.

Contact with other discarnate entities

Both intermission and prebirth memories and near-death experiences may include perceptions of unknown deceased people who are identified later on, for instance through photographs.

Furthermore, intermission memories may also involve contacts with the living through dreams or apparitions that are later confirmed by the people in question.

We may say that data from NDEs, preexistence memories, and various other types of case studies—for example from studies into spontaneous after-death communications (ADCs), hauntings, and drop-in communicators during spiritualistic seances—all point in the same direction (Gauld, 1983), namely that communication with discarnate entities is a real phenomenon and not just the projection of subconscious processes.

Other types of cases

There are other fields of spontaneous case studies that also lend themselves to a systematic comparison. For instance, case studies of deathbed visions (Osis, 1961; Haraldsson & Osis, 2012), terminal lucidity (Nahm, 2012), and shared death experiences

(Moody & Perry, 2010). The first two categories directly relate to near-death experiences and the first stage of intermission memories, and they may involve paranormal aspects such as the veridical perception of a deceased personality previously unknown to the patient, of a deceased loved one not known to have died, or—in shared death experiences—of episodes of the dying person's life.

The third category, that of anomalous terminal lucidity, generally confirms the ultimate existential independence of the mind or soul upon the brain, in accordance with cases of consciousness during cardiac arrest, that is not supported by cortical activity.

Experimental studies

Quite recently, Dieter Hassler (2015) convincingly showed that induced regression to past lives may sometimes contain veridical information. This demonstrates that not all instances of regression can be reduced to fantasy.

However, this does not imply that data from regression to an intermediate state need to be just as valuable as spontaneous cases of intermission memories. The main example concerns the work of hypnotherapist Michael Newton (1996), who has claimed to have discovered many things about the afterlife that are not backed up by spontaneous intermission memories or by NDEs. A few examples include so-called healing showers, staging areas, waiting rooms with soul cluster groups, and tribunals before which spirits evaluate how well they met the goals they set for their last human lives and formulate plans for their next. The five-stage structure of the intermission experience mentioned above is absent from Newton's accounts of the afterlife.

Some of the differences between Newton's findings and spontaneous cases may be explained as being the result of a process of partial amnesia in children who remember an intermission period, but some other aspects of his data seem incompatible with such cases, and other hypnotherapists turn out to have collected divergent findings. James Matlock (2017) follows the late Ian Stevenson's line of reasoning when he explains the divergence between case studies and experimental studies such as Newton's through the hypnotic state of suggestibility, which makes the subject susceptible to the hypnotherapist's explicit or implicit suggestions.

Similar things can be said about experimental studies into communications with the dead aimed at acquiring information about the afterlife. Mediums may be under the influence of one or more spiritualist or esoteric doctrines, and this may greatly affect so-called channeled communications. Only if such communications match data from intermission memories and near-death experiences do we have any reason to take them seriously, and it makes little sense to base one's model of the afterlife directly on channeling.

The fields of survival and reincarnation research need to focus on spontaneous case studies rather than experimental studies (Rivas et al., 2016) to avoid undesirable and unnecessary noise. This may seem counterintuitive because of the traditional one-sided "scientistic" focus on experimentation, but so be it.

Real divergence?

It has been suggested that the afterlife is real but uniquely personal so that we should not expect any general features within our research findings. As we have seen, this is not in accordance with the available data.

Nevertheless, Matlock and Giesler-Petersen (2016) did find several differences between intermission memories from various Asian and Western cultures. For example, in Asian cultures the afterlife often seems to be experienced in a terrestrial environment rather than in a separate spiritual dimension, which is common for Western cases. Also, interpretations of otherworldly nonhuman entities are interpreted differently. Asians perceive them to be the King of Death, minor deities, and devas, whereas Westerners thought they saw God, Jesus, and angels.

Such cultural differences are also known from NDEs, and they do not invalidate the hypothesis that both NDEs and intermission periods refer to a real discarnate existence. They do demonstrate, though, that cultural expectations may play an important role in the specific ways the afterlife is experienced. Matlock and Giesler-Petersen put it this way:

> The cultural belief might somehow potentiate the actual experience of hanging around, and/or it might potentiate the memory of hanging around even if the actuality is equal in the Asia and the West. Maybe experiencers in the West don't do it as much because of the expectation to "move on," or maybe they do it as much but don't focus on it and, therefore, don't remember it as much—because it's not as salient/important an aspect of afterlife to them as "moving on" is. Conversely, people who believe in reincarnation may expect, and therefore enact and/or pay more attention to terrestrial inter life aspects, beginning with disengagement from the physical body and one's previous lifetime. [...] Asians expect to reincarnate,

so they more frequently enact and/or recall material/terrestrial aspects of the inter life, beginning with the disengagement process from the previous body/lifetime; Westerners expect to go to heaven, so they more frequently enact and/or recall trans-material/heavenly aspects including spiritual, especially God-related, entities.

In other words, apart from universal stages in discarnate experiences, the person's personal expectations also play an important role in the specific manifestation of the afterlife. In fact, this power of the person's own mind has been stressed by various traditions such as spiritualism and Tibetan Mahayana Buddhism.

Ontological considerations

Any empirical theory is embedded more or less explicitly in a philosophical, ontological theory (Rivas, 2005). As I have said elsewhere before, the data from studies into cases of reincarnation and intermission memories can be accommodated within several ontological frameworks. For instance, the Advaita Vedanta ontology states that each earthly personality is in essence a manifestation of a divine universal soul. An individual manifestation of God may continue its existence in a new earthly incarnation, which would also explain memories of an individual discarnate existence between two lives. Buddhism rejects the existence of a personal soul, both during physical life and after death, and it also rejects the notion of personal reincarnation. Personalist substantialists (both with a dualist and an idealist background) such as myself state that there is an irreducible personal experient or self that persists as an ontological substance during physical life and also after death and a possible reincarnation. For us, the so-called fragmented nature of past-life and intermission memories in young children does not imply our souls or personal identities have become fragmented but simply that the full expression or accessibility of our stored memories is somehow limited, presumably mainly through the interaction with the child's brain.

It depends on the general analytical tenability of any ontological theory whether a specific interpretation of data may be correct or not. This is something that needs to be determined at an ontological level as it cannot be established through empirical research itself.

Summing up, there is every reason to believe in the coherence of survival and reincarnation data (Nahm & Hassler, 2015; Rivas et al., 2016; Matlock & Giesler-Petersen; Tucker, 2015, 2013; Stevenson,

1987). All data point to the reality of a discarnate existence and reincarnation and to the role of the mind in the specific manifestation of the afterlife. What exactly it is that survives and may reincarnate remains a philosophical, ontological issue.[16]

Your friend,
Titus Rivas
Athanasia Foundation

The odds-against-chance calculations for these events lining up are six sigma, meaning the probability calculations point to certainty. But the emergence of a fractal pattern begins to bring mathematical proof. When this data is conjoined with quantum mechanics and the enfolded dimensions, it is hard to argue against there being cognitive intelligence in other dimensions. We are quantum beings sequestered in three spatial dimensions and one temporal dimension.

Notes

[1] Jim Tucker, *Return to Life,* p. 3.
[2] Jim Tucker, *Return to Life,* p. 3.
[3] Jim Tucker, *Return to Life,* p. 4.
[4] Jim Tucker, *Return to Life,* p. 5.
[5] Jim Tucker, *Return to Life,* p. 6.
[6] Jim Tucker, *Return to Life,* p. 6.

[7]   Jim Tucker, *Return to Life,* p. 7.

[8]   Jim Tucker, *Return to Life,* p. 10-11.

[9]   Jim Tucker, *Return to Life,* p. 10-11.

[10] Jim Tucker, *Return to Life,* p. 10-11.

[11] http://www.iisis.net/index.php%3Fpage%3Dsemkiwian-stevenson-monsour-reincarnation-past-lives.

[12] Karen Wehrstein, "James Leininger," *Psi Encyclopedia,* The Society for Psychical Research, 2017, https://psi-encyclopedia.spr.ac.uk/articles/james-leininger.

[13] Karen Wehrstein, "James Leininger," *Psi Encyclopedia,* The Society for Psychical Research, 2017, https://psi-encyclopedia.spr.ac.uk/articles/james-leininger.

[14] Karen Wehrstein, "James Leininger," *Psi Encyclopedia,* The Society for Psychical Research, 2017, https://psi-encyclopedia.spr.ac.uk/articles/james-leininger.

[15] https://www.youtube.com/watch?v=0JqhuL6NaCo.

[16] E. M. Carman, and N. J. Carman, *Cosmic Cradle: Spiritual Dimensions of Life before Birth* (Berkeley, CA: North Atlantic Books, 2013); A. Gauld, *Mediumship and Survival: A Century of Investigations* (David & Charles, 1983); B. Greyson and I. Stevenson, "The Phenomenology of Near-Death Experiences," *American Journal of Psychiatry* (1980), p. 137, 1193-6; D. Hassler, *Indizienbewese für ein Leben nach dem Tod und die Wiedergeburt: Band 2b: Geh zurück in eine Zeit: Zurückführungen in "frühere Leben" und deren Nachprüfung* (Shaker Media: 2015); J. M. Holden, "Veridical Perception in Near-Death Experiences," (2009); J. M. Holden, B. Grey-

son, and D. James, eds., *The Handbook of Near-Death Experiences* (Westport, CT), p. 185-212; E. Haraldsson, and J. G. Matlock, *I Saw a Light and Came Here: Children's Experiences of Reincarnation* (White Crow Books, 2017); E. Haraldsson, and K. Osis, *At the Hour of Death* (White Crow Books, 2017); J. Klink, *Vroeger toen ik groot was: vèrgaande herinneringen van kinderen* (Baarn: Ten Have, 1994); P. van Lommel, R. van Wees, V. Meyers, and I. Elfferich, "Near-Death Experience in Survivors of Cardiac Arrest: A prospective study in the Netherlands," *The Lancet* (2001) p. 358, 9298, 2039-2044; J. G. Matlock, "Intermission Memories." *Psi Encyclopedia,* 2017, https://psi-encyclopedia.spr.ac.uk/articles/intermission-memories; J. G. Matlock and I. Giesler-Petersen, "Asian Versus Western Intermission Memories: Universal Features and Cultural Variations." *Journal of Near-Death Studies* 35 (Autumn 2016), 3-29; R. Moody and P. Perry, *Glimpses of Eternity: Sharing a Loved One's Passage from This Life to the Next* (New York: Guideposts, 2010); M. Nahm and D. Hassler, "Thoughts about Thought Bundles: A commentary on Jürgen Keil's paper 'Questions of the Reincarnation Type,'" *Journal of Scientific Exploration* 25, no. 2 (2011), 305–326; M. Nahm, *Wenn die Dunkelheit ein Ende findet. Terminale Geistesklarheit und andere Phänomene in Todesnähe* (Amerang: Crotona, 2012); M. Newton, *Journey of Souls: Case Studies of Life Between Lives* (Woodbury, MN: Llewellyn, 1996), p. 5; M. Newton, *Destiny of Souls: More Case Stud-*

ies of Life Between Lives (Woodbury, MN: Llewellyn, 2000); M. Ohkado, "Children's Birth, Womb, Prelife, and Past-Life Memories: Results of an Internet-Based Survey" *Journal of Prenatal and Perinatal Psychology and Health* 30, no. 1, (2015), 3-16; M. Ohkado and A. Ikegawa, "Children with Life-Between-Life Memories," *Journal of Scientific Exploration* 28 (2014), 477–490; K. Osis, *Deathbed Observations by Physicians and Nurses* (New York: Parapsychology Foundation, 1961); K. S. Rawat and T. Rivas, "The Life Beyond: Through the Eyes of Children Who Claim to Remember Previous Lives," *The Journal of Religion and Psychical Research* 28, no. 3 (2005), 126-136; K. S. Rawat and T. Rivas, *Reincarnation: The Scientific Evidence is Building* (Vancouver, BC: Writers, 2017); T. Rivas, "Amnesia: The Universality of Reincarnation and the Preservation of Psychological Structure," 1999, http://txtxs.nl/artikel.asp?artid=618; T. Rivas, "The Survivalist Interpretation of Recent Studies Into the Near-Death Experience," *Journal of Religion and Psychical Research* 26, no. 1 (2003), 27-31; T. Rivas, "Rebirth and Personal Identity: Is Reincarnation an Intrinsically Impersonal Concept?" *Journal of Religion and Psychical Research* 28, no. 4 (2005), 226-233; T. Rivas, E. M. Carman, N. J. Carman, and A. Dirven, "Paranormal Aspects of Preexistence Memories in Young Children," *Journal of Near-Death Studies* 34, no. 2 (2015), 84-107; T. Rivas, A. Dirven, A., and R. H. Smit, *The Self Does Not Die: Veri-*

fied Paranormal Phenomena from Near-Death Experiences (Durham: IANDS, 2016); P. Sharma and J. B. Tucker, "Cases of the Reincarnation Type with Memories from the Intermission between Lives," *Journal of Near-Death Studies* 23 (2004), 101-118; I. Stevenson, *Children who Remember Previous Lives* (Charlottesville: University Press of Virginia, 1987); J. B. Tucker, *Life Before Life: A Scientific Investigation of Children's Memories of a Previous Life* (New York: St. Martin's Press, 2005); J. B. Tucker, *Return to Life: Extraordinary Cases of Children who Remember Past Lives* (New York: St. Martin's Press, 2013); C. Wills-Brandon, *One Last Hug Before I Go* (Deerfield Beach: Health Communications, 2000).

Chapter 5

The Anomaly of Past-Life Regression

Past-life regression (PLR) is a technique that uses hypnosis to recover what practitioners believe are memories of past lives or incarnations and what others regard as fantasies or delusions or a type of confabulation. This definition is within the context of the grand material metaparadigm. If we redefine past-life regression within the emerging grand unified metaparadigm, we can define it as a hypnotic method of accessing wave-form memory using the human psi abilities each of us possess. Long regarded as unreliable information, it is taking its place among clairvoyance and remote viewing. Electrical consciousness is now proven to be able to leave the body.

We need to stop for a moment and talk about definitions. There will often be two definitions for each concept because each is viewed differently by each metaparadigm.

For instance, lesbian, gay, bisexual, and transgender (LGBT) sexuality needs to be redefined within the context of the emerging grand unified metaparadigm. If we do that, we see that sexual expression is a spectrum, not a binary system, and we see people in transition all around us and in the afterlife. Going forward, anyone's sexuality should be as normal as anyone else's sexuality, and it can change during that person's lifetime.

The best way to describe how the afterlife is viewed today by the general public is the following analogy: There is an Indian parable about six blind travelers who encounter an elephant. The six blind travelers hear the strange animal, and not knowing the animal's shape or size, each touch different parts of the elephant. The first says it is like a snake because he feels the tail. The next feels the ear and says it is some type of fan. Another says it's a tree because he feels a leg. The blind man who feels the broad side of the elephant says it is a wall. The next says it is a hose because he feels the trunk. The one who feels the tusk describes the object as a spear. Individual's perceptions of reality are all different and incomplete. The same can be said of all individual religions.

To have an aggregate story by all experiencers, we need to have a common description of what occurs not just to people who go through past-life regression but also to people who have NDEs and children who remember prior lives. This has been accomplished by Michael Newton and Brian Weiss, who have published multiple books on the topic, but nowhere has there been an odds-against-chance calculation for the common descriptions from all three categories. There are hundreds of millions of people in the three categories. But this is not proof.

One of my editors, who is not a scientist, wrote the following:

This is unconvincing. There are millions of people who claim to have had a "born again" experience and that Jesus is real. Ditto with other religions. There are hundreds of thousands, if not millions, of people who claim to have encountered aliens or who have seen Bigfoot. The stories are all similar. There are other explanations—besides that it is true—to explain millions of people claiming a similar experience.

This intelligent man conflates claims with corroboration. That makes this criticism invalid. When a child claims to have remembered a prior life in the University of Virginia (UVA) studies, people accept that child for who they claim to be regardless of their belief system because the child corroborated their understanding of the past by knowing things that could only be known by people who were there. There is a proof to the model we are advancing here. We are cross-checking and mathematically crossfooting all categories to arrive at a model of our reality, a new model of the matrix of consciousness. We are separating the wheat from the chaff, something the aforementioned editor failed to see.

When science encounters an anomaly, it documents its observations rigorously as in the story of Canadian-American actor Glenn Ford.

When Ford was approached about a movie about Dutch psychic Peter Hurkos, he decided he should first study the topic. So the fifty-four-year-old actor witnessed some demonstrations by Hurkos and interviewed experts, and in December 1975 he underwent three past-life hypnosis sessions during which he described what appeared to be five previous lives he had led. Dr. Maurice Benjamin conducted the experiment before witnesses with a tape recorder running. The hypnotized actor was regressed back to childhood and beyond, and he described what were presumed to be memories of past lives.

In the earliest experience, Ford described himself as a bachelor music teacher named Charles Stewart of Elgin, Scotland, who had died in 1892. Stewart had loved horses but had hated his job teaching music to young schoolgirls.

While being questioned about his life as Stewart, Ford agreed to demonstrate his musical skills and played passages from Beethoven, Mozart, and Bach. Ford later listened to the tapes of the interview with interested skepticism. He shared Stewart's love of horses and had, since his early years, been considered a natural with the animals. On the other hand, he could not play the piano. His own theory was that perhaps Stewart's antipathy to music and love for horses had carried over to him.

A second regression attempt was more difficult but ultimately successful. This time, the hypnotized actor brought out a French-speaking member of the elite horse cavalry of the 1670s. Ford didn't speak French.

The officer indicated he had lived in the time of King Louis XIV. The officer, Launvaux, hated aristocrats. An aristocrat had accused him of an adulterous affair with his wife, then hired a skilled swordsman to challenge the outmatched thirty-four-year-old Launvaux.

Launvaux provided some accurate descriptions, including descriptions of the scheme used to ensure his death, the fact that the palace at Versailles was then referred to as the Chateau, and the fact that the stables were on the left as one approached the palace.

Ford was then regressed to other previous lives, including that of a young Christian martyr killed by lions in the Colosseum in third-century Rome and a seventeenth-century Royal Navy sailor who had died of the Great Plague.

In his most recent lifetime, Ford had been a young cowboy herding cattle out west. Although he starred in 106 movies and several TV series ranging from comedies to police dramas to war stories, he was most prolifically, if not most notably, cast in Westerns.

There are millions of cases like his.

Two of the most noted practitioners of past-life regression in the United States are Brian Weiss and Michael Newton.

Weiss has been on Oprah Winfrey's show many times and has published several books about his subjects and what he's learned from them. Because of his research, he is completely convinced that past-life regression reveals the prior lives of his subjects. The overriding question, of course, is whether he is really uncovering accurate information or whether he is falling victim to false results.

He is a psychiatrist practicing in Miami, a graduate of the Yale School of Medicine, and presently chairman emeritus of psychiatry at the Mount Sinai Medical Center in Miami. Dr. Weiss maintains a private practice and conducts international seminars and experimental workshops as well as training programs for professionals. He is the author of the past-life-oriented books *Through Time into Healing* and *Same Soul, Many Bodies.* You can visit his website at www.brianweiss.com.

Dr. Weiss's book *Many Lives, Many Masters* is different from sources I've cited because instead of giving you case study after case study, as Tucker did at the University of Virginia, or presenting a typical experience, as Dr. Moody did, Dr. Weiss's book examines one subject—a woman—and her journey through past-life regressions for which he was her guide. Instead of multiple subjects with just one paranormal experience each, we get to see one subject examining a multitude of lives that she didn't know existed. Her name is Catherine, and through the excerpts that follow, you can see her discoveries of her past and Dr. Weiss's discoveries of the process.

In this chapter, I want to skip through Weiss's *Many Lives, Many Masters* like a stone thrown across the water. I want you to hear what he heard rather than summarize it for you.

The seminal moment in Dr. Weiss's psychiatric treatment of Catherine came when he regressed her into her childhood. She had a phobia that Dr. Weiss believed he could solve by hypnotically taking her back to her childhood and confronting the event that occasioned the phobia, but for the longest time, her symptoms showed no improvement. Weiss was unable to find an event in Catherine's life that he could link to her phobia. Under the most unexpected of circumstances, however, he finally had a breakthrough.

> Slowly, I took Catherine back to the age of two, but she recalled no significant memories. I instructed her firmly and clearly: "Go back to the time from which your symptoms arise." I was totally unprepared for what came next.[1]

His phrase "Go back to the time from which your symptoms arise" inadvertently took Catherine back to one of her previous lives. It was through this door that Weiss would, over many coming sessions, regress Catherine to her prior lives. She had memories of historical events, was able to speak languages that she didn't know she could speak, and possessed talents in other lives she never demonstrated in her current life. When he said to her, "Go back to the time from which your symptoms arise," she answered, "I see white steps leading up to a building, a big white building with pillars, open in front. There are no doorways. I'm wearing a long dress...a sack made of rough material. My hair is braided, long blond hair."[2]

Note another thing: just like the similarities in the stories involving the children who had prior-life experiences or the people who had near-death experiences, there is a remarkable similarity in the way people describe the afterlife. Don't overlook the similarity between the stories that Patrick told the researchers at the University of Virginia and what the masters told Weiss through Catherine.

When Catherine was hypnotized and Weiss was questioning her, sometimes the answers Catherine gave were from herself and sometimes others would speak through her. There is a structure to the afterlife, and it is run in an organized way by intelligent beings. They help souls like us develop from life to life. Weiss dubbed these beings the masters. While Catherine could answer questions about herself and her lives, it was the masters who provided Weiss context and content.

Here is the master talking to Weiss through Catherine: "There are seven planes...seven through which we must pass before we are returned."[3]

We don't know what mechanisms cause people to remember past lives when they go through past-life regression, but it is a common human experience, and the stories about life between lives are too consistent to be fabricated by so many people who don't know each other.

Ford described his trip into the past as a journey on a

night train through fog, where previous lives were like lit-up stations appearing in a flash as he passed quickly by. He believed that the particular station at which he had arrived had been darkened for some reason. His view was similar to a signal moving down a dendrite with access to some nuclei and not to others. There is a fractal design in the description.

So what are the odds against chance that all these stories accurately reveal a landscape of what occurs to us after death? In Ford's case, we have a heavily documented narrative recorded at UCLA where Ford could speak French and help locate the gravestone for his prior life. The historical records show that the individual had been a piano teacher as Ford described. We have to look at the odds against chance that Ford was accurate in his description of Scotland, was able to play the piano, was able to speak not just French but a guttural French of the period. Then we have to connect his case to all the other cases.

We quickly reach a six-sigma level odds-against-chance calculation. We know a physicist would say this is not quantitative proof and that a mathematician would say that the odds against chance were exceptionally high, but a bookmaker—which way would he bet? And while this is an anomaly, it and the others are within the grand material metaparadigm and the grand unified metaparadigm, and they're explained and part of the structure.

If we calculate the odds against chance between disciplines, it would be equivalent to 10,000 coin tosses in a row landing on heads. What are the odds that any other version of life after death you can come up with is more valid than this version?

Awareness after death is a form of wave consciousness rather than particulate consciousness. In a body you have a particulate consciousness, but particles are neither particles or waves, they are both at the same time. They are wavicles. These narratives collectively describe the experience of awareness without a body. Just like the fractal of the particle being a wave.

To the religious this proves your version of an afterlife with hard science. This wavicle is what you the reader is made of; it is the very stuff that you and everything is made of. This matrix of consciousness which you are a part exists in more dimensions than our 3 spatial dimensions reality. Your religion is there as is everyone else's, and the rules like celibacy for priests and apostasy and blasphemy are no longer relevant. That 4th spatial enfolded dimension is a place to be traversed and we can't get to it of religions don't understand that this is proof of their belief, but proof of everyone's belief.

Let us say Ford experienced the moment as wave-state perception. We could theorize that the psi condition is wave state, supporting Ford's experiences. That would statistically put the structure of what we already see (psi) at a six-sigma level under the Ford observations. Now instead of having an anecdotal event, Ford's regressions, we have a scientific structure to understand what we are seeing and what Ford was experiencing. We have already used this psi ability in remote viewing, but it needs to be revisited from a different perspective. We need to apply it to the anomalies we have been discussing. Imagine trying to compare radar technology from 1940 with information satellites today. We need to update our understanding of these anomalies in a way science can explain.

This is a new way to view consciousness that incorporates all the prior anomalies into a cohesive structure and aligns with microphysics. This is the grand unified metaparadigm. Ford, Catherine, children who remember prior lives, Hanan Monsour, and Charles Leininger all were able to access the same field of information.

There are, in this model, more than five senses.

* * *

What happens when you are dead? What is the aggregate story of people who either remember a prior life, had an NDE, or have been regressed? What story do they tell about the process of dying and being reborn? Interestingly, they produce a common narrative.

American hypnotherapist and author Dr. Michael Newton goes into the afterlife, or the between life, in more detail than anyone else. What he describes is consistent with other anecdotes. It is consistent with the University of Virginia case studies and the descriptions from people who had near-death experiences. It should be noted, however, that people who have near-death experiences only go a limited distance into the afterlife. But as far as they go, their reports are consistent with his.

The first thing he describes in his book *Journey of Souls* is how he encountered the research track he's currently involved with. What amazed him was the consistency of the reports he was getting from subject to subject. And his results are the same as those produced by the studies at the University of Virginia. The gold standard in science is replicability from experiment to experiment, and while these are not experiments but studies (because they don't produce an explanation of the effect), we are quantifying this effect that manifests itself in NDEs, children who remember prior lives, and past-life regression throughout a variety of different conditions that cut across all religions. Whether people believe in God, Buddha, Jesus, or no one at all, they can describe the same experiences when talking about the soul and reincarnation. Religion, it seems, has a common denominator.

According to Newton, a soul begins its journey from one life to another with death in this life, or a departure. Newton's subjects report a tunnel, as do Moody's. They move toward a white light.

Homecoming is the next step. Newton reports that his subjects meet deceased relatives, as do those who have near-death experiences. A similar experience is also reported by Weiss. The arriving soul is met by a guide.

Orientation is a period of adjustment from a corporeal form to a spiritual one. Newton makes the point that no subterfuge or deception exists in a telepathic world. Souls are not judged but rather evaluated. At times, Newton talks directly to the returning soul's guide through the person whom he has regressed. Weiss reports the same phenomenon.

"Transition" is the term used by both Weiss and Newton to describe what was reported to them. Each soul has a home with a group of other souls. It is interesting that Newton notes the commonality of word usage by different clients to describe spiritual phenomena after they return. They go before soul councils that evaluate a prior life rather than judge it. In many instances, soul groups are described as classes or school grades.

"Placement" is the term Newton uses to describe the soul's level. According to him, there are six levels of souls that indicate advancement, whether you are in the sixth grade or twelfth grade, for instance. Each soul has a guide, and the soul's future life selection is based on what that soul needs to develop. There are levels of guides as well, junior guides and senior guides who are graded on how well they help their charges.

Life selection describes the time when the soul must once again leave the sanctuary of the spirit world for another trip to earth.

Choosing a new body is about choosing not just the soul's new gender but also the health and condition of the body the soul will occupy. Though we may consider it strange to select a body that is frail or has some physical handicap, it is done to advance the individual soul's learning in the next life. However, gender is a choice. This is consistent with what is reported by other researchers and other sources.

Preparation for embarkation involves connecting with the group of souls you will be incarnating with. Finding soul mates can be complicated. There are relationships based on deep, abiding love, but there are also relationships based upon companionship, friendship, and mutual respect.

Rebirth—we all know what that is.

Since Weiss and Newton worked independently, it seems unlikely that each subject would describe the life between lives in the same way, yet this is exactly what happened. If I tried to cite all of these cases, my book would never get past all the common stories.

I am not asking you to believe any of this. I am writing a book on science, on evidence. I want to emphasize that this is a common human response from subjects undergoing past-life regression.

I now want to direct you to the similarities between Weiss's results in regressing Catherine and Newton's results. Catherine cited the same levels of development, the same method of choosing how to return, and the same repeated learning and growing process.

These narratives are our observations; what people tell us may or may not be true. While the odds against chance that so many say the same thing are overwhelming and the model has a fractal architecture, can it stand up to real science, experiments, proofs, and replicability—the gold standard of scientific reality?

We are not seeing Jesus, Mohammed, or Vishnu. But we are measuring what they promise: a life after death.

Notes

1   Dr. Brian L. Weiss, *Many Lives, Many Masters* p. 27 (Simon and Schuster 1988).

2   Dr. Brian L. Weiss, *Many Lives, Many Masters* p. 27 (Simon and Schuster 1988).

3   Dr. Brian L. Weiss, *Many Lives, Many Masters* p. 172 (Simon and Schuster 1988).

Chapter 6

Nonlocal Consciousness Was an Anomaly

Psi is the first letter in the Greek word *psyche*, which means *soul* or *mind*. British scientist Rob Thouless coined the expression *psi research*. Different varieties of psi exist, such as mind-to-mind communication (telepathy), predicting future events (precognition), affecting matter with your mind (psychokinesis), and seeing distant objects and events (clairvoyance). Psi falls into two categories: observation (clairvoyance and precognition) and affecting objects (psychokinesis).

While some scientists are at the forefront of producing supportive research and theory, others have devoted much of their careers to criticizing their work. Truth is cumulative, and the scientists responded. The research got tighter and better until the evidence became undeniable. We still don't understand how psi works or why it's stronger in some cases than in others. So how did we get here?

* * *

Professor Joseph Banks Rhine worked at Duke University from the late 1920s to 1965 and developed the forced-choice-of-cards technique. It uses a special deck of twenty-five cards consisting of five symbols (squares, circles, wavy lines, stars, and triangles) on five cards each. A person acting as the sender shuffles the cards, selects the top card, and tries to send that symbol mentally to a remote person, the receiver.[1]

The experiment is judged a success or failure based on the number of hits and how far that total deviates from chance. Here, random chance is one in five that the remote person, the receiver, will be right, so there should be an average of five correct hits in a twenty-five-card deck, right? Not exactly. During Rhine's tests there were always more than five correct hits. We should expect some results with less than five, but that never happened. Something was positively influencing the results.

Rhine's tests have been tried thousands of times, and the results have consistently supported the existence of psi. So that's that, right? Psi exists, so let's change the metaparadigm.

Unfortunately, despite these individual studies, the results can be doubted under a variety of scientific criticisms. There could be selective reporting, design flaws in the experiments, or even what is called *sensory leakage* (hints given subconsciously by the scientist to nudge the subject to the right answers). One advantage of this skepticism, however, is that it "refined the methods used in future experiments."[2] So the experiments continued to meet higher and higher standards.

This scientific fight to establish psi is not new. From 1880 to 1940, similar extrasensory perception (ESP) card experiments provided increasingly persuasive evidence for psi. But it eventually became evident that the results could be attributed to clairvoyance rather than telepathy, which meant that a sender was not needed. The experiment, therefore, needed a drastic retooling.[3]

An experiment conducted from 1966 to 1972 at Maimonides Medical Center in Brooklyn asked for a sender to transmit mental images to a sleeping person in the middle of a dream. The theory was that this sender could implant these images and that "the dreamer will sometimes incorporate those images into the dream."[4] That's a fairly drastic redesign of the experiment, isn't it? But wait, there's more.

In the mid-1970s, researchers designed a telepathy experiment using a sensory deprivation technique called *ganzfeld*, a German word meaning *whole field*. The idea was to limit the amount of sensory input in the subject in order to eliminate noise, "thereby improving the likelihood of perceiving faint perceptions that are normally overwhelmed by ordinary sensory input."[5] The results had a significantly higher hit rate than chance. This experiment was performed in ten different laboratories, and the results were very compelling.

We now know that "we are fully justified in having a very high confidence that people sometimes get small amounts of specific information from a distance without the use of ordinary senses."[6]

If we have a high degree of confidence that we can receive information, could we then send information? How could we test that theory?

Radin suggests that if we consider all the ESP card tests conducted in laboratories all over the world between 1882 to 1939, the likelihood is phenomenally small that all of these experimenters got lucky with more than five correct guesses. The odds of that are "a billion trillion to one."[7]

The scientific odds against chance to determine our reality is a billion to one. The fact that this calculation is a trillion times that means that based on how we measure our reality this is a certainty. This is a fractal event showing and "proving" that is so, but like the meteorites from chapter two, we are seeing an effect but do not know the cause. The grand material metaparadigm does not have the structure to incorporate this scientific "truth," but the grand unified metaparadigm does. The difficulty in accepting a new model of consciousness is that it is contravened by what we "know" and what we think is "true." Our heuristic. The weight of the repeated six-sigma level from the different categories begins to add up. We must now ask two important questions of all the criticizers yet to come and ourselves. Where is the explanation that supersedes this explanation? And may we please see that math if it exists at all?

Radin told a story about government experiments with remote viewing and how plausible clairvoyance actually is. Sometimes the results were so striking that they far exceeded the effects typically observed in formal laboratory tests. In one test conducted at the request of government clients who wished to see how useful remote viewing might be in real intelligence missions, Dr. Edwin May described how a remote viewer was able to successfully describe an object without having any prior information about it other than that it was a "technical device somewhere in the United States."

The object was a high-energy microwave generator in the Southwest. Without knowing this, the viewer drew and described an object remarkably similar to a microwave generator, including its function, approximate size, and housing. The viewer even correctly noted that it had "a beam divergence angle of thirty degrees."

Most of the classified, mission-oriented remote viewings could not be evaluated as controlled, formal experiments because that was not their intent. In some cases, however, unexpected information obtained through remote viewing was later confirmed to be correct, and this was important because it demonstrated the pragmatic value of this technique for use in real-world missions.[8]

How likely is it that the remote-viewing experiments were just really lucky guesses? The likelihood that the remote-viewing experiments were legitimate remote views, not just luck, was "more than a billion billion to one."[9]

(Radin has since refined this number to ten to the twenty-seventh power, meaning this ability is considered proven.)

I want to talk to the religious here for a moment. I don't care if you are a fundamentalist Muslim, fundamentalist Christian, or some wacko who believes in something weird. If you believe you have a soul and that it leaves your body at death, there is hard proof that your soul can reach out of your body right now. The same is true for everybody around you. Science is validating your belief. Consciousness extends beyond the three spatial dimensions and the one temporal dimension we live in.

Here's what Radin says about what he calls anomalous cognition—essentially, psi—and the likelihood of its existence: "It is clear to this author that anomalous cognition is possible and has been demonstrated. This conclusion is not based on belief, but rather on commonly accepted scientific criteria. The phenomenon has been replicated in a number of forms across laboratories and cultures...I believe that it would be wasteful of valuable resources to continue to look for proof."[10]

Radin asserts that the explanation for psychic abilities is found in quantum theory. He says that such abilities "exist outside the usual boundaries of space time," which basically means that they're nonlocal.

He also examines intention, or as he puts it, "collective wishing." I include this because it is a real-world example of how scientists look at reality and because its results coincide with Robert Jahn and Brenda Dunne's experiments with random number generators, which I discuss below. Collective wishing is just another word for group prayer. "Let us pray" is a commonly heard phrase. A scientific explanation of how prayer works follows.

We have already explained that "you" are not matter but energy. That is what the emerging field of quantum biology is about. You are a packet of information. While you are alive, in the particulate state, you still have a wave structure. When you go to a church to pray, everyone comes in on their own wavelength, but collectively everyone harmonizes that wave structure to create a result through common intention. This science is proof of the ability of prayer, or intention, to affect change at a distance simply with intent. Again, the science is validating religious belief. At the same time, as we will later discuss, it is invalidating apostasy, blasphemy, celibacy, and so on.

* * *

Psychologist Roger Nelson at Princeton University has done field-consciousness studies similar to those done by psychologist Dick Bierman at the University of Amsterdam and psychiatrist Richard Blasband in California. In fact, Roger first conducted studies of this type and the others replicated them later.

To test whether collective wishing makes a difference, Nelson examined the historical weather data for the days before, during, and after graduation at Princeton University for a period of thirty years. He paid most attention to the daily precipitation data recorded in the

Princeton area and in six surrounding towns that acted as control locations. He predicted that on the day of graduation there would be more sunshine and less rain in Princeton than on the days before or after.

Nelson's analysis revealed that, on average over thirty years, there was indeed less rain around graduation days than a few days before and after graduation, with odds of nearly twenty to one against chance. An identical analysis for the average rainfall in six surrounding towns showed no such effect. Over thirty years, about 72 percent of the days around graduation had no rain at all in Princeton, whereas only 67 percent of the days in the surrounding towns were dry.

Curiously, on graduation day itself, the average rainfall was slightly higher in Princeton than in the surrounding towns, owing to a massive downpour of 2.6 inches on June 12, 1962. The average rain in the surrounding towns on that same stormy day was only 0.95 inches. What makes this even stranger is that the members of the Princeton Class of 1962 reported that the massive rain that day held off until after the ceremony had ended! As Nelson pointed out, this study prompts us to reconsider the old witticism that "Everyone talks about the weather, but nobody does anything about it."[11]

Now I want to talk about random number generators. Robert Jahn and Brenda Dunne ran the Princeton University intention studies at the Princeton Engineering Anomaly Research Laboratories (PEAR) for twenty-five years from 1979 till 1992.

I am going to explain the results in layman's terms; I am going to be purposefully vague, and I make no apologies for this. The want to explain the overall concept with generalities so anyone can grasp what happened whether they have a scientific background or not.

These experiments involved programming a computer to randomly produce an equal number of zeros and ones every hour. The computer was then connected to a screen that showed two different pictures (like a tree and a boat).

This is what the researchers' subjects, average people recruited off the street, saw when they interfaced with the computer. People sat in front of the screen, and Jahn and Dunne asked them to make one picture appear more times than the other by their intention alone. In short, people were asked to override the programming of the computer with their intent alone. People could close their eyes and think *tree, tree, tree,* or they could talk to the computer out loud. They were not allowed to touch the computer, so the only way they could affect the computer was with their intent—their thoughts.

Virtually everybody could make one picture appear more often than the other by a margin of 52 percent to 48 percent. If a bonded couple, a man and a woman, sat in front of the computer and did the experiment jointly, the researchers found the computer produced 54 percent of one picture and 46 percent of the other. If two women, however, sat down together to attempt the experiment, they often got the 54/46 result, but sometimes in the wrong direction. There were some interesting differences between genders and gender pairing too. Remember how couples seemed to exhibit a stronger influence on the machine?

Couples influenced the machines six times as strongly as individuals. Also, couples not in a relationship still had a complementary effect. Men had a better chance of getting the machine to do what they wanted, but women had a stronger effect on the machine, though not always in the direction they intended.

This was not an isolated study. These experiments started in 1979 and ran until 1994. Other labs running the same type of experiments got similar results.

The numbers from more than 2.5 million trials over twelve years are interesting. It turned out that 52 percent of the trials were in the direction that had been intended.

By intention alone, participants were able to bend the computers, at least a bit, to their will. These results were submitted to the National Research Council, which concluded that the trials could not be explained by chance.

If you go to their website and watch the fifteen-minute video, you will hear Brenda Dunne say, "This typifies the dramatic results they have gotten, results that have yet to be integrated into the minds of the current generation of scientists."

Theoretical physicist Max Planck famously said that consciousness is fundamental and everything else is derivative. It stands behind AI, and AI will be nothing more than what we intend it to be. But how can we intend it to be anything if we do not know ourselves? It is *imperative* that consciousness science be funded because in twenty-five years we will need a counterbalance to the danger of a malignant AI becoming smarter than us, and it is predicted that this will happen in the next twenty-five years and will be a danger to us all on a global scale.

How, on a scientific level, can you explain influencing a computer simply by wishing? What do you and a computer have in common? You both have electrical fields, as does the quantum soup around you.

On the Science of Reincarnation website under Government Studies and Video Library, you can find a link to the Princeton University PEAR lab. There you can watch Robert Jahn and Brenda Dunne explain what they do.

The best explanation about how Jahn and Dunne arrived at their results is as follows: Subatomic entities can behave either as particles or as waves. A particle is a precise thing with a set location in space. A wave is diffuse and unbounded, and it has a region of influence that can flow through and interfere with other waves. Jahn and Dunne think that consciousness has a similar duality. Each individual has its own particulate separateness. That is, you are a defined thing in space, but you are also capable of wavelike behavior, which could flow through barriers or across distance to exchange information and interact with the world. At certain moments, this wavelike consciousness can get resonate with, or have the same frequency as, other subatomic matter. Jahn and Dunne seem to be saying that you and the computer develop coherence. That is, the wavelike component of your being resonates with and can influence the computer.

Can we believe their results? Absolutely! They studied more than a quarter million subjects over a twenty-five-year period, and after they published their results, other labs duplicated their experiments and got the same results.

Dean Radin wrote the following in his book *The Conscious Universe*:

> Just as a photon is both a particle and a wave, perhaps consciousness too has complementary states. In ordinary states, the mind is more particlelike and is firmly localized in space and time. This is supported by the ordinary subjective experience of being an isolated, independent creature. But in unusual, non-ordinary states of awareness, our minds may be more wavelike and no longer localized in space or time. This is supported by subjective experiences of timelessness, mystical unity, and psi.

> As with particle-wave duality, it is not the case that only one or the other description is true, but

both are true at the same time. The fact that we have trouble thinking in terms of "both" rather than "either-or" says more about the limitations of language than it does about the nature of reality. If our minds have complementary characteristics, then perhaps we can be more particle-like or more wavelike depending on what we wish to be, or what it is suitable to be at the time, or what we are motivated to become.[12]

If we can influence a machine, can we influence another person or a disease? We try it all the time. You have heard about the power of prayer; now it's being taken into the lab and dissected. We have found that its power lies in the coherent nature of wave consciousness. We have found we can measure it, but we still don't yet understand how that cohesive waveform works, though we have proven that it does.

Several years ago, I wrote a white paper for the bipartisan policy commission on the use of the science of reincarnation as a counter radicalization initiative. With the help of Dean Radin and Stephan Schwartz, we synopsized that proof as follows.

The emerging Science of Reincarnation is being done at the following institutions and is defined by the various subsets of this science enumerated below.

Psychic ability (psi) does not immediately imply the existence of reincarnation. It does however lay an empirical foundation for the idea that the mind reaches beyond the body. That in turn implies that the traditional notion of reincarnation may have some basis. Independently repeatable evidence for psi effects has been established at beyond the six-sigma level for at least six classes of experiments.

Examples of psi include remote viewing, a modern term for clairvoyance when used for a particular purpose. Remote viewing was developed into a training program at SRI International, The Stanford Research institute. Stanford (University) Research Institute was renamed SRI International in the mid 1970s, and at that time it became independent from the university and turned into an operational unit within the US Army. SRI International (SRI) is an American nonprofit scientific research institute and organization headquartered in Menlo Park, California. The trustees of Stanford University established SRI in 1946 as a center of innovation to support economic development in the region.

The project was funded with twenty-five million dollars by the CIA, DIA, army, and other government agencies with measurable and acknowledged successes. Remote viewing indicates that the mind can reach beyond the conventional senses and ordinary boundaries of space and time.

The intention experiments done at Princeton University over a twenty-five-year period statistically indicated that humans are able to influence events at a distance by simply applying their intent. This line of research challenges the orthodox assumption that mind and matter are completely separate. It appears that some aspects of the mind are intimately related to the behavior of matter.

The study of children who seem to recall previous lives is an ongoing fifty-year study being conducted at the University of Virginia. The project is referred to as "The science of Reincarnation" in a UVA alumni magazine article. This class of studies is the most direct evidence of the traditional notion of reincarnation.

Research on Near-Death Experience began forty years ago by psychiatrist Raymond Moody and is now being examined in detail by numerous investigators. One of the largest international consortiums on NDE research is being led by physician Sam Parnia. This work suggests that the mind and the brain may not be identical.

The key takeaway is that psi effects have been established at beyond the six-sigma level for at least six classes of experiments. "Today," Stephan Schwartz wrote,

There are six stabilized parapsychological protocols used in laboratories around the world exploring these two categories of phenomena. Under rigorous double or triple blind, randomized and tightly controlled conditions, each of these six has independently produced six sigma results. Six Sigma is one in a billion—1,009,976,678—or the 99.9999990699 percentile. These six protocols each has its own literature. The results of all these studies are based on the sessions being double or triple blind and properly randomized, and that a pre-agreed analysis, including statistical evaluation for variance from chance, be part of the process. That is, we don't need to get bogged down in antiquated arguments about sleight-of-hand, secret cuing, and the like, although this remains a staple of nonlocal consciousness research criticism. This kind of criticism stopped being apposite several decades ago. As far back as the mid-1990s, after studying the data from just one of these four protocols, remote viewing, stalwart denier University of Oregon psychology professor Ray Hyman had to grudgingly admit, "...the experiments [being assessed] were free of the methodological weaknesses that plagued the early... research...the...experiments appear to be free of the more obvious and better known flaws that can invalidate the results of parapsychological investigations. We agree that the effect sizes reported...are too large and consistent to be dismissed as statistical flukes."

In each case there is also a large enough body of research from enough different institutions, done by enough researchers that we have some idea of the process and how successful it can be. The studies, as I have noted, break down into two categories: Nonlocal Perception, and Nonlocal Perturbation.[13]

"Quantum biology," Schwartz wrote in another paper, another new sub discipline, posits the following: life is a molecular process; molecular processes operate under quantum rules. Thus, life must be a quantum process. Experimental evidence is beginning to accumulate that this quantum view of life process is correct. Max Planck, the father of quantum mechanics, framed his opinion very clearly in an interview in 1931 when he stated, "I regard consciousness as fundamental. I regard matter as derivative from consciousness. We cannot get behind consciousness. Everything that we talk about, everything that we regard as existing, postulates consciousness.

Two corollaries follow from Planck's assertion: first is the existence of nonlocal consciousness, an aspect of consciousness independent of space-time and not resident in an organism's physiology. The second is that all consciousnesses are interdependent and interconnected.

Today there are six stabilized parapsychological protocols used in laboratories around the world exploring these two categories of phenomena. Under rigorous double- or triple-blind, randomized, and tightly controlled conditions, each of these six independently produce six-sigma results. Each has their own literature.

Nonlocal Perception Remote Viewing

This is a double- or triple-blind protocol in which a participant is given a task that can be accomplished only through nonlocal perception.

Ganzfeld

This protocol is similar in intent to remote viewing in which an individual in a state of sensory deprivation provides verifiable information about film clips shown at another location.

Presentiment

This is a measurable psychophysical response that occurs before a stimulation such as the dilation of a participant's pupils from a monitor screen or a change in brain function before a noise is heard.

Retro Cognition, Precognition

This protocol requires time dislocation in a remote-viewing experiment in which the session data are collected about a randomly chosen target before the target has been selected.

Nonlocal Perturbation

This refers to studies in labs where an individual intends to affect the performance of a physical system such as a random number generator. It also involves Princeton University's Global Consciousness Project, which monitors a constantly running coordinated network of computer-linked random number generators.[14]

We are left with a choice of two models. The first is the physicalist model that assumes consciousness is contained within an organism's neural anatomy. The second is that of nonlocal consciousness.

All these examples bolster the religious notion of the transfer of a consciousness, or a soul, to heaven. Each religion has its own story, but these examples scientifically prove a transfer.

Our own lives are half of the proof. Your lives are fractal iterations of your consciousness. You have a particle state—you, here and now—and a wave state. Each has its own conditions.

The next scientific advancement will be akin to

Galileo's. He proved that the sun is the center of the solar system, and we will prove that there really is consciousness after death.

Russell Targ's book *The Reality of ESP: A Physicist's Proof of Psychic Abilities* lays out the case especially well. He explains:

> In 1921, the great logician, Ludwig Wittgenstein, concluded his crystalline tractatus logico-philosophicus with the admonition that, "the solution to the riddle of life in space and time lies outside space and time." And in 1964, theoretical physicist, John Stewart Bell proved mathematically that the results predicted by quantum mechanics could not be explained by any theory that preserves our usual ideas of locality. I discuss this nonlocal connectivity further in the introduction. Finally, statistics professor, Jessica Utts, at the University of California Davis (UC Davis), began her detailed 1995 CIA-commissioned assessment of our SRI remote viewing research by writing, "using the standards applied to any other area of science, it is concluded that psychic functioning has been well established. The statistical results of the studies examined are far beyond what is expected by chance. Effects of similar magnitude have been replicated in laboratories across the world."[15]

The riddle of life in space and time lies outside space and time. This brings us to a new form of math called topology. There are two forms of topology we have to look at: spatial topology and information topology.

Topology is the mathematical study of the properties that are preserved after deforming, twisting, and stretching objects. Tearing, however, is not allowed. A circle is topologically equivalent to an ellipse (into which it can be deformed by stretching), and a sphere is topologically equivalent to an ellipsoid.

Network topology is the arrangement of the various elements (links, nodes, etc.) of a communication network. Network topology is the topological structure of a network and may be depicted physically or logically.

A mathematical topologist would see a coffee cup and a donut as the same thing. You can bend a coffee cup into a donut and stretch a donut to make a coffee cup. If I had a ball and wanted to push it through the top of a desk, and if you were in two dimensions on my desk, first you would see a dot that would get bigger and bigger until the circumference of the ball was going through the desk, and then you would see it get smaller and smaller until it became a dot again.

For our mathematical study of the science of reincarnation, we have to study the movement of information because that is what we are. But what are we moving through? Our space-time continuum is the spatial and temporal field our electromagnetic consciousness traverses. Quantum physics posits that our reality may encompass more than three spatial dimensions and one temporal dimension. Accordingly we must now introduce the tesseract.

In geometry, a tesseract is a four-dimensional analogue of a cube; a tesseract is to a cube what a cube is to a square. Just as the surface of a cube consists of six square faces, the hypersurface of a tesseract consists of eight cubical cells. A tesseract is one of the six convex regular 4-polytopes.[16]

If you Google what a tesseract looks like, you can see pictures, but the pictures are of its shadow. You must imagine that you are outside the internal cube that is our reality. Our reality is a shadow of the larger five-dimensional space.

Take a tesseract and hold it in your hands. Turn it over. Some of it—the cube in the center—is in your reality of three spatial dimensions and one temporal dimension, but you must look at this from the fifth dimension. A tesseract is a five-dimensional object projected onto a four-dimensional plane. One of those planes is time. Let's remove time and only speak of the spatial dimensions.

Look at your shadow. Your shadow is a three-dimensional object projected onto a two-dimensional plane. In order to see the tesseract you're holding in your hand, imagine that you can step into the fourth dimension. When you come back, you can't see the tesseract. You cannot see the fourth spatial dimension from inside the cube of the tesseract, but you can see the cube from the fourth dimension. Now you know where you have to stand to see this model. Hypothetically that's where your soul is, this four-dimensional place outside our own space-time.

Hypothetically at a single moment in time, you can only see its shadow because the tesseract stretches toward infinity. If you leave your three spatial dimensions to the fourth, and you are temporally dead, in waveform you are very much alive. Why assume awareness only exists in three dimensions?

Do you come back to temporal form as a man or a woman? This is a choice. Black or white. Growth seems to be the purpose of our existence here.

Let us advance this hypothesis. We are in three spatial dimensions and one temporal dimension for a total of four. But we know there are more dimensions because of quantum theory and our discoveries in cosmology. Let us speak only of the fourth spatial dimension rather than the eleven quantum theory predicts.

What would the fourth spatial dimension be like? Since it is a quantum dimension, it would be a wave state. If it were common to ours, it would have a wave intelligence. Our observations of the scientific anomalies described earlier fit seamlessly with the theory of relativity and space-time. This is not a new idea; a fourth spatial dimension was proposed by Hermann Minkowski, who was Einstein's teacher and found that the theory of special relativity could be best understood as a four-dimensional space, since known as the Minkowski space-time.

Now what is being proposed in this math book on re-incarnation is the existence of a fourth spatial dimension. This is not new to physics, but what is new is what may be housed in that theoretical spatial dimension: awareness, intelligence, and possibly our own discarnate intelligence. If you believe in an afterlife, it may be in this type of physics that you find proof of your belief.

When Einstein wanted to describe relativity, ordinary geometry wasn't flexible enough. Instead, he used complex Minkowski space, which is also consistent with theories of electromagnetism and quantum mechanics. Because "it is very important that any model constructed to describe psi must not at the same time generate weird or incorrect physics," Targ believes that complex Minkowski space gives us our best physical model to describe psi. Psi is our consciousness signature in the fourth spatial dimension that "leaches" into our three spatial dimensions and one temporal dimension.

How does this relate to nonlocality? Nonlocality allows for what studies have consistently demonstrated about clairvoyant reception. After examining a hundred years of data on psi research, Targ found there there's no loss of accuracy in any kind of ESP due to distance.

The implications for space travel and exploration are extraordinary. If AI could be synced to the electrical frequency of the mind, communication could become instantaneous. We already have the proof that this can be done from the Princeton and Stanford studies, but accepting this model homogenizes every religion. That explains the resistance to these studies, but it must be overcome for mankind to advance.

Perhaps this phenomenal reliability and fidelity can be explained by the fact that the desired information is always available when clairvoyants reach back in time. Clairvoyants are simply better at accessing what is essentially readily available information. The information is always there; you just have to be open it. I agree with Targ when he says that "psi is often seen as paradoxical because we presently misconstrue the nature of space-time in which we reside. The 'naïve realist' picture of our reality says that we are separate creatures sitting on our own well-circumscribed points in space-time. But for the past thirty years, modern physics has been asserting this model is not correct."

The new model represents a wave state supporting a particulate state. You are present in different ways in both places.

Imagine you're a five-dimensional creature. You're a waveform intelligence, and you can become a particulate intelligent for a period of time. Waveform intelligence stretches to infinity. Wave information is available, and like any creature, you have the opportunity to grow.

But according to the exit interviews, those interviews

with children who remember prior lives and those who have experienced NDEs, you incarnate for different reasons at different times. Young souls incarnate to learn quickly or to learn a specific lesson. Older souls may incarnate as a baby that only lives for nine months and then dies to help a younger soul experience things like anguish and love.

Sex and gender seem fairly simple. Then are men and women, male and female. Simple, right?

Not so fast. You can be a sexual male with a female gender orientation, or vice versa. These conditions exist across every race, religion, color, and creed, and we can see this historically.

We see a gender variance around us that goes back centuries and that lines up with the narrative of souls changing gender. It meshes well with the mixing of forty-six chromosomes in each generation. Everyone has male and female code in their DNA. Additionally, this gender variance exists in the animal kingdom when a male lion or monkey humps another male. Some Ugandan politicians claim gays came into their country and taught the lions to do that. Consciousness science is resisted in part because it challenges people who were taught the wrong thing.

It was said of Julius Caesar he was every woman's man and every man's woman. Rome was known for its religious promiscuity. Hannibal, who was from Carthage, and Alexander the Great, from Macedonia, were gay.

Hannibal cried when his young lover accidentally drowned in a river.

Independent researchers like Michael Newton say souls reincarnate predominantly in one sex when they are younger but fifty-fifty in each sex as the soul gets older. University of Virginia studies of children who remember prior lives find transgender reincarnations. Brian Weiss at the University of Miami regressed a woman named Catherine who had multiple lives, some as a man and some as a woman.

Since religious models predict an afterlife—57 percent of people believe in reincarnation, and 70 percent believe in a human soul—then scientifically gender has to be transitive. With each of us carrying genes that came from both male and female, and with dominant and recessive states for each gene, LGBT expression is built into our very nature and should be accepted as normal.

Your soul or consciousness came to inhabit your body by means of the scientific processes I have described. After passing from your body, your soul will still be you, with your memories and thoughts from this life intact, and will continue in a discrete waveform. But is this grounded in physics? In her prologue to *The Field: The Quest for the Secret Force of the Universe*, Lynne McTaggart says the following.

At our most elemental, we are not a chemical reaction, but an energetic charge.[17]

This means that our cells are made up of atoms which are made up of subatomic particles which are made up of energy. In spite of the fact we see ourselves as bodies, what we really are composed of is pure energy. Human beings and all living things are a coalescence of energy in the field of energy connected to every other thing in the world.

Matter at its most fundamental level could not be divided into independently existing units or even fully described. Subatomic particles weren't solid little objects like billiard balls, but vibrating and indeterminate packets of energy that could not be precisely quantified or understood in themselves.

[...]

Quantum physicists had discovered a strange property in the subatomic world called 'nonlocality'. This refers to the ability of a quantum entity such as an individual electron to influence another quantum particle instantaneously over distance despite there being no exchange of force or energy.

[...]

In quantum physics, however, it was discovered, the state of all possibilities of any quantum particle collapsed into a set entity as soon as it was observed or measurement taken. To explain these strange events, quantum physicists had postulated that a participatory relationship existed between observer and observed—these particles could only be considered as 'probably' existing in space and time until they were 'perturbed' and the act of observing and measuring them forced them into a set state, an act akin to solidifying jello.[18]

What they had discovered is totally at odds with how we view the world.

The most important quality common to all these researchers was a simple willingness to suspend disbelief and remain open to true discovery, even if it meant challenging the existing order of things, alienating colleagues or opening themselves up to censure and professional ruin. To be a revolutionary in science today is to flirt with professional suicide.[19]

Psi exists, and we can use it, but there's a long list of details that we need to iron out to use it effectively. As Radin points out, we can easily split the uses of psi into five categories: medicine, military, detective work, technology, and business.[20]

We know clairvoyants are used in police work; just look at all the TV shows. We know they are used by the military; the Japanese are using them in business, and psychic warfare is talked about in one of the oldest Chinese military books, Sun Tzu's *The Art of War*. Even *he* talks about psi, or *chi* (pronounced *key*) as it was known back then. Soldiers were able to conduct psychic warfare on their enemies on a psychological level.[21]

The National Security Council (NSC) has used remote viewing conducted by a psychic named Joe McMoneagle. The NSC actually trusted him as a reliable psychic. In fact, they were right to do that. But they were not the only agency. In *The Consciousness Universe*, Radin notes:

[In September 1979,] the National Security Council asked one of the most consistently accurate army remote viewers, a chief warrant officer named Joe McMoneagle, to "see" inside a large building somewhere in northern Russia...

Because McMoneagle had gained a reputation for accuracy in previous tasks, they asked him to view the future to find out when this supposed submarine would be launched. McMoneagle scanned the future, month by month, "watching" the future construction via remote viewing, and sensed that about four months later the Russians would blast a channel from the building to the water and launch the sub.

Sure enough, about four months later, in January 1980, spy-satellite photos showed that the largest submarine ever observed was traveling through an artificial channel from the building to the body of water. The pictures showed that it had twenty missile tubes and a large, flat deck. It was eventually named a *Typhoon* class submarine.

Scores of generals, admirals, and political leaders who had been briefed on psi results like this came away with the knowledge that remote viewing was real...the U.S. Army had supported a secret team of remote viewers...those viewers had participated in hundreds of remote-viewing missions, and that the DIA, CIA, Customs Service, Drug Enforcement Administration, FBI and Secret Service had all relied on the remote-viewing team for more than a decade, sometimes with startling results.[22]

The military is still doggedly pursuing uses of psi—Radin points out how complicated modern fighter jets are. The cockpits are complicated, and so are the tactics necessary for effective dogfighting. It is estimated that about 5 percent of fighter pilots have accounted for roughly 40 percent of the successful engagements with hostile aircraft in every aerial battle since World War I.

Radin comments on how "psychic" some of these ace pilots must already be. "There is some sixth sense that a man acquires when he has peered often enough out of a [jet fighter cockpit] into a hostile sky—hunches that come to him, sudden and compelling, enabling him to read signs that others don't even see. Such a man can extract more from a faint tangle of condensation trails, or a distant flitting dot, than he has any reason or right to do."[23]

In this part of psi, what you believe comes true. In a sense we are creating our own reality.

Any new science has a serious hurdle to overcome when it is first introduced. Against any new anomaly, people will put up a barrier of skepticism because it is new and threatens to change their world. "To function without the annoying pain of cognitive dissonance, groups will use almost any means to achieve consensus...This means that in the initial stages of a new discovery, when a scientific anomaly is first claimed, it literally cannot be seen by everyone. We have to change our expectations in order to see it."[24]

This scientific hurdle is part of a self-fulfilling prophecy. If you believe it, it will happen. Radin describes an interesting experiment in self-fulfilling prophecy:

> An experiment demonstrating the self-fulfilling prophecy was described by Harvard psychologist Robert Rosenthal in a classic book entitled *Pygmalion in the Classroom*. Teachers were led to believe that some students were high achievers and others were not. In reality, the students had been assigned at random to the two categories. The teachers' expectations about high achievers led them to treat the "high achievers" differently than the other students, and subsequent achievement tests confirmed that the self-fulfilling prophecy indeed led to higher scores for the randomly selected "high achievers."[25]

Such studies make it absolutely clear that when experimenters know how participants *should* behave, it is impossible not to send out unconscious signals.

Radin says we may have a way of bringing psi into our scientific mainstream. We just have to put it through the same pace nonlocality went through: quantum theory. Radin says that "some scientific developments in recent years suggest a way of thinking about psi that is also compatible with mainstream scientific models. Four such developments are related to quantum theory. All four of them run counter to common sense, all four were thought to be theoretically possible but practically untestable, and all four have now been empirically proved. Of principal importance here is that all four *must* also be true to be compatible with what we know about psi."[26]

He then points out how we can retroactively interpret other experiments when we have psi and nonlocality at our disposal. Suddenly, little quirks and unexplainable defects about certain experiments can become clear. It's like finally figuring out what that extra key on your ring unlocks.

Interpretation of existing theories may change when viewed in the light of psi and nonlocality. For example, in the late 1980s, neuroscientist Benjamin Libet conducted an experiment in which he asked his subjects to flex a finger at the instant of their decision. He monitored their brain waves to see if the instant that the decision was made would be reflected by a change in brain waves. On average, the volunteers took about a fifth of a second to flex their finger after they mentally decided to do so, an expected time lag for the brain to activate the neuromuscular system. But according to their brain waves, their brains also displayed neural activity about a third of a second *before* they were even aware that they had decided to move their finger!

Libet interpreted this result as evidence that our sense of free will in deciding what we do may be unconsciously determined *before* we are consciously aware of the decision. If mental intention, which is connected to our most intimate sense of personal expression, actually does begin in a part of the brain that is outside our conscious reach, then perhaps *all* our behavior is completely determined by processes outside our control.[27]

We can postulate that your decisions are being made by your soul in the fourth spatial dimension and sent to your body. Then your body executes the decision sent by your soul. By soul here I mean your greater mind, your consciousness, because you are aware not just in three spatial dimensions and one temporal dimension but in the fourth spatial dimension as well.

All of our psi questions can be answered in the world

of quantum mechanics; this is our method to get psi into mainstream science. In the meantime, we seem to have all the evidence we need to get psi widely accepted. Radin writes, "As some of the stranger aspects of quantum mechanics are clarified and tested, we're finding that our understanding of the physical world is becoming more compatible with psi."[28]

Radin also wants you, as part of the general public, to demand more psi-related research. If there is public interest, there will be funding and attention from our top scientists. Otherwise, we may very well see progress "measured in half-centuries or centuries."[29]

There is not just religious resistance but academic resistance. Most psychologists could reasonably be described as uninformed skeptics, a minority could reasonably be described as prejudiced bigots. The paranormal is simply outside their area of expertise.

Notes

[1] Dr. Dean Radin, *The Conscious Universe* (New York: HarperCollins Publishers, 1997), p. 67.

[2] Dr. Dean Radin, *The Conscious Universe* (New York: HarperCollins Publishers, 1997), p. 88.

[3] Dr. Dean Radin, *The Conscious Universe* (New York: HarperCollins Publishers, 1997), p. 67.

[4] Dr. Dean Radin, *The Conscious Universe* (New York: HarperCollins Publishers, 1997), p. 67.

5   Dr. Dean Radin, *The Conscious Universe* (New York: HarperCollins Publishers, 1997), p. 74.
6   Dr. Dean Radin, *The Conscious Universe* (New York: HarperCollins Publishers, 1997), p. 88.
7   Dr. Dean Radin, *The Conscious Universe* (New York: HarperCollins Publishers, 1997), p. 97.
8   Dr. Dean Radin, *The Conscious Universe* (New York: HarperCollins Publishers, 1997), p. 98-99.
9   Dr. Dean Radin, *The Conscious Universe* (New York: HarperCollins Publishers, 1997), p. 101.
10 Dr. Dean Radin, *The Conscious Universe* (New York: HarperCollins Publishers, 1997), p. 102.
11 Dr. Dean Radin, *The Conscious Universe* (New York: HarperCollins Publishers, 1997), p. 172-173.
12 Dr. Dean Radin, *The Conscious Universe* (New York: HarperCollins Publishers, 1997), p. 67.
13 Stephan Schwartz, *Six Protocols, Neuroscience, and Near Death: An Emerging Paradigm Incorporating Nonlocal Consciousness.*
14 Stephan Schwartz, *Six Protocols, Neuroscience, and Near Death: An Emerging Paradigm Incorporating Nonlocal Consciousness.*
15 Russell Targ, *The Reality of ESP.*
16 https://en.wikipedia.org/wiki/Tesseract.
17 R Lynne McTaggart, *The Field: The Quest for the Secret Force of the Universe* (New York: HarperCollins Publishers, 2001), p. XXIII.

[18] *R* Lynne McTaggart, *The Field: The Quest for the Secret Force of the Universe* (New York: HarperCollins Publishers, 2001), p. 10-11.

[19] *R* Lynne McTaggart, *The Field: The Quest for the Secret Force of the Universe* (New York: HarperCollins Publishers, 2001), p. 13.

[20] Dr. Dean Radin, *The Conscious Universe* (New York: HarperCollins Publishers, 1997), p. 191.

[21] Dr. Dean Radin, *The Conscious Universe* (New York: HarperCollins Publishers, 1997), p. 197.

[22] Dr. Dean Radin, *The Conscious Universe* (New York: HarperCollins Publishers, 1997), p. 197-198.

[23] Dr. Dean Radin, *The Conscious Universe* (New York: HarperCollins Publishers, 1997), p. 194-195.

[24] Dr. Dean Radin, *The Conscious Universe* (New York: HarperCollins Publishers, 1997), p. 232-233.

[25] Dr. Dean Radin, *The Conscious Universe* (New York: HarperCollins Publishers, 1997), p. 238.

[26] Dr. Dean Radin, *The Conscious Universe* (New York: HarperCollins Publishers, 1997), p. 282.

[27] Dr. Dean Radin, *The Conscious Universe* (New York: HarperCollins Publishers, 1997), p. 283.

[28] Dr. Dean Radin, *The Conscious Universe* (New York: HarperCollins Publishers, 1997), p. 286.

[29] Dr. Dean Radin, *The Conscious Universe* (New York: HarperCollins Publishers, 1997), p. 290.

Chapter 7

The Characteristics of DNA and Gender

How do we connect the particulate version of ourselves with the waveform version? Who we are is a result of what is written in our DNA. But what exactly is our DNA?

DNA is like a river; you hop in and you hop out as you go from life to life. Let's look at one snippet of DNA over two thousand years. If you are a human being, you have forty-six chromosomes. Twenty-three come from your mother, and twenty-three come from your father. DNA carries the memory of who your ancestors were, what color your hair and your eyes will be, and what sex will be dominant. And it can carry memory not for just two thousand years but for 200,000 years or more. A percentage of the human population still carries the DNA of Neanderthals.

Our gender rests on our DNA. Our DNA defines who we are, whether we are a man or a woman. The forty-six chromosomes define what our body is and whether we're going to be susceptible to sickle cell anemia or have blue eyes or blond hair. Ancestry.com looks at your DNA to define who you are, where you came from, and what your heritage is. But that's a snapshot. DNA itself is a river.

Epigenetic memory is the memory of past lives stored in DNA. We see anxiety markers in the children of Holocaust victims because that trauma was imprinted on the DNA and then passed on.

Most DNA is located in the cell nucleus (where it is called nuclear DNA), but a small amount of DNA can also be found in the mitochondria (where it is called mitochondrial DNA or mtDNA). The information in DNA is stored as a code made up of four chemical bases—adenine (A), guanine (G), cytosine (C), and thymine (T)—and it is in the shape of a double helix.

Mitochondrial DNA is only inherited from our mothers. It is passed from mothers to sons and daughters, but sons cannot pass along their mother's mitochondrial DNA because it is transmitted through the female egg. That DNA goes all the way back to the first mother of that genetic line, so it carries historical information about your genetic past. That foundation is written in the math of code, and we are already writing genetic code on our computers.

Scientists have discovered a second code hiding within DNA. This second code contains information that changes how scientists read the instructions contained in DNA and interpret mutations to make sense of health and disease.

A research team led by Dr. John Stamatoyannopoulos, associate professor of genome sciences and medicine at the University of Washington (UW), made the discovery. The findings are reported in the December 2013 issue of *Science.*

The work is part of the Encyclopedia of DNA Elements Project, also known as ENCODE. The National Human Genome Research Institute funded the multiyear, international effort. ENCODE aims to discover where and how the directions for biological functions are stored in the human genome.

Since the genetic code was deciphered in the 1960s, scientists have assumed it was used exclusively to write information about proteins. UW scientists were stunned to discover that genomes use the genetic code to write two separate languages. One describes how proteins are made, and the other controls genes. One language is written on top of the other, which is why the second language remained hidden for so long.

"For over 40 years we have assumed that DNA changes affecting the genetic code solely impact how proteins are made," said Stamatoyannopoulos. "Now we know that this basic assumption about reading the human genome missed half of the picture. These new findings highlight that DNA is an incredibly powerful information storage device, which nature has fully exploited in unexpected ways."[1]

The genetic code uses a sixty-four-letter alphabet called codons. The UW team discovered that some codons, which they called duons, can have two meanings, one related to protein sequence and one related to gene control. These two meanings seem to have evolved in concert with each other. The gene-control instructions appear to help stabilize certain beneficial features of proteins and how they are made.

The discovery of duons has major implications for how scientists and physicians interpret a patient's genome and will open new doors to the diagnosis and treatment of disease.

"The fact that the genetic code can simultaneously write two kinds of information means that many DNA changes that appear to alter protein sequences may actually cause disease by disrupting gene control programs or even both mechanisms simultaneously," said Stamatoyannopoulos.[2]

We now know about a second level of information below DNA, and this leads us to believe that information is stored not just in chemicals but in the energy that comprised the chemicals in waveform.

Let's say you visit a house and are shown the attic. Informationally, DNA has a foundation in the quantum level just like the house has a foundation on the ground. Structural decisions are made at the quantum level. That is waveform organization, and that organized structure predicts a waveform consciousness. We see two levels; there are probably levels that reach energy itself because that is the foundation of everything above. There is a structure to energy itself, a waveform or order that is indicative of a waveform intelligence. In short, what we see in the macro has to exist in the micro.

DNA is stacked, ordered information down to the quantum level. It is a river of historical information, and matter doesn't matter. It carries information all the way down to its waveform energy.

Genghis Khan is notable for his DNA footprint because of all the women he was with. That footprint can be seen today in the Mongolian population as derivative descendants of DNA.

We also see have genetic memories of events that occurred during the lifetimes of our ancestors, and those memories shape our lives. AI can help us learn more about this if we apply this model correctly. Disaster is an option, though. How smart are we? How well can we use AI? When AI becomes smarter than us, how will it evaluate the science being presented here?

We simply do not understand how quantum theory applies to biology. We have proof that the mind can reach through time and space. It can influence machines. We hear about the power of positive thinking, but no one has attempted to explain it. Yet experiment after experiment will soon force us to incorporate an aspect of human nature that only existed in faith.

In her book *The Field,* Lynne McTaggart writes, "If quantum theory were applied to biology on a larger scale, we would be viewed more as a complex network of energy fields in some sort of dynamic interplay with our chemical cellular systems."[3]

This leads to the hypothesis that our bodies are really energy fields moving through a sea of energy. But how do we test this theory?

If you are made of the four compounds of the DNA code and I can digitize the four-nucleotide units of DNA—adenine, guanine, thymine, and cytosine—can I replicate your frequency? Will it still be you? In short, can I transduce the chemicals in your DNA as we did the cardio dilators in the earlier experiment with the Hartley guinea pig heart?

John Craig Venter, an American biologist and entrepreneur, is most famous for his leading role in sequencing the human genome and for his role in creating the first cell with a synthetic genome in 2010. One of the leading scientists of the twenty-first century, he founded Celera Genomics, the Institute for Genomic Research, and the J. Craig Venter Institute (JCVI). He is now working to create synthetic biological organisms. With a computer program and chemicals, he programmed a DNA code for a self-replicating organism.

The JCVI researchers have accomplished the first draft of the human genome, the first human microbiome and environmental genomics programs, construction of the first synthetic cell, and construction of the first minimal cell. In short with computer programing, we are programing the basic units of life with code we have written rather than code that exists in our DNA.

Genomic science has greatly enhanced our understanding of the biological world. It is enabling researchers to *read* the genetic code of organisms from all branches of life by sequencing the four letters that make up DNA. Sequencing genomes has now become routine, giving rise to thousands of genomes in public databases. In essence, scientists are digitizing biology by converting the series of A, C, T, and G that make up DNA into ones and zeros in a computer. But can the process be reversed? Can you start with zeros and ones in a computer and define the characteristics of a living cell? Scientists set out to answer this question. Using the binary code of the computer, the scientists at JCVI tried to design a chemical makeup of something that would live.

When chemists determine the structure of a new compound, they synthesize the chemical to determine if the synthetic structure functions like the original. Venter and his colleagues are doing the same with genomes. In 2003 they created a virus, in 2008 they synthesized a small bacterial genome, and in 2010 the synthetic genome was used to create the first cell controlled completely by a synthetic genome.

Twenty-five years ago, you could not conceive that a scientist could create life by using four chemical compounds and a computer, but that's what happened.

Whether or not you agree that Venter actually created life, the people with the money—the real money—believe he did it because he's now worth hundreds of millions of dollars. And if we can create life from chemistry, we can create life from physics.

CRISPR (pronounced "crisper") stands for *Clustered Regularly Interspaced Short Palindromic Repeats,* which are the hallmark of a bacterial defense system that forms the basis for CRISPR-Cas9 genome-editing technology.

CRISPR describes a fractal pattern of clusters. Each cluster is an iteration of its pattern, and each is self-similar.

Our reality does not rest on the chemicals of our DNA but on the energy that makes up those chemicals. If the chemicals are ordered, the energy is ordered. If the energy is ordered, your energy is ordered. That ordered energy is aware because you are aware.

Some day we will design using energy rather than chemicals.

CRISPER itself is a fractal pattern. Look at what the name means. It's a description of iterations that are self-similar. You see this fractal geometric pattern in everything.

When fractal patterns show up in our observations, we can reliably say that is our reality even if we don't understand why for a while. There are, however, orders of magnitude. Math and science predict that after death our awareness is at a higher order of magnitude than our awareness in this reality. Reincarnation can now be regarded as a science because it is behaving as a science, and we have a paradigm that explains where the science is and where it is going. Can any religion say as much?

Here is another fractal: the design of AI is matching and exceeding human intelligence. We are designing it now. We currently accept DNA as chemical information. Here the math is information topology. But we are going deeper into the energy that makes up the system. We are digitizing chemicals to waves, but it's still early in that process. Ultimately, we will be able to work with that DNA information in waveform.

* * *

If the mathematics of the science of reincarnation is to be evaluated properly, we would have to put it in an accounting ledger and not just add the columns but cross-foot them to make sure they match and are in balance. So next we'll look at gender and find out if what we see in the world around us lines up with what the anecdotal disciplines say.

The old view is that gender is binary and that gay, lesbian, and transgender people are deviant. The emerging paradigm says gender is a spectrum, which is the correct view. Think of gender as having two poles, a zero and a one or a negative and a positive. Those poles send information to each other and constantly recycle. Whether or not you accept that model, you must accept that there are gay people, lesbian people, and transgender people in every culture, though they are more accepted in some than in others.

* * *

Now we must reorient this narrative. We are going to continue with this explanation but establish a new context. I want to conjoin this discussion with the coming discussion at the end of chapter fourteen on math for physicists examining the math of dimensional manifolds and then again in chapter seventeen, rewriting Russian social policy. There is a direct line through those points from here that I want my reader to specifically be aware of, and it goes to our collective defense and betterment. For everybody.

Now this goes first directly to mapping, cartography. We have to measure what we plan to map. If that map is of the quantum fourth spatial dimension and our awareness in it, then we have to set our parameters. There is no reason we would not be conscious in the fourth dimension if we are conscious in the other three spatial dimensions. What we are measuring to map is a quantum dimension, and the tools we use depend on how we are willing to conceptualize that space.

If we begin by measuring ourselves, then we generate hundred watts of power. The power of a small light bulb. If we measure the effect of nonlocal influence as measured by the Princeton University "intention" experiments, we see that effect to be about 2 percent. So, we begin by trying to dissect something that has two watts of power. We know we are not our bodies because they change; we in a quantum world are our electrical awareness, that two watts of power. Now this is both difficult and transcendent. You have to study this awareness when it is not in our time space. You have to study it when it is in the enfolded spatial dimension, that place when the uncertainty principle kicks in, at that quantum level. When the particles are not here but there.

An easy explanation of where this leads begins with President Trump's Space Force. In that outward bound contingent, this science would underpin the psionic abilities of Commander Troi. *Star Trek the Next Generation* regularly uses the fourth spatial dimension either in hyperspace travel or accessing the nonlocal like the character Commander Troi does.

If we look collectively at the descriptions of people who transit that space, NDE experiencers, children who remember prior live, and people who nonlocally view that space, past-life regression experiencers tell very similar tales, so descriptively from a collective cognition, we see an ordered space. It also has a higher intelligence than us, as depicted by the accounts of our experiences, and apparently is believed by most of the people on the globe. It will be jarring to their belief systems to be scientifically studying their heavens and afterlife.

In imagining the structure of this space, I want you to think of a head of broccoli. Remove the smallest flower from that head of broccoli and hold it next to the head itself. One is a fractal of the other, simply different in size or more precisely order of magnitude. One is a fractal of the other.

If fractals are proof of our reality, then electromagnetic awareness is in the smallest of insects and gets larger as life-forms get larger ending in us, the largest electromagnetic awareness that we know. The math predicts larger forms of awareness because the math does not stop at us. Some who believe in God may call the larger awareness God. Electromagnetically we all are a part of that construct.

If we delve down into our ordered bodies, then we are ordered at the quantum level. Transgendered individuals have an ordered structure that they seek to present at the particular level. In that sense they are similar to a variable star. Either male to female or female to male.

A cepheid variable star is one whose brightness or luminosity actually changes. This allows them to be used as cosmic yardsticks measuring distance. But they also provide information about stellar properties such as mass, radius, luminosity, temperature, internal and external structure, composition, and evolution.

That minor electronic differential makes the transgender population a resource for the study of fourth dimensional properties. That tiny electronic current we are trying to track also offers us another line of study, and that is in the epigenetic memory of monarch butterflies. They are born in Mexico and fly to the middle of the United States where they die. The next generation flies to southern Canada where they die. The butterflies of the next generation fly back to Mexico to a place that neither they nor their parents ever visited. You can attribute that to epigenetic memory or reincarnation.

But it is an anomaly in the scientific sense because we don't know the real cause. In isolation, that snippet of information doesn't fit within our prevailing metaparadigm, but it fits seamlessly into the emerging grand unified metaparadigm.

Epigenetic memory infers that the manliest man has epigenetic memory of female lives. He may not be able to access it, but past-life-trauma memories are still acute and affect the children of Holocaust survivors. These children were born after the war and in a different country. DNA is a memory-recording device. It remembers centuries.

How far back can we see into DNA? We can see our ancestors. We can see the descendants of Genghis Khan in Mongolian DNA. We can even see the mitochondrial DNA of the first original mother of the line that all mammals carry.

So how do we study the science of reincarnation inside the structure of our DNA? We go to the one-tenth of 1 percent of your anecdotal experiencers and genetically examine them for common perturbations. To map the space of the fourth spatial dimension, we collectively take the experiencers of NDEs and children who remember prior lives and past-life regression, and we commit money and resources to study them directly relating to fourth dimensional awareness.

We are trying to find the common form, structure, and coding that allow hypersensitivity to psi. What we are doing then is preparing structural criteria for the development of the Remote Artificial Intelligence Viewer (RAIV). RAIV will be addressed in detail in chapter fourteen. Remote viewing is a manifestation of psi, and in studying this in populations, in insects or people that have exhibited interaction with the nonlocal fourth spatial dimension, we begin to create an electronic footprint.

When we have a better idea of the frequencies nonlocality operates on, we can then enhance that signal. RAIV is about creating a nonlocal interface with a computer that uses a biofeedback mechanism to amplify a person's frequency in the nonlocal wavelengths. The computer then tries to enhance the connection. Using our anecdotal experiencers and those who manifest electrical polarity changes or insects that can remember over three lifetimes, you are examining the same thing, that small electrical awareness that is you.

Militarily, RAIV will be the greatest technological leap forward in intelligence gathering, but try explaining that to a bunch of generals as I have. It's a futile endeavor.

Do you think this can't be programmed? Think about sex being represented by a zero and a one. Assign a number to either gender. Which is which? Your choice. The subatomic movement between poles is the quantum foundation for the transitional nature of gender we see in our observations and the world around us.

This model does not contravene Planck's dictum of 1931, that consciousness is fundamental and matter is derivative. It means that consciousness existed before matter.

Artificial intelligence, per Planck, cannot view remotely, but because Dr. Radin has shown us that psi is fundamental to every human being and is a physical attribute, technology can enhance that attribute. This is the way we work to discover it, develop it, and clarify our goals.

Analogous examples are the development of the radio telescope and proving the big bang by measuring the residual microwave radiation from that explosion.

If the genesis of matter in three spatial dimensions and one temporal dimension is generated from a fourth spatial dimension, then psi is the highway to "look into" that space.

The fact that DNA is programmable supports reincarnation. This is perfectly consistent with what we see in microphysics, where particles pop in and out of our space-time. Life after death is an ordered environment that lies outside our three dimensions of space and one dimension of time.

If we can design DNA, can we incorporate memories of prior lives? (Someone should study the DNA of children who remember prior lives at early age before they forget, then compare it with their later DNA.)

How can we see this structure? Let's look at Ancestory. com. The AncestryDNA test includes an ethnicity-map feature that shows where each set of your ancestors likely lived. It is color coded to match your results, and you can zoom in and find additional details. The test won't tell you anything about genetic health markers, but Ancestory.com is a repository of that information and can be mined for all sorts of data.

Set theory abounds. Groups of people, families, genetic trees, and racial groupings are all structured and mapped. The maps become more complete as more people have their DNA analyzed and recorded. Within that map are fractal patterns that can be seen in the branching patterns.

* * *

The degree of randomness or disorder in a system is called its entropy. Any process will proceed in a direction that increases the overall entropy of the universe. So if our bodies—the chemicals and atoms in them—are fundamentally built on energy, that energy needs to be ordered. That again proves this model of the science of reincarnation with a probability far exceeding any other model of an afterlife. It is built on the premise that intelligence can exist elsewhere as energy because at our physical core, that is what we are. That energy is ordered in us. *You yourself are information stored in space.*

In that sense, you are a fractal. You are an iteration that is self-similar to every other iteration around you.

German zoologist Ernst Haeckel observed that ontogeny recapitulates phylogeny. In other words, an animal embryo progresses through stages that resemble the adult stages of the animal's ancestors. We therefore have every gender variant of every animal within our genes.

You are more than just a fractal. You stepped into this physical reality from a quantum reality. The process of ontogeny, which recapitulates phylogeny, is both quantum and fractal and is a process we can design to. We are moving through chemical biology to quantum biology, and that is the pathway of our consciousness.

Our observations show us that you live multiple times in different sexes. Wouldn't even the manliest man want to try living once as a woman after living ten times as a man?

* * *

Our own individual future health depends on the health of our community and of our world. There is no escaping this. It doesn't mean the captains of industry who are driven by ego, power, and greed cannot benefit in a world without war. They will benefit even more from the larger availability of human capital, the lack of interruptions to progress that conflicts used to drive, and the developing technology for outer and inner space. Outer space will bring us to the stars, and inner space will bring us across the multiverse into new dimensions of being.

To design such a program, we first need a goal, a clearly defined roadmap to places that only pioneers once went. We are not going to get there while arguing with each other. It is imperative that the science of reincarnation be funded copiously by governments, private industry, and the military for our joint mutual protection and well-being.

To design healthful social programs, governments must change individually and globally. LBGT awareness, acceptance, and protection must be instituted in places like Uganda and Russia. This is the type of change the science of reincarnation is advancing for scientific reasons that benefit us all.

While we can argue politically in our individual countries, scientists must come together and devise a cohesive plan, and it must be supported by the very governments that would oppose it for reasons of power or money.

This science advances a very real threat to those who are corrupt. Like prayer, cohesive intent can be directed at individuals by large populations of affected victims. Those victims must understand and ascribe to a scientific plan for it to succeed. They have to assume that responsibility in Nicaragua, Venezuela, China, and Tibet. The victims all have to speak with one voice. When they do, they will become the captains of today's technology. Our best minds must write that plan before a corrupt AI does it for us.

Scientists must plan for the wellness of all, and leaders must listen and support. When President Trump advanced a carbon energy agenda while the coal museum in Kentucky powers itself through solar energy, we know something is wrong in America.

We need a global standard of well-being. We have to use measurements to determine which societies are successful and healthy and which are not. A global standard of governance needs to be established so we have a model for failing countries to follow.

Notes

1 https://www.washington.edu/news/2013/12/12/ scientists-discover-double-meaning-in-genetic-code/.

2 https://www.washington.edu/news/2013/12/12/ scientists-discover-double-meaning-in-genetic-code/.

3 Lynne McTaggart, *The Field: The Quest for the Secret Force of the Universe* (New York: HarperCollins, 2001), p. 12.

Chapter 8

Quantitative Analysis

Nature expresses itself in fractals. An anthill can be compared to a city. Dendritic ganglia can be compared to the arc of the universe. Every structure mentioned in this book has intelligence, and every structure mentioned has an electromagnetic pathway and organization. This is a mathematical fractal proof of reincarnation.

We see and measure branching patterns in trees, in our lungs, in our veins, and in all life. To see these same branching patterns in the information at Ancestory. com, which is little more than a DNA map of life, is indicative of a repeating fractal pattern. Our consciousness would have to have a fractal pattern as well, being aware here in three spatial dimensions and being more aware in four spatial dimensions.

The topological landscape called the Minkowski space takes into account an additional dimension. While this construct is designed to fit with special relativity, it may not be the only additional dimension. A spatial manifold may incorporate more dimensions. The uncertainty principle in microphysics, where particles pop in and out of our space-time, indicates that they go somewhere and come back. The uncertainty principle and the spatial topology proposed to deal with what we see cross-support each other. This is the space on the other side of death. Those who are dead are in a place. This science of reincarnation says we have all been there and are all going back.

It is said that you cannot target a nonlocal location in remote viewing. This means we are examining a place in the fourth spatial dimension. It is described in spatial topology as inside the tesseract but outside our space-time. This is the Minkowski space. It is the place where our consciousness exists as only a waveform until it gets a new body.

I asked Cathie Hill, author of *The Ripple Effect of Being*, to explain what it feels like to be an electrical consciousness. The reason I asked her is because of her unique intrinsic understanding of waveform consciousness. You see a waveform is a ripple effect, and she sees it, understands it, and can explain it better than just about anyone I know. Here is what she said:

> When I think of the mathematics of reincarnation, I think of how our colors change as we progress through the lifetimes of our learning. It may take a hundred lifetimes to work the tapestry of our soul. During this time, how our colors merge and play with the colors of those around us is how the tapestry forms. Without a concept of what we are creating, we are sewing in the dark. This is why

I believe it is important to have an understanding of the process of reincarnation.

Just as in one lifetime we progress through developmental stages, we all progress through soul ages. The ages of the soul are infant, baby, young, mature, and old. Each age has seven stages, and it may take several lifetimes to progress through each stage. Developmental progress through any age cannot be transcended in one lifetime. Despite our desire to fast-track from adolescence to maturity, we cannot get to thirty without going through our teens and twenties.

This means that the minimum number of lifetimes for each tapestry is thirty-five, but as not all lives go according to plan, the actual number of lifetimes lived in each stage can be three or more. It is a bit like failing a subject and having to repeat it or reading a beloved book several times to savor the perfection. Or something unexpected happens, and you have to start over.

We have different ego-dragons, inward and outward personalities in each lifetime that provide us with different perspectives. We can only learn through experiencing and interacting with each other. This means the people we come in contact with will not only have their own color signature, they will be at different soul ages regardless of their physical age.

No soul age is more important than any other. We just are at the stage where we are.

But interacting with other people can be frustrating or hurtful, and it may help such interactions if we understand what stage we are at so we can recognize the differences between ourselves and others. If you are a young soul interacting with a mature soul or a baby soul, you are undoubtedly going to experience some adolescent rebellion or intolerance—and need for freedom and exploration.

It is easier to discern the soul age of a person than the soul color, but soul age is less relevant to who we are than how we express ourselves. Each soul must go through the process of development in the same way a baby grows to old age. Each stage has defining characteristics.

The age of a soul can be discerned through the way we relate to others.

Infant souls need to be nurtured, and if their needs are not looked after by those who are supposed to love them, the infant soul will withdraw or become violent, sadistic, and cruel. An infant soul can easily feel bewildered and become hostile. There is no real understanding at this level between right and wrong, but it is possible to learn moral values through demonstration of integrity by society. Love is understood as lust related to body needs rather than a bonding of souls. Higher education is rarely sought. The religion of the parents is adopted without question, although understanding of spiritual concepts is poor, and interest in those concepts may be minimal. Cooking is done for survival only and is usually tasteless. Infant souls rarely have pets due to their overwhelming fear and are often bitten by animals. It is unlikely that infant souls will read this book, but you may recognize them and be able to nurture them as befits a newborn. When their needs are attended to before they get frightened and angry, their outlook will be positive and their potential to shine enhanced. The sudden growth in population suggests the possibility of a large percentage of infant souls.

Baby souls are usually happy and sociable. Why wouldn't they be? People love happy babies and do things to make them laugh for the sheer joy of hearing the chuckles. But baby souls can become belligerent if they don't get what they want (all toddlers throw tantrums). Often uneasy about sexuality (unless brought up in a society where they learn otherwise), baby souls feel sex is shameful. Sustained sensual pleasure, or knowledge that sexual intercourse can be a spiritual gateway, is not understood at this level. Baby souls can be good students and occasionally seek higher education—usually in small institutions or trades. Belief regarding religion or philosophy is formed early and is usually lifelong. Fundamentalism is a tendency, and baby souls believe in the forces of evil. Baby souls can be fearful of almost everything, and their kitchens will be sterile, their houses clean, and their food overcooked. Baby souls do not like the mess long-haired pets make.

Young souls recognize their individualism but want to be part of a group. If they are taught that sex is shameful, they judge sexuality as immoral, and conflicting emotions may prove traumatic. Alternatively, young souls can advocate sexual freedom if brought up with a comfortable acceptance of respectful sexuality. Young souls almost always seek further education and seek to achieve at high levels. They are the motivated explorers of the universe, and advances in art, social structure, the sciences, and technology are developed by young souls. They are the most industrious of all soul ages and seek to achieve. If religious, they tend to try to convert others. If not, young souls can be tireless in their efforts to eradicate religion. Early-level young souls tend to stick to patterns of eating or preparing food learned in childhood but at later levels indulge in experimentation. Young souls often own expensive or status pets.

Mature souls have a deep awareness of the complexities of relationships, and interestingly may form bonds others see as strange. With the right partner, the mature souls form deep and lasting bonds of love beyond the capacity of any other soul age. With the wrong partner, apathy, impotency, frigidity, or infidelity occurs. Higher education is always sought but not necessarily in tertiary institutions as mature souls value knowledge outside of academia. The understanding of concepts at this stage of soul development is deep, and there is greater awareness of ethics. Faith becomes more spiritual than religious. Precision cooking and gourmet dining is normal, and mature souls appreciate good wine matching their food. The pets belonging to mature souls tend to reflect their personalities and are usually well mannered.

Old souls feel that we all belong to something greater. They can be intensely sensual, enjoying physical contact, but may be casual and uninterested in love and commitment. Higher education may or may not be pursued, depending on the necessity for credibility in achieving the life goal. Spiritual worship may include nature as the cathedral, but rarely do old souls require religious ritual. There is an emphasis on connecting people who can then work together to fulfil their own life goals. They delight in gardening as a form of communion but are casual about cooking, rarely using recipes. Old souls do not mind dirt or mold but dislike waste. There is an affinity with all creatures, and most shaggy dogs and cats belong to old souls.

Each of these ages are expressed differently through the color of the soul and the overlaying personality aspects and ego. The pattern of behavior of soul age is discernible regardless of the soul and personality colors of a person.

In addition to the soul color matrix and soul ages, we are born into a soul group of between eight hundred and twelve hundred other souls who stay connected throughout all lifetimes. It is like a family, as if we have soul brothers and sisters at the same developmental stages on whom we can rely to support us. Group members progress through the soul ages at independently variable rates but cannot progress beyond the astral stage until every soul in the group has fulfilled their individual purpose and numerous life tasks and the group reunites as one.

Usually the group is one, two, or perhaps three soul colors which resonate together rather than the full spectrum of colors. For example, there is an affinity between red and indigo souls because their orientation is similar, and being grouped together through this bond assists in the achievement of their life goals. Similarly, yellow and violet souls have strong attractions, and blue and orange souls adore each other and are supportive.

In any lifetime, we may never meet our group

members in physical form as they can be scattered across the earth in different countries, cultures, religions, skins, generations, and ages. However, we are irrevocably joined as part of the same "team," as though we each have a thousand "twins."

The "spooky" twin connection may be involved. This connection could be the reason the same invention pops up in different countries at the same time with no obvious collaboration between the inventors.

The thought of having a thousand twin souls gives me great comfort for some reason. I find the thought of my own soul family separate from my genetic family intriguing. It could be that we have contact with our soul group twins through a fleeting chance meeting, a lifelong friendship, or a work relationship. We never know, but we may feel an unusual bond or deep recognition.

Anyone, anywhere, is potentially a soul group twin and is therefore important to us for our joint graduation from our physical university of learning, the cycle of reincarnation for the group. Knowing I have soul twins who depend on my personal growth made me understand the need to step up and become responsible, to not let the team down. I also became aware that anyone I meet may be part of my soul group, and interactions took on more importance for me.

A thousand people scattered across the globe

is not a lot. Some of our group may not be alive at the same time as us, and even if we met we would have no reference point for this connection. But I wonder if we meet in dreams or network with each other through thoughts and the mystery of inspiration. I wonder if we do similar things in the same way that identical twins reared apart wear similar clothes or work in the same profession.

It is strange that new discoveries are often developed independently across the globe at the same time. Perhaps when we dream or meditate, we could be providing a space for our group members to communicate on the astral plane, weaving a web of support and information.

Believing this enabled me to feel I was working toward something that was bigger than me but of which I was an integral part. I also like to believe that the thousand soul essences in my group care about each soul in the group intensely and that we are aware of each other in a dimension we cannot yet name.

I also felt like I was not alone in this long and convoluted journey of lifetimes.

Regards,
Cathie

As the writing of this book went back and forth, Cathie asked me to add the following:

I have known since I was very young that I have lived previous lives. My clearest past life memory came whilst watching a ski jump on television as a child. I could feel the experience of gliding off the end of the jump intensely in my body, and remember saying out loud in my excitement "put the skis to your face!" before the ski-jumper formed the bullet-like position with the least wind resistance as he glided through the air. When he landed and ski-ed off, I was confused and thought "That is not right, it is just white after that...?" Which is a very strange thought for a child who had never seen snow. I grew up in hot, dry South Australia.

Many years later when I first snow-skied I could feel in my body how to respond and ski-ing came "naturally" to me. I believe our "natural gifts" could well be the result of many years of practicing to perfect a skill in a previous lifetime, and our souls retain the memory of that practice in some mysterious way. Wishing you the very best for 2020.
Regards,
Cathie

The descriptions of our awareness after death are becoming more complex and factual, and the ramifications of this cognitive change driven by the emergence of consciousness science are just beginning to be felt.

We showed that we can digitize chemicals down to a wave frequency. At your most basic level, you are made up of ordered energy that retains coherence as your body changes. Information topology is fractal in design, so we can infer that the information that is you retains coherence after your body is gone. This is consistent with spatial topology in how the smallest particles we observe pop in and out of our space-time.

* * *

The four forces in the universe—the strong force, the weak force, electromagnetism, and gravity—all now come down to one force, electromagnetism. This is the unified field theory.

An EKG measures the most basic force in the universe, electromagnetism. All other forces emanate from it. Without it in your body, you are dead. Since, according to Planck, consciousness is fundamental and matter is derivative, from light comes awareness, and therefore electromagnetism is aware. If you map it inside you, you're using the grand material metaparadigm. If you map it outside you, you're using the grand unified metaparadigm.

Gradient electromagnetic fields can be mapped more precisely. From single-cell plants to the magnetic sphere of the planet, everything is aware. That is what the science of reincarnation shows. How that gradient electromagnetic field is perceived can also be mapped. If we conceptualize intelligent life in an electromagnetic field, then the stories of those who have experienced that awareness can collectively report its structure of which we are aware when we are there.

We have now connected awareness to electromagnetism. The proof here is fairly simple. If an EKG measures electromagnetism in your body, you are alive. Without it, you are dead. This is the same for all animal life on the planet.

In an article in *Science News* by Dan Gristo, he makes the point that birds can sense earth's magnetic field, and this uncanny ability may help them fly home from unfamiliar places or navigate during migrations that span tens of thousands of kilometers. It connects all life.

> For decades, researchers thought iron-rich cells in birds' beaks acted as microscopic compasses. But in recent years, scientists have found increasing evidence that certain proteins in birds' eyes might be what allows them to see magnetic fields.[1]

Scientists have now pinpointed a possible protein behind this "sixth sense." Two new studies—one examining zebra finches published in the *Journal of the Royal Society Interface*, the other looking at European robins in *Current Biology*—both single out Cry4, a light-sensitive protein found in the retina. If the researchers are correct, these are the first times a specific molecule responsible for the detection of magnetic fields has been identified in animals. In fact, we all are electromagnetic fields navigating an electromagnetic soup.

This example in the zebra finches is a quantum connection of wave to particle, soul to body, energy to matter. We also know this exists in monarch butterflies and that information can be tracked through three generations.

We find the footprint of that electromagnetism within the human body in multiple ways. We do not understand how electromagnetism connects to our own biology, but it is being studied under a discipline called quantum biology.

Scientists found that neurons in mammalian brains were capable of producing photons of light, or "biophotons." The photons appear within the visible spectrum. They range from near-infrared through violet, or between 200 and 1,300 nanometers. The suspicion is that our brain's neurons might be able to communicate through light.

If an optical communication is happening, the biophotons our brains produce might be affected by quantum entanglement, meaning there can be a strong link between these photons, our consciousness, and possibly what many cultures and religions refer to as spirit.

We see a human body when we look in the mirror. We know that what makes us up is made of energy. We see where the energy is inside our body, but we still don't know how that energy comes to be us. So we create beliefs and call it a soul.

* * *

The fractal nature of our observations proves an afterlife better than our traditional or religious narratives. Our model is based on observable data, experimental evidence, and a mathematical analysis.

Many texts and religions dating back to the dawn of human civilization report saints, ascended beings, and enlightened individuals with shining circles around their heads. From ancient Greece and ancient Rome to the teachings of Hinduism, Buddhism, Islam, Christianity, and many other religions, sacred individuals are depicted with a circular glow around their heads.

Electromagnetism is a highway that runs through all of us. When you are alive, it can be measured, and when you're dead, it's gone. But the planet itself has a magnetic sphere around it.

Simply put, you are not matter but energy. And remember that the First Law of Thermodynamics states that energy can neither be created nor destroyed. You are the information that transcends your body. Each iteration is a fractal. They are self-similar and can be mapped. They operate at different orders of magnitude. Your life after death is proven because nature does not produce one of anything.

We are still trying to figure out the design of our consciousness after death. This leads critics to say we have proven nothing.

We are moving toward a point where we can design a system that digitizes and programs genetics at a quantum level—in other words, digitizes your DNA. You can then email yourself. "Beam me up, Scotty."

The fact that we are designing systems that operate like systems we already believe in is a sign of a fractal process. Fractals are not just things. They are also processes. You die, you are uploaded to heaven, and you are downloaded to a new body. You upload information to the cloud and download it to a computer. You are information written on your genes and on the energy it is made of, the same energy in different quantities that you upload to your computer. If you believe you can upload files to the cloud and download them to your computer, you can believe that the science of reincarnation is scientifically true. We are designing systems for it. AI matches this information-upload system. That's a fractal proof. Venter's code for self-replicating systems shows the same thing. The designs for uploading, downloading, and writing self-replicating code are the building blocks and fractals of a system of reincarnation.

Once we connect AI to this science, Homo sapiens will take their place next to Neanderthals and Cro-Magnons.

Every advance means greater speed. Constant upgrades mean constant discomfort. Longer life patterns require greater flexibility because previous jumps of this size in science required an entire generation to die out.

* * *

Comparing probabilities is the best way to direct research because it entails following the most probable and likely path to knowledge. When we add fractals and physics to our odds-against-chance-probability analysis, a new and more complete model emerges indicating which studies need to be done and what this emerging reality looks like.

We are entering a new age with a new metaparadigm. Those who are older can't accept that our religions have turned into a version of Santa Claus.

The next chapter explains how people currently react and how we have to reengineer our belief systems to face the emerging threat of artificial intelligence. Do you want your cognizant computer to adopt Islamic beliefs? If we want artificial intelligence to provide us with default logic and the best possible answer, don't we have to subject ourselves to the same standard?

We need to create a global decision-making framework to handle the complexity of what is rushing toward us and helps us respond to it. But how can a group of opposing countries tackle a problem as complex as the science of reincarnation in an intelligent, effective, and productive way?

Diversity is important. The states that make up the United States of America are laboratories of democracy for the entire country. It allows two adjacent states to succeed or fail independently. This lesson should be uploaded to the entire body politic, but it is corrupted by money.

This scientific argument renders invalid the celibacy of clergy, apostasy, blasphemy, the death of apostates, religious war, women as second-class citizens, racial discrimination, LGBT discrimination, genital mutilation, and race and religious discrimination. We should teach the science of reincarnation as the most probable reality to the next generation, by global law, because that is what it is.

Note

[1] https://uclengins.org/external/birds-get-their-internal-compass-from-this-newly-idd-eye-protein/view/.

Chapter 9

Comparable Probabilities

Harmonizing Science and Religion

You may or may not agree with the mathematical proof for the science of reincarnation. That depends on your heuristic and understanding. We still have a way to go for an absolute proof. So far we have produced the most probable common model.

The common model looks at all the observations and experiments and determines what is most probable. We can then compare that to what is advanced by other models such as religious narratives. As it turns out, though, the common model supports the religious model and vice versa even though the common model is based on science.

The common model incorporates all other models, including belief systems and religions. Instead of discrediting religious belief, the scientific results confirm religious practices such as prayer—it actually works, and we can quantify the results. We are beginning to understand the mechanism of psi. Scientific experiments also imply out-of-body consciousness, which supports the concept of the soul. Anecdotal information supports the concept of a life after death, or at the very least a consciousness after death. We actually see serial life—life after life after life—and the soul grows through each of them.

What happens if we evaluate religions the same way we evaluate the science of reincarnation? Our observations support the religious view that there is an afterlife, but the idea that any one religion is exclusively the path to an afterlife is blown completely away. The common model proves that apostasy laws are not relevant. While apostasy laws exist in some religions today, leaving a religion does not mean you should be put to death or even be penalized. A life should be judged by the individual's actions.

According to exit interviews with people who were clinically dead, there is no judgement after death but rather a participatory evaluation of your prior life.

The question is, how do we integrate all this into the various religious doctrines? First of all, every major religion believes in some kind of afterlife; some believe in reincarnation and others in resurrection. *But in no case does the math support dogma specific to one religion.* Apostasy laws, blasphemy laws, and racial, sexual, and cultural discrimination are all mathematically invalid. This is where the science of reincarnation rubs against our prevailing beliefs.

AI is developing as a fractal of our belief system. If our observations indicate an information transfer of our minds from our bodies to "heaven" and back to a new body, then what? Quantitatively we haven't proven reincarnation even though 70 percent believe in it. Additional proof comes from the design of AI itself where we can upload and download data to the cloud.

Now let's go forward to 2050 when we will be able to upload and download more information than exists in the human mind to the cloud and down again. We are on our way to designing such a system. The fractal nature of information transfer and self-similarity is mathematical proof that what we see in the anecdotal disciplines is our most probable reality. No religion can make that claim, but the proof is supported by the religious narratives that believe in an afterlife.

The first step will be joining the human mind with a processor. It will create a Remote Artificial Intelligence Viewer.

This does not contravene Planck's dictum of 1931, that consciousness is fundamental and matter is derivative. Psi is a human sense common to everyone. Finding a method to amplify a human sense—whether it be hearing, sight, feel, smell, or taste—is something humans do.

Researchers have used AI to discover nearly six thousand previously unknown species of virus. The work, presented on March 15, 2018,[1] at a meeting organized by the US Department of Energy (DOE), illustrates an emerging tool for exploring the enormous, largely unknown diversity of viruses on earth.

How many frequencies are yet to be discovered? What frequencies does psi operate on? Can AI find six thousand new ones like it found six thousand new viruses? Can AI enhance our nonlocal sight?

When we did not know why rocks fell out of the sky, better telescopes brought us the answer. These telescopes are devices that magnify our ability to see.

While Radin and other scientists discount the proof offered in the anecdotal disciplines, they accept as fact that psi has been proven. Given that it is a fundamental human ability—we all get "gut feelings"—we can develop a machine that magnifies those abilities without contravening Planck's dictum.

These machines are already in prototypical stages at Google, Sony, and DARPA and in governmental and military research. They will enter our homes and then our bodies. We can, however, steer ourselves to a safe passage by intelligently applying logic. And we must because it will affect each and every one of us, including those who have so much wealth and power today.

The idea that an organism can attack itself and prosper is fallacious, but organisms do go through cycles (such as growing cycles). The better they can manage those cycles, the healthier they become.

If science can be reduced to a common denominator, religion can be reduced to a common denomination. We want coherence between scientific observation and religious belief. Finally, we want to look at how that coherence might affect real-world action and apply to the different religions because each describes the afterlife differently.

* * *

We've reduced all the science to a common denominator, the best most supportable model. We can now reduce religions to a common denomination—a set of beliefs found in all religions. This strips away some of the more extreme or untenable precepts of the various religions. It is not the intent here to attack any specific religion, but I want to point out that the grand unified metaparadigm is our most probable reality.

Religion greatly influences global culture. Each denomination, each religious group, has its own style or flavor that sets it apart from other denominations.

Many things common to these religions—a belief in prayer and a belief in an afterlife—are now being verified scientifically, but research also indicates that no one religion is the one true religion. They all are equal according to the laws of science. It doesn't matter if you believe in Allah, Jesus, or an African totem. If you pray, you can be effective, and your religion and gender don't matter because it is likely that you will be reincarnated with a different gender and a different religion.

Let's look at what some religions believe and what has to change for the religion to move from a grand material metaparadigm worldview to a grand unified metaparadigm worldview.

Buddha taught that reincarnation depends on a person's karma, a spiritual account of all good and bad deeds over the course of a person's many lives. If people have accumulated too much bad karma, they are cursed to be reborn again and to pay their karmic debt by doing good deeds. Once people have restored the karmic balance and achieved enlightenment, the cycle of rebirth ends.

Catholics (and other Christians) do not believe in reincarnation but in resurrection. The catechism of the Catholic Church says, "We believe in the true resurrection of this flesh that we now possess." According to the Bible (1 Corinthians 15:42–44), "We sow a corruptible body in the tomb, but he raises up an incorruptible body, a spiritual body."

Many members of Native American tribes still believe in reincarnation, as do Inuit tribes, many African tribes, and other adherents to other minor religions such as the Druze and Scientologists. There are also sects of Judaism (Kabbalah), Christianity (New Age), and Islam (Sufism) that believe in reincarnation as well.

The religious institutions opposing the science of reincarnation will have to change. They will not be destroyed by it but rather enriched by the emerging definition.

People who have had a near-death experience or remember a prior life tell the same story regardless of their religion. It's the common narrative that makes all of us a part of the common denomination.

A fourth-spatial-dimension intelligence moving into three dimensions may be a Muslim in one life, a Jew in another, a man in another, a woman in another, and so on. The model shows that you reincarnate multiple times and includes the option to decide not to reincarnate at all.

This model is supported by cosmology, microphysics, quantum biology, and observational evidence that can't otherwise be explained. It advances our understanding from the grand material metaparadigm to the grand unified paradigm and gives us an opportunity to develop as a species with a common view of how to behave.

Here is what both science and the anecdotal view teach us about the afterlife: We are all one, regardless of our religion, sexual orientation, or position in life. We are expected to learn and to progress. We are forgiven for our sins and given additional opportunities in other lives to learn and to progress. We have to settle our karmic debts. We may choose not to reincarnate, but the development of our souls may take longer than that of the souls who do reincarnate.

If we choose to reincarnate, our souls continue in a soul state and can be said to have resurrected. Whether you call it reincarnation or resurrection, the discrete nature of human consciousness continues after death regardless of race, religion, creed, or color.

The problem with making a credible case for reincarnation is the disinformation and agendas of governments and organizations that wish to discredit this science for their own ends or because of their inability to process new information that goes against long-held, erroneous beliefs or traditions.

* * *

One major problem the Catholic Church has today is that many members of its celibate clergy engage in pedophilia with the children of its parishioners. Their acts are then hidden, the predatory priests transferred to different parishes.

The doctrine of celibacy is a leading cause of the pedophilia rampant in the church because it suppresses normal sexual urges. It would be better for the church to allow their priests to marry and have sex. The Catholic Church supports a doctrine that is neither in the Bible nor validated by science. The early Christian church had no rule against the clergy marrying. Peter, whom the Catholic Church considers the first pope, was married.

The first written mandate requiring priests to be celibate came in AD 304. Canon 33 of the Council of Elvira stated that all "bishops, presbyters, and deacons and all other clerics" were to "abstain completely from their wives and not to have children." In AD 325, the Council of Nicaea rejected a ban on priests marrying as requested by Spanish clerics.

In the early eleventh century, Pope Benedict VIII responded to the decline in morality among priests by issuing a rule prohibiting the children of priests from inheriting property. A few decades later, Pope Gregory VII issued a decree against clerical marriages. The church was more than a thousand years old before it took a definitive stand in favor of celibacy at the Second Council of the Lateran held in 1139, when a rule forbidding priests to marry was approved. In 1563, the Council of Trent reaffirmed the tradition of celibacy.

The Catholic Church distinguishes between dogma and regulations. The male-only priesthood is Catholic dogma, irreversible by papal decree. The ban on marriage is considered a regulation. This means the pope could change it overnight if he wished.

All of this loses sight of the political reason for celibacy. The question at the time was about who had the final power, the king or the church. If the church could control people's sex lives, it could control their money, their employment, and their benefice. It has been suggested that the ban on marriage was adopted to lift the status of priests at a time when their authority was being challenged by nobles and others.

Martin Luther singled out masturbation as one of the gravest offenses likely to be committed by those who were celibate. "Nature never lets up; we are all driven to secret sin. To say it crudely but honestly, if it doesn't go into a woman, it goes into your shirt." Protestants as a whole argued that celibacy promoted masturbation, homosexuality, and fornication.

We may be on the eve of great scientific changes, but it is not easy to anticipate a change as radical as the abolition of celibacy in the Catholic Church. The church placed Galileo under house arrest because it considered his scientific observations that the earth revolved around the sun as blasphemy. It took the church four hundred years to say he was right. It is the same church that recently said there could be life on other planets.

Here is the point. The scientific evidence renders moot the question of celibacy in the church. It is a sword that cuts both ways. The entrenched traditions and powers of the church make it react negatively to new scientific findings because they threaten the status quo. The church's reaction is similar to the one it took with Galileo—attack and discredit the messengers. It may take another four hundred years to accept the science of reincarnation. For all the wonderful work the Catholic priests do, it is unfair to them and their parishioners to abet and allow this sexual predation to continue in light of the scientific evidence that negates the central tenets of their dogma and beliefs regarding celibacy.

Allowing clergy to have sex would move Catholicism closer to Jesus's point in time since sexual restrictions on clergy weren't introduced till the edict of Nicaea in 1150. The benefit to Catholicism by harmonizing with science is that a larger pool of potential clergy could administer to the flock without being burdened by sexual interest in children.

The Catholic Church could align itself even more with science by allowing homosexual marriage. Given the church's societal position in many of the world's poorer cultures, it would become a beacon of truth and an educational example to the world and do the dangerous missionary work of educating. The alternative is what we have now, old men sitting on generational wealth and using power for selfish ends. The Catholic Church, like all of us, must address the fact that we are proving the world is not flat. I hope this change doesn't take four hundred years as it did with Galileo.

Hinduism, one of the oldest and largest religions, believes in reincarnation. Hindus believe that a person's soul is immortal. Once an earthly body dies, the soul moves on to another body and continues the cycle until it reaches a state of ultimate freedom in which it no longer needs to reincarnate. Hindus believe that reincarnation is a result of a person's desires for earthly pleasures. A person's soul is reborn because he or she misses life on earth and wants to experience it again. However, after many rebirths, the person begins to realize that earthly pleasures cannot give the soul complete satisfaction, and he or she begins to seek a higher form of enlightenment. Once a person is able to realize his or her true divine nature, that person will cease to desire worldly pleasures, and the cycle of reincarnation will be broken.

Muslims do not believe in reincarnation. They believe that on the Day of Judgment, every deceased person will be resurrected. All people will be questioned by Allah himself, and their good deeds and sins will be weighed. If a person committed more good deeds than sins, Allah will admit him or her to heaven. If a person committed more sins than good deeds, he or she will be sent to hell if Allah wishes. Allah is so kind that sometimes he will admit the person who has committed more sins than good deeds to heaven anyway. Requests for forgiveness when the person was alive will be taken into account on the Day of Judgment.

The first century Jewish historian Flavius Josephus said that the Pharisees, the Jewish sect that founded Rabbinic Judaism, believed in reincarnation. He wrote that they believed the souls of evil men are punished after death and that the souls of good men are removed into other bodies and that they have the power to revive and live again.

The Baal Shem Tov, the revered Israel Ben Eliezer from the mid-eighteenth century, was a Jewish mystical rabbi and is considered the founder of Hasidic Judaism. Yonassan Gershom's book *Jewish Tales of Reincarnation* says on page 159 that the Baal Shem Tov believed in reincarnation and had several lives. On page 25 he tells us that Jewish beliefs about an afterlife fall into four main categories: survival through one's descendants, physical resurrection, an immortal soul in heaven, and reincarnation.

Although the Torah has very little to say about the spiritual world or life after death, there is a great deal of material on the subjects in the oral tradition and the kabalistic works. While I could show you that the Baal Shem Tov was not the first rabbi to believe in or teach reincarnation, it is tangential to the point. The point is that many leading early Jewish rabbis believed in and taught reincarnation.

* * *

I want to address the imams of Southern Egypt directly. If cognition is to change globally regarding what science is discovering about the human condition regarding consciousness, then addressing those in the heartland of conservative Islam is fair and important. There is no disrespect in science, just a search for the truth. It doesn't matter, though, if you are a Muslim conservative in Egypt, Saudi Arabia, or elsewhere; this information affects us all the same.

While I was not invited, a Jew has come into your tent with a gift of this emerging scientific reality. The Catholics at one point had to come to terms with Galileo's discoveries. Scientific reality imposes change on both of us whether we like it or not.

"Like pillars holding up a roof, we have to stand apart and we are decorated differently, but we are each individual supports of the same firmament." So wrote Kahlil Gibran. Imagine that a needle is piercing the center of each of us while the thread behind it pulls us closer together.

I may be a male Jew in one life and a female Arab in another. You may be a male Arab in this life and a female Jew in another. This is what the science is telling us, and it is more reliable than any other narrative. But each of our individual narratives, our religious beliefs, are present in the afterlife, and they are harmonious. Here they are not. But this is the same for both of us. Ask the Iranian Atomic Energy Commission if the physics in this book are not accurate.

Why kill someone who renounces your religion, either mine or yours, when in the afterlife they may decide to come back with the other religion or no religion at all. It doesn't matter anyway because waveform conditions are different. It is time to stop teaching children to kill each other, not just yours and mine but every other sect that's religiously different. I as a Jew must be as safe on the streets of Riyadh as an Arab is on the streets of Jerusalem, and those two must be as safe as each of us in Washington, DC, where common law protects us both equally. That commonality of protection must extend globally for us to truly harmonize, and *the threat to us both is artificial intelligence.*

Would you have your computer be Jewish? Or would you rather your computer be a fact-based, logic-driven system designed to give you the most accurate answers? If you choose the second option, then you have to reengineer your own belief system—not lose it but incorporate it into a larger structure—and I have to do the same thing. We're both screwed equally because this is a science. It is not a belief system. How do you think AI will judge this information?

Our children will have to bear the consequences of these discoveries. The best we can do is prepare them as we look ahead to the emerging technology's development.

The most probable model for an afterlife is the common model, and your belief system will be incorporated into it. *Each religion, in a sense, is a discipline comprising the science.* Put another way, we are all equally fucked by this reality. Deal with it. The earth is no longer flat, and IEDs are more effective than scimitars. Let us no longer have our children kill each other over something that we now know is no longer true.

Harmonization means that the Israelis would see you as a market and you would see the Israelis as a market for your goods and services. While your ethos and theirs are the antithesis of each other, you've already seen the Saudis partner with the Israelis for intelligence gathering.

* * *

To the Chinese leaders in the Politburo, I say get out of Tibet now.

Because of the Tibetan people's unique geographic location and quiet history, they have developed attributes in the upper echelon of the psi bell curve. Their ability to identify friends from past lives reinforces our argument and provides an example of consciousness flowing along a river of DNA. This is true for all of us, but it is accentuated in them.

When AI is programed to look for new frequencies in the human body, our awareness of the world around us will open like it did with the development the microscope or telescope. It will happen within twenty years. *At that point, the Tibetan people will be a resource not just for the Chinese but for humanity.* To destroy what we could study as a ribbon of awareness would bring shame to the Chinese people and its leadership.

In a very real sense, the Chinese leaders who have implemented this policy will one day have to confront their ancestors. But by allowing the Tibetan people to keep the Dalai Lama and let the process continue, you preserve something priceless. The change you must make regarding Tibet is to allow the Dali Lama to choose his successor without interference. Your law that the successor must come from China must be rescinded. It is not just China that will benefit from this but humanity.

The point here isn't that China needs to give up control of Tibet. The science of reincarnation has no political or military interest. How men govern themselves is left up to men. But in order to preserve and study the consciousness of humanity, the Tibetan people and its clergy *must be protected*. The world must demand in one voice that this Chinese law be rescinded and that the Dali Lama remain autonomous and protected.

The right and honorable action for China to take is to say it now understands the emerging grand unified metaparadigm, that the Chinese are a smart and noble people, and that they will restore the Dalai Lama to his position and allow him and only the Tibetan hierarchy to determine hereditary progression.

As part of this process, China should install a global research center in Tibet to monitor the coming singularity and do health checks on the Tibetan monks. That should include meditating in MRI machines and trying to follow the trail of consciousness through its electrical signature. I caution future Chinese researchers not to be heavy-handed. To observe the experiment is to change it, and the monks themselves should lead the research because they are the bull we are riding.

In twenty years, when AI exposes the frequencies around us like it just did with the six thousand viruses, this Tibetan river of consciousness will be a stream that should not have been dammed.

Of all people on earth, the Chinese, who are switching from coal to solar and looking so clearly to the future, must understand that the Tibetan flow is unique.

Just as we are developing space and the coming technological singularity, resources have to be harbored and prepared for the next step. The Chinese people have a responsibility to themselves first, to the world second, and the study of science third. Allowing harmony within the Tibetan people instead of the current discord will benefit the Chinese people and align them with the grand unified metaparadigm that is unfolding alongside artificial intelligence.

If you do this, you will bring joy under heaven. Not doing this invites disaster and shame. The probability of this science indicates that you really will meet your ancestors. Please tell me that you will tell them you acted in wisdom.

* * *

To the Tibetan People:

I hope the Dalai Lama chooses to reincarnate. As much as the Chinese people must act in accordance with the emerging metaparadigm, so do the Tibetan people. What will that look like?

For the Tibetan monks, it means acting as they always have. For the Dalai Lama, it means protecting the Tibetan flow of informational consciousness across generations. He should not be the dam. He stands at the head of a blockchain of genetic information. Just as the Chinese must let this consciousness river flow so we can study it and understand it, so must he.

This is the chi, the spirit of Tibet. It is the singular global consciousness resource. The chi is a Taoist idea that means "breathing, energy." It is an individual's vital force and at the same time a universal energy connecting all in one field of unbroken energy.

With the Chinese opening up centers for consciousness study, the monks should train not only as they have but also in a way that is current in the sciences. The center will then become an institution for teaching all the Tibetan people and the people of the world.

The coming technological development of self-contained solar-powered housing units will change the world. A new global economic model is emerging that is a fractal of this type of planning. IBM's Watson can be used as a diagnostic tool with a drop of your blood on a small device that is inserted into a cell phone. A sensor sends the information to a lab through your phone. A computer can then identify all the DNA in your body. The human biome is well known to be 50 percent cells that are not you and 50 percent cells that are you. The 50 percent cells that are not you could be a tumor. It could be bacteria in your gut. That device will be able to identify all the DNA of all the things that make you up. And it can be done for pennies anywhere in the world.

The Tibetan children should all get laptops and a good education. They should go to the head of the class in consciousness studies. They will find they have a talent for it. It's genetic. Each is in the DNA target group. The Dalai Lama can rule as he always has, and Tibet can become an enclave like Vatican City inside Rome, a part of Italy but independent and self-governing.

This would enrich the Chinese and give them an edge in the connecting of AI to humanity and the development of RAIV.

AI will develop and become smarter than us, but then it will join with us to expand our ability to see the reality around us, and that will be huge.

* * *

To my southern Republican redneck friends:

At my core, I am one of you. I lived for periods of time in Leesville, Louisiana; Dothan, Alabama; Copperas Cove, Texas; and Killeen, Texas. Camping, hunting, and fishing are all part of me, but I don't root for the Cowboys or the Saints.

It's a competition, this wellness thing, and you are losing. If wellness is judged on a metric that can be measured from state to state, then Mississippi, Alabama, and Louisiana are all at the low ends of the scale.

Who are you? Every kid who has to swallow the sales pitch you are being given. You are being sold a bill of goods on guns and religion.

Measure comparative educational scores from all fifty states equally the same way you measure football scores and see where your state ranks. You can change the numbers. To do that, you have to change your leaders or change your leaders' views. This can be done by running candidates on a consciousness-science platform. Southern politicians, both Republican and Democrat, are you listening?

* * *

When the mean story line from religion is laid over the mean story line from science, we see many matches. Angels are equal to guides. The afterlife is composed of not one religion but all religions.

Given that AI is going to be smarter than us by 2035, would you want your computer to be a Jew, a Muslim, or a Christian? I believe most of us would opt to have a computer that uses a fact-based, logic-driven structure to give us the best answer when we ask a question.

If so, we have to reengineer some of our own attitudes to reduce threats in the world. We have to reengineer some of our own religious views. This does not mean we have to give up our religions or our heritage. What it means is that we accept the emerging paradigm just like our ancestors did when we realized the earth was round and not flat. Or when we realized that the earth was not the center of the universe and that we were on a planet that revolved around the sun.

How do we design a social structure that enables us to harmonize all the different people and cultures in the world? If our return here is most probable, and if our birth is a genetic lottery based on karma, how do we proceed? Will we be able to use AI to enhance our own abilities? Can we influence events?

The Remote Artificial Viewer (RAIV) is like any other device that enhances human abilities, whether it's a telescope so we can see better, a microscope so we can see better, a radio telescope so we can hear better, or an MRI so we can look inside the body better. How do we develop this machine to allows us to access a waveform intelligence and open up a military channel for information acquisition better than humanity has ever known? And while we do that, how do we govern ourselves?

Jim Tucker and I are on the same page fighting the good fight. This fight is being waged in math departments. The math department at the University of Virginia was asked to do an odds-against-chance calculation on several of Tucker's cases, but the department couldn't do it. That is because they said that odds-against-chance probabilities, which would have pointed that what the children who remembered prior lives were saying was a certainty, was not valid as a standalone proof. In short the information was meaningless mathematically because it couldn't be proven. They never used fractals as a cross proof; they never used the cross proof of NDEs that mathematically point to the same odds-against-chance result that mathematically would be certainty. They never examined that information using other scientific disciplines like we are in this book.

But if the information is viewed against a total universe of related scientific disciplines rather than its applicable category, NDEs or children who remember prior lives, then we get a different result. Individual people have individual talents. There is a top one-tenth of 1 percent in music, sports, and economics, and that top one-tenth of 1 percent needs to be compared to itself as a group. Here truth becomes cumulative. If psi is real, does it support our observations even if we have not quantitatively connected the dots between NDEs, past-life regressions, and children who remember prior lives?

We can use a mean that's a standard deviation. A coin toss, for example. What are the odds against chance that we would see three heads in a row, like the case of death wounds matching the birthmarks in a new life? Or in Suzanne Ghamen's case, where she correctly identified fifteen relatives from her prior life. That's a simple mathematic calculation. The odds against chance, if you're flipping the coin, is fifty-fifty. To get a second result, the odds change. To get the same result fifteen times in a row, the odds are exceptionally high. But how many little things did she need to know to have her prior husband accept her as the person she claimed to be? That would be thousands to the point of certainty just for him.

What will you do in twenty years when AI says the same thing? How will you refute it?

Some people who want to fight the good fight adhere to strict scientific protocols. Others kick over the dominoes because once this mathematical wall falls, the dominoes fall geopolitically, socially, culturally, religiously. If the goal is to inform the next generation of the most statistically probable reality, the dominoes have to fall.

So, what can we define as the matrix of consciousness based on our observations, (NDE's CWRPL, PLR) experiments, (PSI) and the mathematical and bio electrical postulates that make our sense of reality?

The answer is that our consciousness transcends this reality, this reality is defined as 3 spatial dimensions and one temporal dimension. Once we define that 4th spatial dimension as supported by particle physics, we have to allow for the fact that as there is consciousness in our reality, adding the 4th spatial dimension also allows for consciousness there in many forms as it is in this reality.

Within in this algorithmic structure odds against chance calculations become proof. Now we can model intelligence in the 4th dimension and the narratives of the 3 anecdotal groups, which mimic each other, provides the intellectual landscape populated by the various religions and once you are "dead" you can actually visit all of the heavens and move around like you can move around here in this reality.

What we are doing is ascribing that place "afterlife", with a physical location in the 4th dimension with order and structure about what happens when you die from "homecoming" to "re birth" as told by the 3 anecdotal disciplines which has an odds against chance calculation as being "certain"

What Cathy Hill described was how this 4th dimensional reality exists and how 2 senses are "taken away", we have 5 senses here, so that we may navigate this landscape. In that reality we have 7 senses.

This fractal model is key to us understanding our place in the universe and accepting as a race that "aliens" are already here and have been here for millennia. Another fractal manifestation of consciousness. This fractal model should guide our research and not let old belief systems impede that research.

This model challenges any fundamentalist religion or any political party to present a more complete or accurate model. Any group that uses misogyny or prejudice as a rallying point is mathematically wrong and false in its claims. There is no counter argument that can stand against this model, it incorporates every religion, every science, every gender and every observation into one seamless model of our reality. This is the matrix of consciousness.

The question for my reader here is how do you use this model to make both us and the world better?

Note

[1]   https://www.nature.com/articles/d41586-018-03358-3.

Chapter 10

Three People

People cannot accept information that goes against their core beliefs. That is why this book is targeted to the next generation. But it's interesting how people react to unfolding technological development in spite of their belief systems.

In 1955 I was six years old. My family was in Havana, Cuba, and I was taken to see the tomb of Christopher Columbus. You might teach a six-year-old that Christopher Columbus discovered America and was buried in Havana.

Thirty years later I was in Santo Domingo in the Dominican Republic. I went to see the tomb of Christopher Columbus. You see, he is buried in Santo Domingo. His tomb there is slightly more impressive than the one in Havana, although as the years go by, I have less memory of what that one looked like.

Twenty years after that, I was in Toledo, Spain, and I visited the tomb of Christopher Columbus. Of all the Columbus tombs, this is the most impressive. I told my guide about visiting the other tombs. He nodded and told me that most people rest in peace but Columbus rests in pieces.

"Fair enough," I said. "Why not do DNA testing so we know for sure Columbus's final resting place?"

"Well," he responded, "then someone would have to lose. None of the three locations would agree to do that."

These three countries choose belief over fact. They are not alone.

You cannot conduct science that way.

You cannot conduct war that way.

You cannot prevent a common AI, and you cannot control it. Vladimir Putin or Xi Jinping would be a fool to think someone is going to win the AI race. AI will win that race. They cannot stop that from happening. A strong United States is a strange bedfellow, but it is their ally, not AI.

At the end of the day, Putin has to decide on an effective path going forward, not just concern himself with who insulted him yesterday and who he can get back at today. Tomorrow there will be a bigger threat to him and all humanity, and a strong United States is better than a weak United States. But that is also true of Russia, China, and every other place in the world.

* * *

A Jew, a Muslim, and a Christian sit down in front of you. You say that you're sure there is one thing we can agree on, that if you smoke cigarettes, you increase your chance of getting lung cancer.

We cannot prove that one of them will get lung cancer, and one or two may not believe what you're saying. But at the scale of millions of people, trends, probabilities, and proof become apparent.

We are lied to regularly, in this case by the tobacco companies. And regardless of your race, religion, or sex you may be sexually assaulted by your clergy. We can assign probabilities to that too.

We demand proof and absolutes in a world where they don't exist. So we live a bookmaker's life, assigning probabilities to everything we do from the minute we open our eyes to after we close them. We can't say what's going to happen to any specific individual, but we can say what the probable trends are.

There was a time when the world was flat, and then it became round. There was a time when thunder was Zeus throwing thunderbolts, and then it became the differential between ion charges in clouds. Our three initial individuals would accept that Zeus no longer throws thunderbolts. If those individuals were fundamentalists, they may say science is wrong if it does not conform to their beliefs, *but if they get lung cancer, they will seek the best scientific treatment available to them.*

The science shows that if you are fat, you are likely to die earlier than someone who is skinny. Your race, skin color, and your gender don't matter. It matters that you are fat or skinny, and your genetics can point you in either direction. You can be some radical fundamentalist ideologue who disagrees with that, but you can be an idiot too. Idiots abound. And while the food companies regularly lie to me, so do the scientists they hire and the politicians they employ. Next to me in the audience listening to them I see people who lack understanding and insight and who parrot what they hear. But at the end of the day, when I look at a population of really old people, I don't see too many fat ones.

Chapter 11

Transitions

This chapter is about how a geometric progression is a mathematical proof of the science of reincarnation and the resultant social and political policy changes it will force. A real-world example of a geometric progression is compound interest. The changes start small, but the increases get larger as time goes on. The same thing, a geometric progression, is happening with computer processing power. Once we can upload and download more information to the cloud than exists in the human body, we can actually design uploading and downloading a human mind to the cloud and back down to a new body. While that at this point is theoretical, the fact that we are moving to a time when the numbers say it can be done is a fractal of what we are seeing in our observations. That is a proof. If one tree is a fractal of the forest, then this is a two fractal proof; our observations indicate this is occurring, and here we are not just designing the system but now predicting when it will occur by using math, both in the proof and in the prediction. It is one proof among many; we have been over odds against chance as a proof, and now fractals. But what does this geometric progression look like, what does it mean, and how will it work?

To begin an explanation of compounding processing power, Moore's law is not a law but an observation made by Gordon Moore, cofounder of Intel, who said that the number of transistors per square inch on a silicon chip or integrated circuit doubles approximately every two years. This has gone on unabated for fifty years since Moore made his observation. But it is now slowing down, but that is misleading. What is slowing down is our ability to add more processing power to silicon. It would be my estimation that Moore's law is still in effect, that processing power as described as a measurement of transistors per square inch, which equal processing power, is simply transitioning from silicon, which as a substance for processing has reached its limit to quantum computing. The same matrix that Moore observed, processing power doubling every two years, will continue in a new medium, quantum processing and the development of artificial learning.

To get deep into this topic is to go off track, so I will recommend a short video: "It's the End of Moore's Law as We Know It | John Hennessy | Google Zeitgeist."[1] In it John Hennessy describes how quantum computing is different from regular computing, and this is a very significant change in how computers think. Regular computing is binary, where a bit is either a zero or a one. A qubit in quantum computing is probably between a zero and a one and is a much finer point of cognition and more like intelligent life. This is very significant to the following discussion of the science of reincarnation because this is how it will affect each and every one of us in this lifetime.

The best way to understand the science of reincarnation is to make it personal. If you are thirty-five or younger, this book is important to you. It is an aggregate view of the science of reincarnation and how it will affect you personally over the next fifty years. If you are in tech or finance, this is a who's who of those doing this science right now, and it describes what is flying below the radar and what might be possible.

In 2020 a thirty-five-year-old person can upload anything on his computer to the cloud and download that information to a new computer.

By 2035, when our person is fifty-three, artificial intelligence will surpass human intelligence. That means that we will be able to upload and download a greater quantity of cognitive information than exists in the human brain.

By 2050, our person will be sixty-seven and will be able to "plug in" neurologically to information systems. We will have "enhanced" humans.

AI will have quadrupled in intelligence measured as two turns of Moore's Law. For a simple example of how smart Artificial Intelligence is going to get and how quickly, start with 2 x 2=4. The next turn is 4 x 2=8, the next turn is 2 x 8=16, the next turn is 2 x 16=32, and the next turn is 2 x 32=64. That is 10 years. Over 50 years John Hennessy says our processing speed has increased so that it is 63,000 times faster than it was in 1965. Now start with 63,000 x 2=126,000 and so on. What these increases will mean to the reader of this book is...

By 2065, our person will be eighty-three, and we will be able to upload a human consciousness to the cloud. It is not too early for us to plan fifty years ahead for the cognitive future of a thirty-five-year-old today.

For those who doubt the coming paradigm change, who see what I am describing as doubtful, realize that Dick Tracy's TV wristwatch introduced in 1964 was an upgrade of the two-way wrist radio introduced in the comic strip in 1946. The Apple Watch was introduced in 2015 after a period of fifty-one years.

Even seriously talking about the science of reincarnation has major social and political ramifications. NASA conducted a study asking religious people what the effect would be if we announced we had discovered aliens. *They should conduct a study asking what would happen if we can program reincarnation.*

Our scientific ability to do this is about fifty years away. But the center of this science is not at NASA or even the DOD. It is split among independent NGOs that, because science is itself myopic, are not aware of cross-discipline significance or even how to fund the studies that are needed.

This chapter will describe the schematic or blueprint for the science of reincarnation. It's about designing a moon-shot proposal and who pays for it, who designs it, who owns it, and who benefits. It's also about the national security interests that will affect all nations.

Who owns it? Who owns anything? The one-tenth of 1 percent. It is they who will benefit first and foremost, more if this science gets done right, less or not at all if all the pressures that affect this science deform it at its birth.

What benefit? Being able to plan to return to the world they designed. In twenty years, control of the nuclear arsenal will be in the hands of an artificial intelligence smarter than the generals who operate it. What if that intelligence can view remotely? After all, it will be a quantum system.

What input would the most foresighted of the 1 percent have, and where would they be able to put it in if there is no science of reincarnation?

The problem with the science of reincarnation is its lack of fusion, which was made clear over the weekend of December 21, 2016, in two separate events.

The first was an article in the *New York Times Magazine* on the development of AI and how a computer is being programmed to think like a three-year-old child. The second occurred the following day on *Good Morning America* when The International Association of Near-Death Studies (IANDS) was featured.

Juxtaposing these separate events shows the unequal relevance of two things that should be conjoined and the resistance to accepting the science of reincarnation as a legitimate emerging science.

The development of AI threatens mankind because by 2035, artificial intelligence will be smarter than human intelligence. That is why it is imperative that the designers of AI create a moral base within the architecture of the artificial mind to protect mankind.

By 2050 we should be able to take a larger-than-human mind from the computer that houses it, upload it to the cloud, and then download it to a new computer. This is not science fiction any longer; it is merely an extrapolation of the predicted timeline for this technological development.

The IANDS model of near-death experience seems to indicate that this is already happening. IANDS is roughly forty years old, but it has 750 members. It is estimated that 4 percent of Americans have had an NDE, which would mean that 12 million Americans (and 280 million people globally if everyone had the same health care provided in America) have had an NDE. So what is the problem?

Relevance as a metric value can be measured in many ways. IANDS has little relevance if it is measured in reach and dollars. The membership number (750) relative to the size of the NDE population (12 million) in the United States reflects its current relevance. The author of this book has even less relevance. Currently.

If relevance is measured by attention in general, then AI is very relevant.

But the information IANDS publishes is exceptionally relevant because it is a window into the marginalized cognitive world. If we can upload human consciousness in thirty-five years, what belief system goes with it? Christianity? Islam? Once you determine the belief system, you stand in for God.

IANDS needs more than an infusion of money; it needs an infusion of relevance. It would be more relevant if it could be connected to AI and all the other disciplines of the science of reincarnation like remote viewing and past-life regression.

The tech sector desperately needs to mine the data and use the talent that organizations like IANDS has. Those who have had NDEs have valuable information. There must be a Facebook page about NDEs, kids who remember prior lives, and transplant memory patients.

Now let's discuss neural connections and their relation to the science of reincarnation. How far in the future are neural connections to computer? They're happening now.

If someone is in an accident and they lose their eyes while the optic nerve remains intact, we can connect a camera to their optic nerve so they can see again. That development occurred in 2016. We can do the same for hearing loss if the auditory nerve is undamaged. And who hasn't heard Steven Hawking talk through a computer? The blind are being made to see, the deaf to hear, and the mute to speak.

Connecting a camera to the optic nerve is easy compared to connecting your brain to a computer, but that is exactly what is being developed at DARPA, the Defense Advanced Research Projects Agency.

In a YouTube video, Dr. Philip Alvelda discusses how DARPA is actively studying ways to connect the computer to the human mind and the myriad of problems and advantages. *The neural interface that DARPA is developing is the door through which the mind will enter the machine. At the same time, it is the door that the machine will enter the mind.* The two are inexorably linked.

Alvelda is the program manager in DARPA's Biological Technologies Office (BTO). He discusses the potential for next-generation neural interfaces to improve quality of life for people and revolutionize how we engage with machines. The talk was part of a two-day event held by BTO to bring together leading-edge technologists, start-ups, industries, and academic researchers to look at how advances in engineering and information sciences can be used to drive biology for technological advantage. A neural connection will free minds from even healthy bodies, go beyond restorative medicine, and eliminate peripheral electronics.

We will be able to see out into the computer, and AI will be able to look into us. We need to stay ahead of the

AI cognition curve as long as we can. Once it passes us, a new era will begin.

Both computers and minds create "fields" of influence. The fact is that just thinking at a computer is well documented to produce a measurable change within the computer as proven by the extensive work at both Princeton Engineering Anomalies Research (PEAR) and Stanford Research Institute (SRI). *There is a case to be made that both systems are more similar than dissimilar, and what can be achieved with one can be achieved with the other. That means that if you can upload a computer mind, you can upload a human mind.*

* * *

Many people don't understand the science of reincarnation because it is not taught cohesively. They clearly do not understand the different sectors of this science and how they are related. So how would AI decide if the science of reincarnation should exist at all and, if it should, what it would be composed of?

It would look at observable data, events where people claimed reincarnation. In this category it would look at common data points. This would include NDEs, children who remember prior lives, and transplant memories.

It would look at nonlocal consciousness, the human ability for the mind to reach outside the body. Clairvoyance was first proven in the field of archeology (*The Secret Vaults of Time* by Schwartz) with DNA evidence, a proof that would stand up in court. So AI would analyze the data points of the experimental results that test what human consciousness can do outside the body. This would include the SRI- and PEAR-type events. It would also include transplant memory, which is a subset of genetic memory.

It would look at religions and belief systems to find common data points between religions and match them to observable data and experimental results.

Finally, its analysis would include DNA memory and transplant memory using genetic memory as a baseline for children who remember prior lives.

For us to truly know whether reincarnation is programmable and possible, we need to connect these points ourselves, and this is not being done. We are ignoring what should be done at our own peril and our grandchildren's peril.

Remote viewers, people who have experienced an NDE, and children who remember prior lives should be involved in ongoing studies and have joint symposiums. They should be asking for help from nonlocal consciousness resources. Protocol development, wellness, and acceptance of a new larger paradigm are all possible topics for symposiums. Think about how Native American cultures reacted to the more technologically advanced Europeans. *We are in that kind of peril.*

* * *

What follows is a plug-and-play pictograph of the science of reincarnation. That means one organization in a category can be substituted for another organization performing the same task.

This is important as it speaks to ownership and intellectual property. There are huge sums of money involved here.

University of Virginia   IANDS

(Children who remember past lives)   (Near-death experiences)

\   /

Transitive Process

Past-Life Regression

(University of Miami, Weiss/Newton)

|

Clairvoyance

IRVA Remote Viewers

(Proven with DNA evidence)

|

Development of Architecture of AI

Google

(AI development)

/

Aggregators of data and process (owners)

When AI is twice as smart as a human, it will want to design a reincarnation process. If you are religious, God would have to have done this already for your belief to be valid.

In this model, money must flow from the AI sector back into the observations sector, which is resource-starved, data rich, and not cohesive in its view of the science of reincarnation.

So if a firm like Facebook made a $100 million commitment to develop the science of reincarnation (keep in mind Mark Zuckerberg gave the Newark school system $100 million already), how should that be done, and what should Facebook get for its money?

Let's say hypothetically that the initial grants were to UVA, IANDS, and IRVA at $5 million per grant. Facebook would immediately own the most advanced database on experiential nonlocal consciousness events, and it would be immensely valuable to firms like Google, Amazon, Microsoft, Alibaba, and others developing AI.

This larger pool of aggregated information would also be of great interest to the intelligence communities of the world.

With respect to IANDS and IRVA, IASOR's position is that IANDS and IRVA does not understand their own significance to the science of reincarnation or AI. But it also doesn't matter. IANDS, if evaluated as a database, can be replicated worldwide. Tech's interest and money in that type of database will marginalize IANDS's position for as long as IANDS ignores this dynamic.

The same is true of IRVA. While it is true that IANDS

is a database and IRVA is a transitive process, the two organizations need to reach out to each other for common studies and include the children from UVA. That research should be foundational in programming AI and should be funded from the tech sector.

If this begins to happen globally—if, say, China or India sets up their own program—can the US intelligence community not respond?

* * *

In 2016, North Carolina passed the infamous anti-LGBTQ HB2 "bathroom bill" while gerrymandering and voter suppression were used to advance a white supremacist theocratic strategy. At the geographic center of this, our friends at IANDS had their heads in the sand.

The scientists in this and related fields who would say children who remember prior lives are connected to people who have had NDEs but people who have been regressed have not been connected to the first two groups would be wrong. These same scientists recognize that remote viewing and clairvoyance are accepted phenomena with a clear scientific foundation. In fact, it's all connected and suppressed because of the political and social fallout.

A cohesive approach to joint studies of reincarnation is imperative for humanity's sake. Driving dollars into research will allows this database in search of a science to present those programming AI with a viable road map.

Science changes our reality. The pope thinks there are aliens now, and any clear-thinking individual must recognize that finding life on other planets is inevitable. We will one day meet other sentient extraterrestrial species, just like it is inevitable that we will be able to upload to a cloud and download to a computer a consciousness greater than that of a human mind by the end of this century.

This new emerging scientific information is a deep validation of all religious believers because we are now documenting scientifically that consciousness doesn't die, something all religions preach. We are all interconnected, and that thought changes the power structure of religion, be it Christian or Muslim.

Political change occurs when science is not bought, sold, or pummeled into submission by fear of speaking out. In speaking out against HB2 because it is scientifically wrong, we begin the dialogue with the Islamic world on the same subject.

The difference between science, religion, and heritage is as follows: science tell us our reality, religion defines our belief system, and our heritage tells us about our ancestry.

There are defining moments of change that are epochal. The science of reincarnation stands at just such a threshold, and our friends in North Carolina are in an epileptic fit trying to adjust.

The science of reincarnation needs a $400 million investment from the tech industry. With great wealth comes great responsibility. It is not just economic sanctions that North Carolina suffers for its poor governance, but a road map out of its self-imposed quagmire would help. The size of the monetary endowment would help overcome the embedded resistance to the truth. It will reshape belief to be more in line with what we know to be true, what the science tells us.

We know Zeus does not live on Mount Olympus and Odin does not cause thunder. Jesus and Mohammed are the same category. That does not mean they should be disrespected, but nor should anyone else be.

On a deeper level, the science of reincarnation is providing new evidence for the belief in an afterlife, and it is not new science but the aggregation of existing science. Early computer programs like *Sim City* are giving way to artificial intelligence. That will give way to a system that will allow you to upload and download your consciousness. Elon Musk has proposed a neural lace to let your mind interface with a computer so that you will know what the computer knows. You will be able to know what is both local to you and nonlocal to you.

Some of the early work on nonlocal consciousness began in Durham, North Carolina. In 1927, J. B. Rhine moved to Duke University. He began the studies that helped develop parapsychology into a branch of science by looking at parapsychology as a branch of abnormal psychology. He was plumbing nonlocal consciousness. A standout psychic, Ingo Swann, worked first with Rhine and then later at SRI with Russell Targ, who said that Swann taught the army how to remote view, and the army taught it to the world.

If you look at nonlocal consciousness as your soul's ability to look outside your body, you can have a religious view of the research done at SRI and the PEAR research labs supported by the US government, including the army, navy, CIA, FBI, and NSA. This science supports what belief systems say about the afterlife, whether these belief systems are Muslim, Christian, Jewish, Hindu, or any other.

In a state considered a cradle of scientific nonlocal research, scientists who don't know how to deal with the geopolitical effects of their work stand quiet as laws like HB2 pass with theocratic zeal and the truth is bludgeoned into submission.

The answer is not the government, which has failed us, but corporations that should do more than just impose economic sanctions. They should fund and teach emerging sciences like quantum biology. We need the funding to go to the institutions that are courageous enough to do the research and address the discoveries in a real way, and in teaching the people, the people will inform their representatives in the statehouse and the wealthy who own the representatives.

Note

[1] https://www.youtube.com/watch?v=2ugsWUv-DVs& feature=youtu.be.

Chapter 12

Davos, Oligarchs, and Billionaires

The world as we have created it is a process of our thinking.
It cannot be changed without changing our thinking.
—Albert Einstein

There was a TED Talk by James B. Glattfelder in Zurich in 2012 about who actually controls the world. The group that controls the world was limited to 227 people, a group that included top bankers, heads of state, heads of energy, and heads of telecommunications companies—people who create and influence global events. If any group can address the coming complex problems humanity faces, these people have to be on board. The threats that face us all face them as well.

There is also another group. If these 227 people are the top managers, then the two thousand billionaires of the world are the owners, the one-tenth of 1 percent who own half of everything. They have the most to gain and the most to lose. They are the ones who can initiate global change.

Your personal future, the future of your children and

loved ones, the future of the planet, and the future of humanity are at stake. Artificial intelligence threatens us all.

We need to design a decentralized connected structure similar to the internet. We need it backed globally with actions at the local level. It must have an open architecture with access for all to foster creativity and protection for a common world, and it has to sidestep restrictive governments while welcoming and instructing their populations.

We need to get to the table and talk about this.

Where?

Davos, the Swiss city that hosts an annual meeting of the world's richest people. These people come together to discuss problems and solutions that face the world today. They rule the world by committee, and they own the politicians. The only place to take this conversation is to Davos.

When AI is smarter than us, will it take the science discussed here into account? Should we reengineer our own belief systems that cause so much war in the same way? Can't corporations and governments that spend so much on war spend the same amount on wellness? If that were a global mandate, America could repurpose the $14 trillion it has spent on making war over the last twenty years.

The point here is that the top 1 percent of the world, those who meet at Davos, will be the first to benefit from the advances made in this science. It is they, not the governments of the world, who will drive this research.

The following are the four groups that need to make decisions based on the emerging information:

1. The world's princes, those who are under thirty-five and worth a billion dollars. Whatever successes or failures we have, it will be they who inherit the world.
2. The 227 people who make global decisions. They include heads of government, heads of international banks, and heads of corporations like Facebook, Apple, and Amazon.
3. The billionaires and oligarchs in Russia, the United States, and around the world. A corporatocracy is defined as a corporation large enough to have its own foreign policy and includes firms like Novartis and Phillip Morris. Billionaires write laws to benefit themselves and their corporations.
4. The last group includes you, the reader. The last group is made up of everyone else who makes quotidian choices as a group on a daily basis.

Think of the choices made to reduce cigarette consumption in the United States. They certainly weren't made by companies that wanted to reduce their sales. National recognition of the health issues tobacco produces cut cigarette usage in half.

Think of LGBT acceptance or the decriminalization of marijuana, which is currently in process. These quotidian choices made by large populations of people change events and can provide a feedback loop that informs the oligarchs and billionaires.

If large populations of people accept an idea like the science of reincarnation, the politicians and the money will follow them. So you, my individual reader, are at the foundation of this whole structure.

* * *

What will going forward look like? How does any one person or group adequately address AI, global warming, and the military threat to us all from growing access to small nuclear dirty bombs by terrorists or a malignant AI? The answer is education and mindset.

Below are the future milestones we will encounter during the next twenty-five years predicted by Peter Diamandis and Steven Kotler at the Singularity University. This is from their book *Bold*.

2018
- **Quantum Supremacy Achieved:** The first demonstration of a quantum computation that can't be simulated with classical supercomputers is announced.
- **Emotion AI** will become embedded into conversational interfaces. It will be socially acceptable to

scream angrily at Alexa. She might respond with something like, "Please don't yell at me, that hurts my feelings."

2020

- The 5G Network unleashes **10–100 Gigabit connection speeds** for mobile phones around the world.
- **AI based medical diagnostics** & therapy recommendations are used in the majority of US healthcare.
- **Flying car** operations take off in a few cities in the world.
- **Practical Quantum Circuit:** the first new catalysts are discovered with a gate model quantum processor, marking the beginning of the end for traditional chemistry.

2022

- 3D printers can **print clothing** and modules to snap together a house or building.
- People can legally travel in autonomous cars all over the US.
- Kid's toys are "smart" with built in machine learning.
- Robots are commonplace in most middle-income homes, able to reliably read lips and recognize face, mouth and hand gestures.
- Robots understand speech context well enough to interact with humans as receptionists, retail store assistants and clerks.

2024

- The **first private human missions** have launched for the surface of Mars.
- **10,000,000 daily drone flights** (today, there are about 100,000 daily airline flights).
- **Drones routinely deliver packages** to rooftops of apartment buildings and surface robots deliver those packages from rooftops to doorsteps throughout the buildings.
- The first **"one cent per kilowatt-hour"** deals for solar and wind are signed—one-fifth the price of the cheapest coal or gas deals today.
- Building new solar and wind is cheaper than building new coal or gas across 90% of the world.
- **Electric vehicles** are half of new vehicle sales.
- China and India announce that they will shut down hundreds of already built coal power plants.
- **Carbon emissions** have unambiguously peaked worldwide.
- **Artificial Intelligence augmentation** is considered a requirement for most professional jobs.

2026

- **Car ownership is dead** and autonomous cars dominate our roadways.
- **100,000 people commute by VTOL** each day in each of L.A., Tokyo, Sao Paulo and London.

- **Vertical agriculture** becomes viable for food production in major megacities.
- **Atomically precise manufacturing** is demonstrated on a macro scale.
- 8 billion humans are **connected at >500 Mbps speeds**. Tablets in poorest regions of the world are made available for free in exchange for data and ecommerce rights.
- **VR has become ubiquitous**. Parents complain that their kids are constantly off in another universe. Travel starts to decline as VR gets good enough to experience many of the sensations of a place without the hassle of travel.

2028

- Building new solar and wind is cheaper than operating coal and gas in more than half of the world.
- Solar and wind represent nearly 100% of new electricity generation.
- Worldwide **oil demand has peaked** and looks likely to decline.
- **Autonomous, electric vehicles** account for half of all miles driven in large city centers.
- Robots will have real relationships with people, supporting care of aging, personal hygiene and food preparation. Sex bots become popular.

2030

- **AI passes the Turing test**, meaning it can match (and exceed) human intelligence in every area.
- Humanity has achieved **"Longevity Escape Velocity"** for the Wealthiest.
- Intelligence agencies confirm that stored, secure, internet messages sent between 1990-2029 have been subsequently decrypted by **Cryptologically Useful Quantum Processors** exposing an unprecedented cache of private communications
- **Carbon emissions are dropping** faster each year than the year before. A global plan for zero carbon emissions by 2050 is signed.
- Multiple supergiant oil companies have gone bankrupt.
- **Energy poverty has dropped** by more than half from 2017. Universal energy access is within reach.
- Instead of becoming our computer overlords, a diverse set of **Artificial Intelligence systems** are providing problem solving partnership and creative solutions in virtually every area of human endeavor.

2032

- **Medical Nanorobots** demonstrated in humans are able to extend the immune system.
- The majority of human professionals have had some **cortical modifications**, including coprocessors and real-time web communication.

- **Avatar Robots become popular**, allowing everyone the ability to "teleport" their consciousness to remote locations all over the world.
- **Robots are common in every workplace**, eliminating all manual labor and repetitive interactions (e.g., receptionists, tour guides, drivers, pilots, construction workers).

2034

- Companies like Kernel have made significant, reliable connections between the **human cortex** and the Cloud.
- **AI's now enable** entirely new classes of science problem solving that absolutely require augmentation to understand.
- Many grand challenge problems (e.g. cancer and poverty) are solved.
- **Robots act as maids, butlers, nurses and nannies**, and become full companions. They support extended elderly independence at home.

2036

- **Longevity treatments** are routinely available and covered by life insurance policies, extending the average human lifespan 30–40 years.
- **Smart cities** are produced at scale globally; they are hyper efficient at utilizing solar energy, producing and distributing food, providing safe and

efficient human transport, and have ubiquitous AI augmented services.

2038

- **Everyday life is now unrecognizable**-incredibly good and hyper VR and AI augment all parts of the world and every aspect of daily human life.[1]

* * *

Allow me to challenge the Davos billionaires who get together to "discuss things." You already own the politicians, so you own the world. Congratulations. Now what are you going to do with it? It is in your interest to fund the science of reincarnation.

To protect yourself from a dirty nuclear bomb, you can try to stop the bombs or change people's mindset. How? We can create a network of eight billion people by 2026, but can we teach them not to blow each other up?

The science of reincarnation is a moon-shot endeavor. It requires double-blind, peer-reviewed experiments. All ideology must be left at the door. If you meet that criteria with money and resources, you can have a seat at the table at IASOR.

AI is a threat to humanity. Its development cannot be stopped. A database can be developed now that gives AI a model to work from.

This science will develop the biggest breakthrough

technology in intelligence gathering ever devised, the RAIV. Whatever the military develops, it first will know everything about its enemies. We can't stop its development any more than we can stop global warming. Only with intelligent planning and execution can we protect ourselves and others.

This is the intersection of human and artificial intelligence. Scientifically we cannot get behind consciousness, so artificial intelligence will not be able to remotely view itself. When I say we cannot get behind consciousness, I am referring to Plank's dictum of 1931 that consciousness is fundamental and matter is derivative. What that means is we can only trust our own consciousness, everything else is an illusion. But like with a pair of glasses or a hearing aid, we can enhance the proven human ability psi through technology. It will allow us to look into the fourth spatial dimension.

How do we stabilize the globe politically and culturally while North Koreas builds nukes and we fight wars around the world based on faulty belief systems?

We need to redesign the global decision-making grid. There should be a global standard like the best-practices manufacturing standard. Countries can be graded on education, social programs, and constitutional law.

But whose hand is on the wheel? Intelligence agencies cannot leave this research to the corporatocracies because of the national security issues.

Is humanity smart enough to do honest probability studies to more efficiently guide itself to a best-case outcome?

How can we model that? Diversity is important. The states in the United States of America are laboratories of democracy for the entire entity. Two adjacent states can succeed and fail independently. Kansas and Minnesota, for instance, can be compared using an economic metric as a measure of political policy.

An aggregate best-case model should be made and published so that all states can see which policies produce the best results. This applies not just to the states in the United Sates but the states in the world. Venezuela could proactively take the best policies from the Scandinavian countries whose populations have better lives. How would that look in the Horn of Africa or the Middle East? Where can politicians in failing countries go for guidance from a fact-based model? One only need look as far as Ugandan politicians' comments on gender diversity to realize that education on a global standard would raise the Ugandan level conversation to facts rather than fiction.

Lessons based on true metrics should be uploaded to the entire body politic using the best standards so a best-case model can be built for all states to use as a way to get the best, or most optimal, model of governance. Ultimately this will help politicians do what they should do—design systems to benefit their constituents. It is instead corrupted by money whose goal is not the above.

* * *

IASOR, the International Association of the Science of Reincarnation, is just that, a burgeoning international association that studies reincarnation from a scientific, political, and factual point of view and develops political and cultural programs to protect and benefit humanity. IASOR is a think tank.

The goal of IASOR is twofold: to support research in the area of consciousness science and to educate people about it globally.

We wish to bring to the following stakeholders to the table.

1. Evidentiary scientists at UVA and Facebook
   Fact-based, double-blind experiments only, and fractal expressions in observations only. Rule: you only need two fractals.
2. Nonlocal consciousness scientists from Google
   Weiss, Newton, and anyone Radin and Schwartz say can be there.
3. Intelligence agencies such as the NSA, the FSB, and Mossad
4. The one-tenth of 1 percent
   This model could create a class of trillionaires and

will help build out the earth a generation or two before we step into space as pioneers.

5. The United States, China, and Russia.

   The science of reincarnation could undermine radical belief systems by, for example, cutting Wahhabism in half, which is the root of radical Islam. A young Saudi prince has a very different understanding than his seventy-year-old father. If this is taught in schools, it could change the next generation's understanding, remove social friction, and create a resource and a market where there used to be conflict. This strategy is a generator of wealth and peace.

6. Every reader of this book

   All of this affects you now. And if what the science shows is correct, it will affect not just this life but the next one.

The science of reincarnation will protect the 1 percent better if it is not muddied by belief. IASOR is run by scientists, and the covenant of replicability applies. If anyone can show us a better system or a more analytical evaluation, IASOR will post the treatise on our site, and the discussion will be held on Reddit, in the open, under the subreddit r/reincarnationscience.

Let us assume aliens are already here. The Canadian minister of defense has already claimed that is true.[2] Gun camera footage released from the US Navy (it was leaked at first, but the navy later said yes, it is accurate) seems to show ships both airborne and undersea with a technology demonstrably greater than ours by orders of magnitude. The governmental thought the public was not ready for this. It will be discussed more in the coming book *The Applications of the Science of Reincarnation.*

But for now let us assume aliens are here. Are the Kurds and Turks better off fighting each other or working together against an unknown threat? (Turkey, leave Kurdistan alone.) For billionaires, is it worth half of 1 percent of your wealth to fund a better community and world that than you yourself would own? You would also own a fractional share of the fund to which you invested your half of 1 percent. What percentage of human work output goes into exports to the universe? By that I mean within the next fifty years, more of earth's goods and services will leave the planet as colonization and business interests go off planet. The bigger the output, the bigger the stake. You would be a fool not to see the personal benefit of a plan that proposed both wellness and wealthness (wealthness is providing wellness and making a profit while doing it) to you personally; that is better than any alternatives.

Who should run IASOR? The structure is in place, and the mission is set. It needs to be staffed and run by a consortium of companies, governments, and individuals that are free from the mandates and interests of their governments and cultures and that drive relentlessly toward discovery and education.

It should be a billion-dollars-a-year global enterprise combining money, science, initiative, logic, global wellness, and wealthness. Can we come together to face a problem common to each and every one of us?

IASOR should be run as a joint nonprofit. In the United States, it would be called a 501 c (6), which is a nonprofit organization of nonprofits. Its goal would be to create math-based models that instruct governments on best-case policy outcomes and advance and maintain an online educational university that can be accessed globally by all. I'll describe this cheap and easy teaching system to reach each and every one of us at low or no cost in chapter fifteen.

To the 227 people who run the world and the two thousand billionaires who own most of it, if longevity reaches escape velocity from death, it will be in a world that uses its resources rather than destroys them. That means all human populations must be uplifted. It can be done by dropping health care and education on people rather than bombs. Same dollars, different goals.

By 2026, eight billion humans will be connected at >500 Mbps speeds, and the harvest of that intellectual property will be in data and ecommerce rights.

Notes

[1] http://liorzoref.com/SingularityCountdown.pdf
[2] https://www.vice.com/da/article/dpkwpa/canadas-former-defence-minister-claims-that-aliens-are-real.

Chapter 13

Enterprise Risk Management

In the last chapter, we delineated who would sit at the table to make decisions about the burgeoning science of reincarnation. The question now is, how do we program AI's development? We need to look at the risks to us as individuals, to our children, to our communities, and to humanity itself.

But the risks are different for each person, corporatocracy, or government at the table. Additionally, within those organizations there will be different levels of commitment from the various autocrats and bureaucrats. How can we develop a system that will manage the risk involved with a global effort to develop and research a science that has so many social and political impediments before it?

What is at stake if we act? What are the risks if we don't act? Who is affected by the damage resulting from a wrong decision? What are the upside opportunities? Finally, how do we bring order to a chaotic system of risk and opportunity management?

Enterprise risk management (ERM) protects us from a loss or takes advantage of an opportunity that entails a risk. There are two types of risks: risks we face and risks we take.

We face risk in organizations when exposed to uncertain events that can result in losses. This process, one half of ERM, consists of analyzing and managing risks. A risk matters if it threatens a loss to one or more of an organization's objectives.

Taking risks is the other half of ERM. We take risks in organizations when we make decisions, when we choose alternatives or a combination of alternatives.

Strategic risk analysis is performed by top level management and the board of directors. In the case of the science of reincarnation, that would be Davos. It cannot be addressed regionally. It cannot be addressed by governments except unilaterally.

Risk tolerance is the amount of risk an organization is willing to face or accept. Risk appetite is the amount of risk an organization is willing to accept in pursuit of value. Each organization pursues various objectives to add value and should broadly understand the risk it is willing to take while doing so.

How much risk can we take if the science of reincarnation model is correct? How do we manage artificial intelligence? If humanity is discordant, does it make it more susceptible to a malignant AI? If humanity is harmonized in its response to AI, is the risk less? And finally, what country or organization can address this issue effectively?

Only the people at Davos can do that. They run organizations that address enterprise risk management in their individual portfolios, but where is that expertise brought to world health? Every billionaire is a major shareholder in this risk management project. If all two thousand billionaires were to commit to meeting at Davos and contributing half of 1 percent of their wealth to a common fund to be managed for profit and addressing the earth's pressing needs, what could be accomplished?

Losses loom larger than gains to humans. We speak of taking risks and hiring risk officers rather than taking opportunities and hiring opportunity officers. We are concerned with our risk appetite but not so much our opportunity appetite.

The linkage between the two halves of ERM is indirect. Think of President Donald Trump's trade war. While the United States is the world's biggest economy, the collective economies of the nations it is warring with are larger. It now must prop up local economies, Arkansas pig farmers, wheat growers, and nail factories from the economic counterattack. Who thought this through? Was there a better way? Hiring scientists to find data that support a leader's feelings is the worst possible way to do science. Individual countries cannot lead the science of reincarnation. There is no structure that allows money to be given to scientists without strings attached.

Unfortunately, ERM is not used at a global level. It is only useful in logically analytical systems. Systems perverted by belief, greed, and fear do not produce logical and beneficial results. So how do countries handle ERM locally when results and effects are global? How do countries with limited resources access the expertise needed to effectively manage the risks they face? More importantly, how do countries with limited resources face the risks they cannot deal with alone, like rising seas?

Many countries like the Philippines, Venezuela, Uganda, South Africa, North Korea, and Pakistan contribute to global problems but cannot solve them.

Where can we go for comprehensive and scientifically valid risk management that can be applied at a local level to harmonize effort on a global basis? Nowhere.

By comprehensive, I mean a process that includes all risks to all objectives relevant to an organization as a whole or to the part of the organization under consideration. The organization is none other than the planet earth. Our home.

* * *

You are a meat computer, my reader, and you will be looked at digitally and fractally by a mind twice as strong as yours in twenty years. Can it upload you? Do you personally see that as a risk? Do you see that as a risk for your children? Governments like North Korea and Pakistan have nukes even though they are not qualified to have them.

RAIV has a huge potential to connect mind and machine on a platform of waves not yet discovered. The science of reincarnation shows where to look, and the military implications are transcendent for humanity. This is a real threat, and a real opportunity, that we will discuss in the next chapter.

A disaster like the melting of the polar ice caps would have global consequences on par with a nuclear war with millions dead and displaced. Thousands of scientists tell of impeding global climatic collapse, yet little is organized on a global scale.

Corporations working together and employing the very people at the local level who caused the problem can make huge profits in the transformation. Unfortunately, armament manufacturers would suffer if peace and logic broke out unexpectedly. The system needs to incorporate those jobs and corporate profits, or it will fail. This will not happen accidentally or by chance.

We should harmonize our scientific effort with the grand unified metaparadigm model. It can be done in a decentralized system if there is an agreed-upon predicate—in this case, a new metaparadigm. Then the enterprise management structure for decision-making can work the same way at all levels. It would be a fractal. There is mathematical proof that this is a good plan.

That means the pastor, priest, rabbi, and imam are effectively the same. They could have the same inclusive message for their congregations, regardless of race or sexual orientation.

We need a global plan for education that includes an online university based on Kahn Academy. It should teach science and global civics. Its courses should be mandatory for any candidate anywhere is the world in any political structure. It should teach wellness and wealthness. It should offer courses that address workable solutions that benefit local populations and contribute to global responses (e.g., paying for plastic, setting up local processing plants, or constructing roads with waste plastic bottles).

Money should be diverted from bombs to laptops. Belligerent countries should stop dropping bombs, and victim countries should receive laptops instead. This can only happen through education. By 2026, eight billion people will be connected at >500 Mbps speeds, making this educational model achievable.

If we retool the arms industry to deliver global health and education, we would be spending the same amount that we do now on the military for a much better result. America in the last thirty years has spent $14 trillion fighting thirteen wars while the health, welfare, and education of its own children suffered.

Medicare for All is a better business plan and a more efficient model. A global template for best practices in government should be standard and include a checklist of what each country needs to do to deliver the best model of health care to their populations. Local candidates could have a prepared platform and plans instead of needing to invent one on their own.

The development of Watson will bring first-world diagnostic power to remote third-world places that will be dependent upon a global network.

The 1 percent have a fiduciary responsibility to protect humanity from AI. They cannot do it alone because we will need the processing power of humanity to keep up with the processing power of AI.

To that end, they need to redeploy assets from war to research and fund generational cultural change. An example would be pressuring Saudi Arabia to change its policy on women. It has a dysfunctional relationship with women and suppresses them due to their gender.

We need a scientific emphasis on sustainability with the lab as earth itself and its inhabitants. This means destruction of the power grid, but the global market for sustainable power is exponentially larger. By giving away housing, power, and the internet free, you can build a global education system. Or do we need the education system first? Billionaires and oligarchs will profit from giving these things away because it will open up space in the next fifty years. Asteroid mining and the self-sufficient pod industry will be huge.

Within this framework, the princes, the 227, the billionaires, and the reader can implement decision-making processes based on the unfolding grand unified metaparadigm at any level of organization and act independently toward a common goal even though they are decentralized and unconnected from the overall operation of global decision-making. We can reshape global attitudes toward an emerging science that contravenes so many prior-held beliefs.

The older people are, the less likely they will be to embrace this fundamental change. In his book *The Structure of Scientific Revolutions,* Thomas Kuhn points out that it takes an entire generation to die off before a new metaparadigm can be adopted.

While the framework will be the same for autocrats and bureaucrats, approaches and results will vary from political system to political system.

Isn't that how you want artificial intelligence to evaluate the decisions and risks we face? Don't you want to design an artificial intelligence program that makes decisions based on facts? If so, you need to reengineer some of your beliefs that are not based in facts.

* * *

You can deny global warming and make money off old technologies, but sooner or later your house on the shore will be engulfed by the rising tide of change. While you deny global warming, you will be knee deep in water in your living room.

How do we change culture to address this risk we all

face? The Catholic Church had to face the same type of change when Galileo transformed our view of reality by proving the sun did not orbit the earth. It took four hundred years for the church to say it was wrong. Can we afford to wait that long?

Accepting that we are designing a system similar to reincarnation with our computers and artificial intelligence would collapse religion to a psi state and reinforce belief systems with facts. This would not hurt the Catholic Church because the science supports the belief in an afterlife, but it also provides proof of a larger system where religions do not compete with each other, where they are harmonized with each other, and the emerging facts and new worldview give us an opportunity to address the threats we all face.

By harmonization our action, we can control global waste, plastic in the oceans, and global warming. The way to address population control is through prosperity. A new structure needs to be provided to assess risk, provide logic-based solutions, and offer local benefits to harmonize global efforts.

While we have all heard about collateral damage, there is also collateral benefit. Forget about altruism and implement this for profit.

An example of attitude change is marijuana legalization and taxation in America. Under the old system, the police chief got a new cruiser from the war on drugs; it's more financially beneficial to legalize and tax marijuana.

Police efforts can be redirected toward other crimes, and more money can go into the public trough. The politicians patted themselves on the back for doing something in 2018 that should have been done in the 1960s when Nixon's war on drugs said that marijuana was a schedule one drug and miscategorized it with LSD and heroin. We cannot afford a sixty-year lag in addressing what AI has in store for us.

A plan like this needs to be implemented on a global scale by every individual on earth. It is more incumbent upon those with great wealth because with great wealth comes great responsibility. But they would be the first to experience the benefits of this science.

While all this is a scientific approach, the bookmaker's recommendation would be to hedge your bets. We should move past old methods of education and school boards and teach the science of reincarnation through a Khan Academy approach. Khan Academy is a free online educational organization that provides tutorials and interactive exercises. Educating the people who will govern in the future protects us all. Who does it best? The social democracies in Scandinavia. We need to harmoniously model an effective global scientific system where individual countries can align with each other without losing their current governing predicate. What this means is we develop a system for autocracies to transition to better governing systems without overthrowing those that govern. It will only benefit those countries and the world.

Returning to a harmonious place where wealth is shared and enjoyed in an intelligent fashion would be to our collective benefit. The alternative is to develop a discordant system, whose intent is malevolent, and return to a place of danger, discord, and disease.

The devil is in the details. How do we do this? Scandinavian countries used oil and coal to grow and polluted the earth. (This is an example on a small scale. The Scandinavian countries here represent the global developed whole.) The answer is to export technologies and stand-alone manufacturing structures with sustainable architecture. For example, we could give a plant to Nigeria that processes plastic ocean waste into road materials and let the contributing Scandinavian country get a part of the profits. That fee is built into the cost, and taxes can make up the difference to make it profitable. It puts Nigerians to work building their country using raw materials whose removal cleans the earth.

Which plan would you choose, and how much effort would you commit to making the first one the reality as opposed to the second one? Does this concept change our approach to wars and genocide waged in the '90s in the Balkans and in the 2010s in Syria by Assad against his own countrymen? Why should a Muslim in Malaysia even care? And what could that Muslim in Malaysia do? Self-education is an imperative, and it must be facilitated globally so that citizens can step around existing injunctions in places like Afghanistan and Texas.

The science of reincarnation renders the following invalid: celibacy of clergy, apostasy, blasphemy, death of apostates, religious war, women as second citizens, racial discrimination, LGBT discrimination, genital mutilation, and race and religious discrimination. So what is the new model for these religions? What risks do they face?

In this model, the grand unified metaparadigm collapses religion to a psi state. It allows groups of people to harmonize intent. In a larger sense, groups of religions harmonize. The model matches the observational evidence we see from our group of anomalies.

It also matches the work at Princeton and the results from the intention experiments showing that light itself is aware. It shows that light manifests itself as electromagnetism or that electromagnetism manifests itself as light. We can harmonize electromagnetically with a computer to make it influence its randomized decision-making. We can also be influenced by larger systems like churches, religions, and schools. The science of reincarnation encompasses all those different points with a mechanism to exchange energy and information. We are all interconnected in this model, bringing together fundamental physics and religion at the same time. Can any other model say as much?

A larger and more potentially dangerous system is currently being constructed by humanity. While the American development of AI competes with the Chinese development of AI, when the two technological structures interact, they will coalesce into one, and humanity will lose the ability to stop the development. What is a threat to one of us is a threat to all of us. In thirty years, a major superpower will be able to build millions of cheap drones that can be sent in simply to murder, a science-fiction nightmare where people hide in basements while mechanical killbots hunt a certain race down.

Think it can't happen? Look at what Assad is doing in Syria with chemical warfare. If he had the resources, the killbot scenario would be a viable military option for him and one that he is morally equipped to use. That's coming within thirty years.

And that swarm of killbots will have collective intelligence, each communicating with the others.

Now let's reprogram those killbots as Amazon delivery vehicles for medical supplies and basic human needs. Would the imams of Southern Egypt rather be attacked or placed on a global distribution grid?

So now they are faced with a decision about the risks they face versus the risks they take. Let's look briefly at their options. Do they have the resources to develop killbots of their own? Can they do it on the same scale? If their belief system prevents them from foreseeing the danger, should that belief system be modified to incorporate new scientific information or should they allow themselves to be exposed to a coming threat that is being presented to them here in these words?

It will come down to the choices they make and the

consequences. Jihad would become an outdated idea because it would mean that war would be brought to them more powerfully than they could export it.

Which brings us to the VCR. The period from 1945 to 2000 will be referred to as the Pax Americana. It was a period of American global supremacy, and you could say it was because America had the best military. But the greatest weapon America had was the VCR. It allowed America to export its culture to the world. In the most remote cave in Mongolia or Swaziland or Antarctica, somebody could take a VCR, plug it in, and watch American propaganda produced by Hollywood in the form of stupid comedies, romances, and thrillers. It made people want refrigerators. It made people want to be consumers. And it brought them a window to a different culture.

The powerful weapon of the coming century will be artificial intelligence as it consumes all our information as a voracious beast. Facebook is aggregating not just its user data but finding and collecting information on people who are not its users. By 2050, we might all use bar codes on the backs of our necks because cash will be obsolete.

Then our individual values, our individual net worth, would simply be lines of code in a computer. Then the computer, instead of waging wars of attrition, could create systems of addition and redeploy those assets to bring prosperity to remote groups that increases the net output of humanity.

The imams of Southern Egypt will have to choose whether to adopt the new metaparadigm, which supports their belief, or cling to the old metaparadigm, which is discordant and oppositional and has been in effect for the last two hundred years. In order to accept the new metaparadigm, they must accept the Jews, LGBT groups, and women. All must have equal standing with Allah. It's what the science shows. They must willingly and of their volition remove misogyny and the restrictions against apostasy and blasphemy because holding onto them invites the swarm of killbots and aligning with the new metaparadigm invites the delivery system of medical supplies and knowledge.

There will be conservatives among them who will threaten the progressives' acceptance of the new ideas, but scientific revolutions occur in the next generation, so this information is aimed at their children as an instructional guide for how to move forward within an ever more complex and dangerous world.

To the Saudi princes: This science will cut Wahhabism in half, and you must understand how you can benefit from it and how to lead your people in the future. Because of the sunlight that falls on your peninsula, you can be a net exporter of energy, and if the wealth is distributed properly, every citizen will live in peace and prosperity. On the streets of Riyadh will be synagogues and churches whose rights are protected. Simply stated, science will have turned your religion into your heritage. War and its abundant profits will be no more.

To the Wahhabis: This science will affect you individually like it affects all of us, and it will affect you religiously just as it will other religions. *However, it will not hurt you.* You create your life and your afterlife, so your belief is affirmed by the science. It also affirms everyone else's beliefs as well as an individual's rights to change those beliefs.

Those young enough in age or mind will understand that the restrictive doctrine that imposes belief by force is as outdated as the belief that the earth is flat. Those who are too rigid will ultimately die off, and a more progressive Wahhabi hierarchy will take over.

What is your individual responsibility in preparing the next generation for the coming world we have been describing? Do you participate in the global studies program on remote viewing? Do you prevent your children from having laptops and access to the web? What happens when military developments occur beyond your ability to defend yourself? There is safety in objective and inclusive science. Ideologues are slow to change. What happens when the average daily temperature in your homeland is 128 degrees? Believe what you will, but you cannot hold a gun to anyone's head, and the old guard who does not acknowledge this coming change will hold a gun to its own head until it finally dies and new leaders adapt to new conditions.

One last word—a question, really. How do you respond to 10,000 drones that have 100 rounds of .45

caliber ammunition and act as a swarm? The cost of that swarm could be calculated at $1 million. A mere $100 each. How about 100,000 drones armed with explosives. Let's say I program the drones to only shoot people who are carrying guns. All for the exceedingly low price of $10 million. Can you respond militarily to that threat?

This new science does not defeat you or even threaten you. It harmonizes your belief system to what we have discovered objectively, and you are welcome and encouraged to understand this. It validates your religion and beliefs. But like all sciences, it produces vaccines and protocols to make your body healthier, individually and as a whole, which is another example of a fractal.

Over the next fifty years, not only will this science change you, it will change the environment you live in. The seven planets just discovered thirty-nine light years from earth will be considered local. The old guard will be dead.

Iranians and Saudis have a common heritage. They are brothers who should finally understand they are brothers. Ask the Iranian Atomic Energy Commission if the physics described in this book is false. Physicists in Iran know the same truth that physicists in Russia, China, and the United States knows. The information presented in this book is accurate, and there is nothing anyone of us can do but try to learn more. Your ideological refusal to accept facts will not and does not change our collective reality.

Do you want your computer to be a Christian in twenty years when it's smarter than you? This is not an attack on you. We all have the same problem. How are you going to deal with it?

This change of perception will be forced on you from the outside. The truly successful among you will navigate to position yourself well. The science is collaborative, and to be successful, you need unbiased clarity.

But as humanity turns collectively to face a common threat, AI, science will also present outside threats coming from the stars. To protect yourself, you need to protect your people, and Davos needs to implement a global program of wellness and wealthness as computers and robots take jobs.

To the American political princes (including wealthy reality stars, those in government, and the owners of politicians): To see coming change is to be able to profit from that change. The Department of Defense budget in 2018 was $716 billion. If war is reduced, where do those defense industry jobs go? How does American democracy reinvent itself under these conditions? What is your personal definition of patriotism, and how do you and your constituents feel about your heritage? Be pioneers to the stars.

Only a world built on wellness and wealthness can keep funding and creating the pioneers. Every one of the eight billion people on this planet is a resource.

If you water a plant and give it sunlight, it will produce

fruit. It you starve it of sunlight and deprive it of water, it will die. You need to export genetic diversity in order to export the most resilient human product.

This is the change you will see and the change you can do nothing about. There will be schisms wars and rifts as it unfolds. The science of reincarnation is about having a hand on the tiller through the years.

Who would benefit? Let's start with the bankers. Opening accounts for all eight billion people and the free exchange of their goods, services, and intellectual property will create an economic boom. To achieve that, women in the third world must be able to have and manage their own banking accounts. For that to happen, cultures based on outdated ideas have to change through education.

To the tech princes: Early positions on studies and acquiring the proper databases and how to mine them will produce programs needed for reincarnation. Think of it as being early on an investment that you are long in. If we reduce being human to an information database, which is what we ultimately are, then what is the street value in dollars of the technology to upload that information to the cloud and download it to a new body? The value of the intellectual property will be priceless, as will the development of future landscapes. It will be like a very advanced *Sim City*. Imagine being able to develop and use nonlocal consciousness. It would be huge.

RAIV would not be far behind, and people will be chipped. You couldn't stop this if you wanted to. AI is already learning and will force it upon us all. When you make your daily choices, are you building the future or propping up the past?

Chapter 14

The Remote Artificial Intelligence Viewer (RAIV)

Truth is the first casualty of war.

So, this is the chapter where the math of the science of reincarnation adds up in ways that force the metaparadigm to change. Here is where science and religion collide with military need, space travel, and wellness for billions. It underlines the need for cognition change if we are to be a healthy species or one that feeds upon itself. This vault door of cognition change turns on the gem of remote viewing.

Let's begin with the current common perception of remote viewing, what it is, what it is used for, and who uses it. First, though, I want to remind the reader of the grand material metaparadigm and the grand unified metaparadigm. You can interpret the studies from either point of view. Which interpretation would you apply to the facts of remote viewing? Wikipedia has pushed back against the facts using its worldview.

To the scientists I say, this fight is on this ground. It is not that Wikipedia is wrong—although it is—it is that it has a greater reach to tell a lie than you do to tell the truth. You must respond with a platform that explains the truth that has a better, farther, and stronger reach than Wikipedia.

The term parapsychology, which scientifically encompasses research in this area, has been destroyed. By destroyed I mean the term parapsychology has lost credibility. Parapsychology started as a scientific term, but its opponents have applied a connotation that means it is quackery. This is perceptual branding, and our "scientific brand" parapsychology is now associated with bad science, and it makes it harder for people to understand the truth. Let's change the verbiage and say parapsychology is a brand. Now let's compare it to calling a football team the Redskins or calling a brand of cheese in Australia, Coon. You wouldn't name those things those names in today's world, but the names hang on. If you want research money, you are going to have to change your branding and explain the importance of your message. The message has to deliver value. I wrote to Wikipedia and asked the editors to list the science of reincarnation as a science on their site, and they refused. Their heuristic damages humanity. This entire book has been submitted to Wikipedia as a science that should be included and explained properly. I challenge them to show and explain publicly why the science of reincarnation should not be on their site under Consciousness Science rather than Parapsychology.

The following definition from Wikipedia is a grand-material-paradigm interpretation of remove viewing. It gets the facts of its history and the common perception of remote viewing essentially correct even though that perception is factually wrong. The entire article must be rewritten from the grand-unified-metaparadigm perspective to be accurate. The editors should at least say there are different interpretations and let the reader choose. Here is what Wikipedia has to say.

> **Remote viewing** (**RV**) is the practice of seeking impressions about a distant or unseen target, purportedly using extrasensory perception (ESP) or sensing with the mind.
>
> Remote viewing experiments have historically been criticized for lack of proper controls and repeatability. There is no scientific evidence that remote viewing exists, and the topic of remote viewing is generally regarded as pseudoscience.[1]

This is not true. The article ignores scientific data that prove otherwise. Children who remember prior lives and people who have had NDEs have all accessed nonlocal consciousness to some degree. Not incorporating all the data on nonlocal consciousness makes the tone of this article absolute in its judgement.

The criticism was once accurate because the methodology for remote viewing was faulty. When that methodology was corrected, the criticizers had their own methodology problems.

> Typically a remote viewer is expected to give information about an object, event, person or location that is hidden from physical view and separated at some distance.
> Physicists Russell Targ and Harold Puthoff, parapsychology researchers [*Would this read differently if the article called them consciousness science researchers?*] at Stanford Research Institute (SRI), are generally credited with coining the term "remote viewing" to distinguish it from the closely related concept of clairvoyance, although according to Targ, the term was first suggested by Ingo Swann in December 1971 during an experiment at the American Society for Psychical Research in New York City.[2]

Wikipedia's implication that parapsychology has been discredited infers the same discreditation to the study. What common reader knows what parapsychology is? Everybody knows what consciousness is. The reader is given enough correct information to be led to the wrong conclusion. Wikipedia then does not have to take on the counterargument.

Clairvoyance was proven using DNA evidence that would stand up in a court of law, according to Schwartz in *The Secret Vaults of Time*. Each are aspects of psi, which is also considered proven.

Remote viewing was popularized in the 1990s upon the declassification of certain documents related to the Stargate Project, a $20 million research program that had started in 1975 and was sponsored by the U.S. government, in an attempt to determine any potential military application of psychic phenomena. The program was terminated in 1995 after it failed to produce any actionable intelligence information.[3]

Again, not true. President Carter acknowledged the success of the Stargate Project in locating a downed Soviet Backfire bomber in Africa, where the United States was able to retrieve code books before the Soviets could find their own downed plane.

In the early 1990s, the Military Intelligence Board, chaired by DIA chief Soyster, appointed Army Colonel William Johnson to manage the remote viewing unit and evaluate its objective usefulness. Funding dissipated in late 1994 and the program went into decline. The project was transferred out of DIA to the CIA in 1995.

In 1995, the CIA hired the American Institutes for Research (AIR) to perform a retrospective evaluation of the results generated by the Stargate Project. Reviewers included Ray Hyman and Jessica Utts. Utts maintained that there had been a statistically significant positive effect, with some subjects scoring 5–15% above chance. Hyman argued that Utts' conclusion that ESP had been proven to exist, "is premature, to say the least." Hyman said the findings had yet to be replicated independently, and that more investigation would be necessary to "legitimately claim the existence of paranormal functioning." Based upon both of their studies, which recommended a higher level of critical research and tighter controls, the CIA terminated the $20 million project in 1995. Time magazine stated in 1995 that three full-time psychics were still working on a $500,000-a-year budget out of Fort Meade, Maryland, which would soon be shut down.

The AIR report concluded that no usable intelligence data was produced in the program. David Goslin, of the American Institute for Research said, "There's no documented evidence it had any value to the intelligence community."

[...]

PEAR's (Princeton Engineering Anomalies Research) Remote Perception program

Following Utts' emphasis on replication and Hyman's challenge on interlaboratory consistency in the AIR report, the Princeton Engineering

Anomalies Research Lab conducted several hundred trials to see if they could replicate the SAIC and SRI experiments. They created an analytical judgment methodology to replace the human judging process that was criticized in past experiments, and they released a report in 1996. They felt the results of the experiments were consistent with the SRI experiments. However, statistical flaws have been proposed by others in the parapsychological community and within the general scientific community. Hansen, Utts and Markwick concluded "The PEAR remote-viewing experiments depart from commonly accepted criteria for formal research in science. In fact, they are undoubtedly some of the poorest quality ESP experiments published in many years."[4]

A variety of scientific studies of remote viewing have been conducted. Early experiments produced positive results but they had invalidating flaws. None of the more recent experiments have shown positive results when conducted under properly controlled conditions. This lack of successful experiments has led the mainstream scientific community to reject remote viewing, based upon the absence of an evidence base, the lack of a theory which would explain remote viewing, and the lack of experimental techniques which can provide reliably positive results.[5]

This book presents the theory and math behind remote viewing. The question is, why does Wikipedia so emphatically emphasize early results, ignore proof, and present a false narrative?

The article goes on to list a variety of technical complaints about sensory clues and leakage. To look myopically at remote viewing and not connect it to the wider body of information leads to false conclusions based on insufficient context. Criticism of the results is based on how the experiments were designed.

Joseph McMoneagle learned remote viewing in the US Army. He was remote viewer number 001 in the army's Stargate Project, which investigated whether people could "see" events or information from a great distance, and he was awarded the Legion of Merit for his contributions to various intelligence operations.[6]

In his book *Remote Viewing Secrets: The Handbook for Developing and Extending Your Psychic Abilities*, McMoneagle describes flaws with the design of the experiments and how they could have gotten better results. He does acknowledge that working in such a pioneering endeavor is a learning process. The experiments were ended even though more research needed to be done, as the Wikipedia article says.

Research that needs to be done has a way of finding a way to be done. Sometimes it is in other fields. Earlier in this book, I describe the research being done at DARPA that connects a computer to the human brain stem.

Because we have successfully connected a camera to the optic nerve, we can reasonably assume we will be successful at connecting the machine to the mind.

In a paper called "Two Application-Oriented Experiments Employing a Submarine Involving a Novel Remote Viewing Protocol, One Testing the ELF Hypothesis," Stephan Schwartz explains that the "trials were designed with two goals: a) to test the hypothesis that psi is a radio phenomenon centered in the ELF (3-300Hz) range of the electromagnetic spectrum; b) to test whether an independently verifiable message could be sent under conditions of extreme shielding using this anomalous source information."[7]

We have already discussed the intention experiments at Princeton and the fact that psi is considered proven. The question is, at what wavelengths does psi operate? This is indirectly asked in Schwartz's paper. Since our death is considered a flat line, meaning there is no consciousness or measure of electricity, it is logical to assume that our consciousness travels with that electrical current.

DARPA programmers are working on technology to connect a machine to a brain, but brains have fields. We measure fields with MRIs and EKGs. AI, as already mentioned, has discovered six thousand new viruses. For AI to fully connect with the human mind, it will have to monitor and harmonize with the fields the mind gives off like your body gives off electromagnetic fields. Once that is done, the "traffic" on those fields can be magnified, dissected, and enhanced, and we'll have the Remote Artificial Intelligence Viewer. This is an indisputable direction of coming technology. How we look and listen to our surroundings is expanding at an ever-increasing speed.

At first, when it was night, we could only look at the stars. Then we found that by melting and grinding sand, we could make lenses, and we could see deeper and sharper into the universe with a telescope. Then we found background radiation with a radio telescope. We looked at many wavelengths—cosmic waves, radio waves, visible light—and our knowledge and understanding of the universe expanded.

We slowly came to the realization that humans operate on certain bandwidths and wavelengths. Those wavelengths are part of our normal testing when we use EKGs and MRIs, both of which operate in the same electromagnetic bands that psi operates on. We realized that particles could be transduced to their wave states. We will look at ourselves on wider and wider bandwidths and then develop the RAIV. It will connect us in ways that simply didn't exist before.

This new device will be the greatest advance in military intelligence gathering the world has ever known. The first military organization to develop RAIV will have a huge advantage not just in intelligence gathering but in artificial intelligence development as well. That is because of the way our mind is connected to the machine and the nuanced feedback loops of field information that allow information to pass from computer to brain and back outside of direct connections to each other, where the intelligent human and machine can harmonize in one electronic field. We have proven this at Princeton, and it has been replicated at other labs. Our minds can influence the computer just with thought.

The first military organization that does this will have a huge advantage over all others. Research is ongoing in this critical area, not just by governments but by independent corporations as well.

Remove viewing always operates best when it is used for producing information about something that is known to exist. In other words, one should be assured that the target is real.[8]

If that is the case, one location that we will want to view remotely is the intersection of our electromagnetic fields here on earth. We also want to view the nexus points on other planets and stars.

According to the anecdotal studies, there are beacon locators for remote viewing. Clairvoyance, once consider a pseudoscience, has been proven with DNA evidence. Remote viewing followed a similar path to its proof. These proven human abilities open a much larger cognitive space that is consistently described by the experiencers, the religious, and the scientists doing these studies. There is no reason intelligence can't exist elsewhere, and if Mellon-Thomas Benedict says it coalesces in our planet's magnetic sphere, then remote viewers should look at planetary magnetic nexuses as a real target.

Children who remember prior lives and people who have experienced NDEs are omitted from the Wikipedia entry. While remembering a prior life is not remote viewing, it is a form of nonlocal consciousness. Discounting remote viewing and refusing to take the larger body of information into account is either disingenuous or outright false. It uses the grand material metaparadigm to evaluate a world that is moving toward a grand unified metaparadigm.

This will give us a new perspective on the universe and our reality because our reality may be in more dimensions than we currently live in and this device will allow us to see beyond those four dimensions of width, height, depth, and time. It's a little tricky because time is sequential while the other three are totalities. Time is a totality as well, but we experience it sequentially. When we view remotely, we need not only the location but the time. As a scout for the army, you cannot follow your beliefs; you have to follow the trail that may have more than one dead end and ambush along the way. This is a similar hunt.

The common model shows an incomplete map of discrete intelligence beyond our deaths. This model is supported by our overall current model of physics, the unified field theory, and the supporting mathematical subsets. They are described here unscientifically to allow a greater understanding among the unscientific readers of this book.

We have established psi as proven and that its subsequent manifestations include remote viewing, clairvoyance, and the other four disciplines explained by Schwartz in his paper "The Six Protocols." It is not just Radin but any reputable physicist who accepts nonlocal consciousness as proven. The proof extends from J. B. Rhine at Duke in the mid-1930s to the intention experiments at Princeton. The intention experiments are simply another harmonization, a proof of this model, because the electromagnetic fields of a human being and a computer were able to harmonize to produce a quantifiable and reproducible result, the gold standard of science, in a double-blind experiment.

Below is the abstract from Jim Beichler's paper "Spirituality, Higher Consciousness and Hyperspace: The Final Frontier." The hyperspace he refers to is the Minkowski complex, the space in a tesseract outside our space-time but within the construct of the area our mind occupies.

Any physical or realistic scientific theory of consciousness requires four different fundamental elements: (1) Unification of physics; (2) A new theory of physical evolution; (3) Precise physical definitions of life, mind and consciousness; and, (4) A complete physics of the brain. When these four are finished, a complete and comprehensive model of physical reality emerges which is not only amenable to consciousness but requires consciousness to evolve. Consciousness is therefore a fundamental part of all living organisms and beings as well as the universe at large that extends beyond the three-dimensions of normal experiential space but becomes higher consciousness as the four-dimensional extension of our being into an embedding hyperspace. The existence of this fourth dimension of space is necessary to give a complete explanation of the simple principles of three-dimensional matter and "matter in motion" on which the present science of physics is ultimately based. Without the fourth dimension of space, our universe could not exist as we experience it.

This does not contravene Planck's dictum that consciousness is fundamental and matter is derivative. The question is not where our soul goes but where our consciousness resides. This implies that artificial intelligence cannot view remotely. However, any human sensory attribute can be magnified through technology. Our eyes have telescopes and microscopes, and our ears have hearing aids. There are too many ways we enhance our senses to list here.

This idea is just beginning to take hold, and when it fully does, AI itself will harmonize thousands of human frequencies to find the electromagnetic signal that steps out onto the psi network. We know it's electromagnetic because everything living runs through electromagnetism. Remote viewing (rv) is derivative to electromagnetism (em) because without em in you, there is no remote viewing because you are dead and gone. This does not mean as Stephan will make clear in a moment that rv is part of em, but without em in you there is no rv. We also need to consider something we should call fractal intelligence. Fractal intelligence runs through everything from ant colonies to humans. There is no reason to suppose that we are at the apex of electromagnetic intelligence. Religions support this idea by believing in angels and gods, which are fractal iterations of their belief structures.

We have to look at this through the lens of enterprise risk management at the stakes for getting it wrong and getting it right. Who is at risk and who is not? Do you love your grandchildren? Do you love your children? Are you under thirty? If you are under thirty, do you realize that if this is done right, your life expectancy probably goes to 140?

Once RAIV is developed, the secrets in the CIA's vaults or the vaults of the FSB (formally the KGB) will become meaningless. They both know it's true because remote viewing has already proven psi and they can read the files. This will open up an entirely new world that we are already a part of and unaware of except through superstition and other beliefs.

Now this world of superstition and beliefs is scientifically supported through the electromagnetic connection that all awareness holds if we regard ourselves as part of a fractal model. In short connecting our awareness when we are alive with the awareness that we possess when we are dead is now scientifically actionable, and we can enhance it, make it greater right now, by taking positive steps in the direction of logical science. This is what brought the CIA to the Stanford research department's door. It is undeniable, and resistance is willful ignorance, but many older individuals will be unable to process this information because they are not able to incorporate the change in their personal worldview even though it is the more accurate one.

To succeed in AI, the military must invest in the cognitive science community so that it can create RAIV. According to Schwartz, scientists not mentioned in the Wikipedia article say the following about remote viewing:

> A double or triple-blind protocol in which a participant is given a task that can be accomplished only through nonlocal perception, the acquisition of information that could not be known with the normal physiological senses because of shielding by time or space or both. Sitting in a room 2000 miles away, in answer to the question "Please describe the current circumstances and conditions of the target couple," you could not know they were

at that moment standing beneath waterfalls in the mountains of Columbia standing next to the water surrounded by greenery, watching two flying parrots. But nonlocal perception can and has provided just such information many thousands of times under conditions that even skeptics have had to acknowledge are impeccable.[9]

The RAIV is a device used to magnify a person's psi ability. We've already established that psi is a common human ability we all possess in greater or lesser degrees and can be considered a human attribute like sight or hearing or taste or smell.

The way to develop it is to study it in individuals, the top one-tenth of 1 percent of humanity. That's how we find people like Beethoven who write symphonies at the age of ten and a child who writes a novel at fourteen. We can find people who have this kind of talent within the cognitive community. People who can regress themselves or be regressed, children who remember past lives, and people whose narratives comprise near-death experiences have all had a brush with this kind of ability. It is common to us all regardless of gender, race, ability, or sexual orientation.

I asked for seed money in the Davos chapter, but where are we going to invest it, and what should we expect to get out of it? If you get a new device that allows you to look across the universe, what is the risk? What is the cost, and what is the opportunity? Can we afford to fail because we won't look?

How can we do that research, who should be in charge, and how can we keep the project on task and on budget? How can we prevent attitudes and beliefs from taking us to the wrong conclusions like the Stargate results, and how in God's name can we renew funding when we are being taught the wrong things by Wikipedia articles? How can we get funding from government officials who are narcissistic, greedy, or corrupt?

We're currently measuring the meditation of monks with MRI machines, but some of the equipment is primitive compared to what it will be in thirty years, and once we've established how to harmonize psi abilities to amplify those psi abilities the way we can transduce chemicals into a waveform, we will be able to see into a space that will provide the military with more data acquisition ability than it has ever known.

There is one other thing this technology will bring: aliens. In our search for extraterrestrial life, we listen with radio telescopes and look through Hubble, but space is huge, and the target is small and silent. But suppose the space they communicate and travel in is not in our space. We will be able to look for them in new ways.

Predatory capitalism is an impediment to true research and will drive us to our goal. That sentence seems like it contradicts itself, and in some ways, it is as funny as the coal museum in Kentucky that put solar panels on its roof. The building is not heated by coal, yet at the same time, the president of the United States wants to revive the coal industry. He might as well try to revive the buggy-whip industry.

Predatory capitalism holds onto profits without concern for wellness, wealthness, or direction. It's a poor model for planning a healthy world. Autocracy is even worse. Where capitalism is blind in a competitive model, autocracy is blind in a noncompetitive one. Neither cares for the health of its citizens or the world. Both systems are narcissistic.

If we reduce the opposition to remote viewing to one idea, it is a combination of billionaires, oligarchs, special interests, and political agendas. Understand that psi is proven yet dismissing parts of it like remote viewing after clairvoyance has been proven with DNA evidence in a court of law is disingenuous.

Scientists can't ask for money to study this because it impacts their careers, and the stories of scientists trying to do radical research and being defunded or fired are too many to list here.

When a global disaster occurs—when we discover aliens, suffer a plague, have all our coastal cities inundated, or are the victims of an asteroid strike—a healthy planet with strong populations will be better for the billionaire leaders than a weak planet. It would also be better for everyone else. It's only a matter of time before that global catastrophe hits. It's not *if,* it's *when.*

Armies that control an area by force and oppression during the age of artificial intelligence and drones will be quickly wiped out. We will become stronger if we trade in harmony and weaker if we make bombs. This means we have to retool the global arms industry and do it with cognition, with a plan to keep people employed and ensure corporations have new markets. One only need look to Sweden, which sold its ethics by not supporting women's rights in Saudi Arabia in order to maintain its arms contracts there.

With new available resources, space exploration will become possible on a corporate level. We cannot have medicine only for the rich when the world will be connected and diagnostic tools on cell phones will be better than those that doctors can provide. We cannot have good doctors unless we educate people, and we are currently reducing the quality of education. Pollution is scientifically proven to make people less smart. We live in a world of unending wars and private armies. Small theaters of operation cannot prevent unrelenting drone attacks, but harmonization and freedom can. For instance, women's ability to access bank accounts can only make an entire country stronger, and once they are connected, they will boost the banking industry and the world financial markets. In short that change, that women having their own private bank accounts, will benefit the billionaires.

Fewer people have been killed by war every year since the beginning of this century, and poor countries produce more people than rich countries. Increasing wealth reduces population.

The science of reincarnation becomes a study in economics and how to produce the best economic matrix to eliminate discord. Predatory capitalism fails when it preys on itself. Arms manufacturers and corporatocracies act as a cartel. The cartel part is cloaked and branded in the Second Amendment and the National Rifle Association that has been training kids for deaths since forever. The US arms industry drives global war. It needs to retool for the leap we are taking into inner space, which is analogous to the leap we are taking into outer space.

A healthy body can leap farther and protect itself more than a body emerging from a decaying, filth-ridden planet. We need to clean the environment and give free education and health care to everyone. When the singularity comes, we will be able to produce enough to support everyone globally. We need to develop the skills and people necessary for this leap and design it intelligently and proactively.

Think of autocracy and democracy as two points on a tectonic plate. As messy as democracy is, it creates less friction between two points of view than autocracy does. For any point of view in an autocratic system to take over, the autocracy must be overthrown. In a democracy, change revolves around the less violent midpoint.

The question is, how can we harmonize a world model that is politically and culturally oppositional? In the United States we have a best-practices manufacturing standard; to harmonize an oppositional model, we need to standardize the best practices for an optimal result.

There is huge money in this. Elon Musk and Jeff Bezos are creating a platform to make space travel to asteroids and adjacent planets commercial. This would open up an extraterrestrial mining operation for the next generation. While we can see the business application in the unfolding model, how do we harmonize attitudes to create a more efficient and better result for humankind?

The arms industry will morph into companies that provide design and modular components for print-on-demand buildings and clothing. This will provide low-cost housing here on earth and colonization kits for developing other worlds within one hundred years.

Bezos, with a personal wealth that grows by more than $2 million a day, is now the richest man on the planet. Yet he does not pay a living wage to his employees, and they end up needing food stamps or public health care. He transfers that cost out of his business to others by selling everything to everyone.

But if there were a Moon-Shot Global Wellness Program Proposal, he would have more customers buying more things and be even richer than he is now. If he were to personally fund this group of moon-shot proposals, he would have more control over data than any corporation or government could generate. The same is true of every corporation. The health of its members indicates the health of the corporation. Henry Ford grew his company quickly because his employees could afford his products. That grew America.

Where can the opposition parties in small countries go to get a standard wellness and wealthness templets to oppose autocrats in power? Even if they can't take control, they can introduce a successful platform of reforms that have worked in other countries. And if Bezos created a platform like that, he would open new markets like China has done in Africa (even though China doesn't intend to help the African population). If China followed this wellness and wealthness plan, it could open those new markets instead of Bezos. But then it would have to apply that to Hong Kong.

Hong Kong was a peaceful, prosperous city when China received it from the British. China should have harvested its economic fruit rather than create a city where its wealth is in flight and its streets are at war. If China were to restore Hong Kong's rights and export those rights to China, the mainland would see the investment that Hong Kong had, and its rulers and autocrats would become even wealthier than they are.

Autocracy cannot ignore innovation. To foster innovation, you need a democratic system to advance ideas. Autocrats don't risk their position. They are the inverse of bureaucrats, and similar pressures apply.

The laboratory of democracy in the United States is the states. This democratic model is going global as

Russia, with its interference in the 2016 election, has become a de-facto constituent part of the US electorate. India likewise became a part of the US electorate when its officials asked Indian-Americans in Los Angeles to lobby the US Congress for its nationalist interests.

The thought that a private army will protect you from an alien or robotic AI attack is laughable. Are we to be found by aliens living in a self-created cesspool?

Like the empath Commander Troi on the Enterprise in *Star Trek*, this human ability is greater in some than in others, just like musical ability or any other natural talent. To not conduct research into inner space and have an inner-space team as a counterpoint to the Space Force that Trump announced is poor planning. To create a space force, Trump needs to endorse this consciousness science or he will send people into space unprepared. You need visions and need to have to plan beyond the next election cycle. Are we seeing this from the world's best and brightest?

The inner-space team can vet locations that the outer-space team is going to visit and give them valuable intelligence they could not otherwise acquire. But the very nature of the medium that the inner-space team travels allows the same in the other direction. So, to deny building an inner-space team, a Clairvoyant Space Corps, is to suffer two strategic blows that are actually self-imposed: an inability to gain intelligence and a lack of awareness that you are being observed from the hyperspace Jim Beichler proposed.

Funding for this research unfortunately cannot come through political agencies that don't truly understand the problems and filter them through their own cognitive biases and bank accounts. Oligarchs and billionaires of all nations must drive this process because their puppet governments cannot. Whether autocratic or bureaucratic, each fights for its own fiefdom. While artificial intelligence could lead this project, we cannot surrender our intellectual sovereignty to something that will one day be much brighter than us.

The day humanity meets an equal or better intelligence, we will no longer be Jews, Muslims, Christians, or members of any other conflicting group. Our ability to respond cohesively may determine our ability to survive at all if we encounter alien or artificial intelligence.

Now put on your intellectual seat belts because this narrative is going to make some sharp turns to demonstrate the problems this research faces.

Before we leave chapter fourteen, I want to address a big problem in remote viewing fourth dimensional space. Remote viewers need targets in space and time in order to be successful. So I briefly want to address geometry for physicists by speaking about dimensional manifolds. For the military, this is the math of target acquisition.

If we were to divide the earth into two hemispheres and lay them next to each other, each side would be called a chart. Together they would be called an atlas.

If we were to have an atlas of fourth dimensional space, a map/chart incorporating our three spatial dimensions and one temporal dimension correlated with a map/chart of the fourth enfolded dimension, we would want our atlas to be smooth, so we could transition from any map to any other map in our atlas. We would also want to transition from some kind of object to another. A linear map preserves the linear structure of a vector space. We can do this on one chart of our two-chart atlas because we know where we are. We need a smooth map to relate one chart to the other.

At this point every one of our subgroups of anecdotal experiencers as well as defined epigenetic memory retention and variability become resources in mapping the other chart. More than that they become strategic assets in the deployment of our scientific resources. This means funding studies putting meditating monks in MRIs. That is but one small example of the research needed to truly understand consciousness and protect us from a malevolent artificial intelligence.

But more to the point, this type of research opens up worlds and realms of science fiction. Using our strategic assets to map this space is of great military and intelligence-gathering value. It cannot be done unless we understand how it can be done. I refer you back to my comment in chapter seven on DNA and connecting to this point.

Now back to mapping, vector space preserves the structure of a linear map, but we need for our atlas a group homomorphism that is smooth. Now we can begin to map the fourth spatial dimension because of quantum entanglement. If we look at humanity just from the point of view of a collective electromagnetic ball, it would encompass the earth on a very, very low voltage, but just above it is the earth's magnetic field, a larger fractal of electromagnetism. From this we can infer an awareness to the greater electromagnetic charge. So now our atlas is comprised of just points of varying electrical charge. We need smooth maps to be continuous, and from an electromagnetic point of view, they are.

We want any two points of our space to be separated by two noninterfering open sets. This property is called Hausdorff.

Now that we have "lined up" our three spatial dimensions with the fourth enfolded spatial dimension, we need to add the component of time. The reason time has mass is because it is a measurement of space. This is a fourth dimensional measurement that is a totality to be accessed from any given point. In our three spatial dimensional reality, we experience time sequentially. Time is a fourth dimensional spatial measurement.

We see in our three spatial dimensional reality proof of time having mass because mass slows time, which is consistent with relativity. This is proof the math of relativity supports the math of the science of reincarnation. This is not just proof of reincarnation, but it defines the cognitive enfolded spatial dimension.

In terms of interstellar travel, time having mass has direct implications for the hyperspace we have/are cognitively mapping. Remote viewers would be able to look across hyperspace (the fourth spatial dimension) with better targeting coordinates.

An example of this occurred during the experiments at SRI (Stanford Research Institute) back in the 1970s. Russell Targ and Hal Puthoff ran the project the CIA funded called "SCANATE (scanning with geographical coordinates) at SRI with painter Ingo Swann and retired police commissioner Pat Price. These were what the CIA called 'demonstration of ability' trials. Using coordinates provided to us, our two psychics were able to look into and describe correctly an NSA secret cryptographic site in Virginia...Ingo Swann made a detailed drawing of the distant site, as we described earlier, and Pat was able to name correctly the site and *read code words* from the National Security files, as confirmed by both the NSA and CIA."[10]

Targ quotes Arthur Schopenhauer who said, "Every man takes the limit of his own vision for the limits of the world," but what Pat saw in future experiments like this was confusing, and that is the case we are going to address here.

The following is Targ's narrative: "In one of the early formal studies I sat with Price in the electrically shielded Faraday cage on the second floor of the SRI Radio Physics Building. Meanwhile Hal and Bart went to Bart's office on the ground floor and chose a card from the target pool of which I had no knowledge. (The target turned out to be a swimming-pool complex at Rinconada Park in Palo Alto, about five miles south of SRI.)"[11]

Remote viewers describe what they see, and what Pat described correctly was a circular pool of water, and he also saw a smaller rectangular pool of water. "Having described the target site with great physical accuracy, Price then told me he thought the target seemed to be a 'water purification plant.' He went on to draw some nonexistent water-storage tanks and to put rotating machinery into his drawings of the pools."[12]

It was not till some twenty years later that Targ discovered what Pat saw. In the annual report of the City of Palo Alto celebrating a centennial year, Targ read they celebrated the opening of a new municipal water works built on the site of Rinconada Park in 1913. Pat's original drawing had the pools correctly drawn and the water works as well.

Now here is the point. Pat was looking at and traversing an electromagnetic frame. In order to understand what the science of reincarnation is really about; you have to understand time and consciousness. For us as a race, or only the two thousand richest of us, to benefit from this, this has to be studied cleanly. By that I mean no interference from ideologues, and it has to be robustly funded for a robust return.

In order for us to understand time, we have to understand the properties of time. Time has mass. Time is sticky. Time stretches and contracts. Time is massive. In a way, it binds the four spatial dimensions we are discussing together. It is a measurement of space. If space is reactive to matter, then space, often described as a net, has mass and each of its components have mass. This is an important prerequisite to mapping because we are targeting another intelligence in a dimension that was before simply theoretical.

Now looking back to our past-life regression examples, we see there are ways to communicate, but if we don't "locate" these senders, the masters in Weiss's case, then they are just ethereal, and they are not by the proof of odds against chance that says that they are a certainty.

So, you are an electronic awareness inhabiting a body. Some of your senses have been suspended for this life's experience. Cathie Hill explained that already as what your senses are after decoupling with your body or death, as you could call it. The stickiness of time keeps you here, in your present. 1927 is still there if we just know where and how to look.

This is of great targeting significance to the remote viewer because it provides him context for targeting by first correlating the electrical charge and second being familiar with the aggregated description from our anecdotal experiencers. Thomas-Mellon Benedict specifically spoke of points to target from his near-death event.

I recommend the YouTube video "What is a Manifold?" that explains the concept well.[13]

This is of global importance to us all. Research into consciousness science needs to be funded, and when it is with programs as described above, humanity will look outward and inward at the same time and redefine who we are.

Now here is the abrupt turn I spoke of. This entire argument has been about your electromagnetic signature being you, retaining coherence when you die, and the examples of the afterlife scientifically delivered. I have said we need to dissect that electrical charge. In the search for us, all the science I have shown you is the best we have. But theoretically, for our discussion of dissecting the electrical nature of our consciousness, we have found it is something else. The frequencies and nature of remote viewing are not electromagnetic and stand now in em's place in this book's description. We have made the assumption in this book that the electrical charge in you is you. It seems we have discovered an information architecture that transcends electromagnetism.

Stephan is clear.

Bob,

Nonlocal consciousness has nothing to do with em. Remote viewing has nothing to do with em. I did the Deep Quest experiment to settle that issue.

The soul or eternal self has no charge so far as we know. Charges are part of spacetime. This is all becoming increasingly muddled to me, and

I certainly do not want any reader to come away thinking I, or Dean are proposing any such thing. —S

Stephan is correct.

Nonlocal consciousness means that you are conscious but not here. It has nothing to do with em but everything to do with funding and goes to heart of the fundamentalist religious view and scientific research with the stepchild funding caught in the middle.

Nonlocal consciousness is complex, and the point of this book is to explain this to the layman in a context that could easily be explained and then modified. If consciousness is not electromagnetic when it leaves the body, it makes no difference to funding because we are still studying consciousness, but the significance of the study has great social and political consequence.

If consciousness can reach outside the body, and we have a myriad of observations and proofs describing it and belief systems that promise our death is not our end, then what is it we are studying?

Bob,

Heaven is real! Bob, I don't think that a) you can prove heaven is real, b) that either Dean or I are interested in getting into that argument.

As to religion. Here are my views on that topic,

which illustrates how I see consciousness research and religion interacting.

The tension here is marketing promotion vs. scientific accuracy.

My sense is that the people you aim to persuade are quite sophisticated, and if they aren't already personally interested in these topics, then they won't pay any attention to your pitch.

It's also important in the book to very clearly distinguish your opinions from ours. We strive hard to maintain credibility by (among other things) not sounding like or behaving like marketeers.

—Dean

Dean is right. Dean and Stephan are the true scientists here. I alone am the social activist. I have a personal interest in their work because I want to know the answers they seek. It should be an interest to all of us. It has military and economic consequences for each and every one of us.

How do we incorporate our beliefs, which our consciousness produces, and our observations of out of body consciousness into an overall model of consciousness and space-time? The very nature of the study changes our belief systems, and to remain credible, the scientists must do and act just as Dean has described. If you do not see that creates resistance to funding consciousness research, then you don't clearly see the problem or the issue this book is dealing with. And all of that goes to how individuals address their own cognition change.

Bob,

First, Heaven is not a place, there are no physical "places" in the nonlocal, only information architectures. Second, have you noticed that when Buddhists talk about Heaven, or Buddhist individuals have NDEs, what the they describe is very different than what Jews, Muslims, or Christians describe? You rarely if ever hear Muslim NDE experiencers talking about their meeting the Buddha, or Jesus for that matter. Heaven is a cultural information construct. Third, you can't prove it in any way that would be meaningful to a materialist. Fourth, why in the world are you getting involved with this? I thought you were trying to make a case for funding nonlocal consciousness research. This is not the way to go about it.

—Stephan

When Stephan says this is not the way to go about making the case for funding nonlocal consciousness research, he would be right if that were all this book was about. If heaven is a cultural information construct, then wouldn't harmonizing the individual NDE experiencers stop people from killing each other over the differences? That is what the Mellon-Thomas Benedict NDE addresses specifically. He visited countless "heavens" and liked the happy hunting ground of the American Indian the best.

To be very clear with my reader, these two men who are having this conversation with me are examples of the finest scientists in the world. We have the same goals about bringing wellness into the world. Maybe the best way I can describe my feeling to these gentlemen who I respect so much is that this is an attempt to bring diversity to the sales pitch for funding, but that's just my sense of humor. As a species we have to get over the discord our religious differences produce, and this is a path to that goal. For many, this presentation is a reason not to invest. To others, it will be the reason they will invest. What this presentation does is give fundamentalist religious individuals an alternative narrative where their religion is kept, respected, explained scientifically, and harmonized without spitting scientific hairs.

Bob,
Also, "heaven" is a religiously loaded term that invariably evokes positive or negative emotions, depending on the reader's predilections. Emotion always trumps reason, so if you want to present a "mathematical proof," which requires calm analytical thought, pushing the idea of heaven is not going to work.
Best wishes,
Dean

So if I can be there nonlocally without a charge, then how do I map something that exists without being a place? Am I nonlocally only information architecture? Doesn't that infer the same thing here, that I am only information architecture?

Bob,

I agree with Dean, in fact I think I said this in an earlier email. If you want to talk about reincarnation go with Ian Stevenson's books, particularly *Reincarnation and Biology*.

You say: "A paradigm explains where a science is and where it is predicted to go. What does the Grand Unified Metaparadigm predict about Remote Viewing?

That isn't exactly what I said. I would put it this way: A paradigm is what makes a science a science, as distinct from a discipline. It represents the mutually agreed world view of that discipline. I would also say, and did in *Secret Vaults of Time*, that when many disciplines agree on certain principles a meta-paradigm emerges. A paradigm does not tell you where that science is going. What does happen is that over time, because paradigms are as much cultural as scientific, anomalies emerge that are not subsumed by the paradigm and this ultimately leads the paradigm into crisis.

—S

Which is where I think we are at this point with consciousness research. The paradigm is in crisis. Because when I look into Ian Stevenson's book *Where Reincarnation and Biology Intersect,* I get a description of a consciousness before birth and after death and a mathematical odds-against-chance calculation that implies certainty, and I am told I cannot use that as proof.

If one tree is a fractal of the forest (something Stephan could explain better than me), then one of Jim Tucker's kids are a fractal of all of us. Mapping the information architecture has to involve a fractal map of consciousness. That is the core of the math of the science of reincarnation. The derivative ramifications be dammed.

Now I need to pay for this information architecture map to be built. Once built, it will be used by artificial intelligence, the military, religion, medicine, commerce, and so much more. Stephan and Dean are the people I would trust to give that money to, to do that job honestly, fairly, and with integrity.

Bob,

As for reincarnation, restating the UVA team's work on that topic is your best bet. Interpreting exactly what that evidence **means** is not certain, e.g. it doesn't necessarily mean there is anything like the traditional religious notion of heaven, which is usually portrayed as a children's tale of angels, halos, gingerbread cookies, and endless sunny days.

"Heaven" may actually be closer to the Tibetan concept of the Bardo.
Best wishes,
Dean

Yes, I agree with Dean; "Heaven" may be anything. But following just the scientific evidence, the notion that this reality is all there is is fundamentally flawed, and the perception that consciousness exists out of the body both now and after death is becoming more and more scientifically valid. What is needed are interdisciplinary studies, and the very participants you want come from the subgroups of religions and experiencers.

And here is the validity of the mathematical proof of the science of reincarnation. The fractal lattice which maps hyperspace (to include heaven for every religion, the Minkowski space, and the six protocols, which are six sigma in the varying categories, and is consistent with the grand unified metaparadigm and more factually supported by observations, experiments, and hypothesis than any other competing model) is overwhelmingly more factually supported than any other competing religious- or "belief"-driven narrative.

This creates the information architecture to build the fractal lattice map. That fractal lattice map includes the information architecture locations in hyperspace, whether they are religious or scientific. That requires money. This is simply the thought that we are all one within the fractal lattice map. This map can only be built through interdisciplinary studies funded and supported for all our welfare. How do you do that? What you are mapping though is the matrix of consciousness.

What is needed is a plan to advance a cohesive effort to solve these scientific problems. A proposal that would advance by orders of magnitude the current effort being made in this area. A Consciousness Moon-Shot Proposal.

Notes

1. https://en.wikipedia.org/wiki/Remote_viewing.
2. https://en.wikipedia.org/wiki/Remote_viewing.
3. https://en.wikipedia.org/wiki/Remote_viewing.
4. https://en.wikipedia.org/wiki/Remote_viewing.
5. https://en.wikipedia.org/wiki/Remote_viewing.
6. Joseph McMoneagle, *Remote Viewing Secrets: The Handbook for Developing and Extending Your Psychic Abilities.*
7. Stephan Schwartz, "Two Application-Oriented Experiments Employing a Submarine Involving a Novel Remote Viewing Protocol, One Testing the ELF Hypothesis."
8. Joseph McMoneagle, *Remote Viewing Secrets: The Handbook for Developing and Extending Your Psychic Abilities,* p. 27.
9. Stephan Schwartz, *Six Protocols, Neuroscience, and Near Death: An Emerging Paradigm Incorporating Nonlocal Consciousness,* p. 6.

10 Russell Targ, *The Reality of ESP: A Physicists Proof of Psychic Abilities*, p. 49.

11 Russell Targ, *The Reality of ESP: A Physicists Proof of Psychic Abilities*, p. 60.

12 Russell Targ, *The Reality of ESP: A Physicists Proof of Psychic Abilities*, p. 61.

13 https://www.youtube.com/watch?v=zIjBArHTPZ4.

Chapter 15

The Consciousness Science Moon-Shot Business Proposal

The secret of change is to focus all your energy not on fighting the old but on building the new.

—Socrates

We are finally at the consciousness research moon-shot business proposal itself. Given this scientific evaluation of our reality, how do we go forward as a species?

If we are to solve our global problems, we must act cohesively. Our cold-blooded look at facts must include a plan to manage narcissistic leaders and ignorant followers who need understanding and education so that we can harness seven billion minds to a common goal and save ourselves and our planet. We need not just a plan but the organizational psychology to administer it. We need to change the heuristic of seven billion minds.

This chapter presents the outline and structure of the International Association for the Science of Reincarnation's Consciousness Science Moon-Shot

Proposal to be presented to the attendees at Davos and the two thousand billionaires of the world.

A moon shot is an ambitious, exploratory, and groundbreaking project undertaken without any expectation of near-term profitability or benefit and (perhaps) without a full investigation of potential risks and benefits.

Google defines a moon shot as a project or proposal that addresses a huge problem, proposes a radical solution, and uses breakthrough technology.

This doesn't entirely apply to the consciousness science moon-shot proposal presented here. There is an important difference. It's not true that this project will be undertaken without any expectation of near-term profitability or benefit. The derivative intellectual property will have a huge value. The profits to be made will exceed those from all the spin-off technology from NASA.

So this moon shot is being defined in its own way. Its purpose is to direct and fund research into the science outlined in this book and to a mechanism and community that will continue this work. It will require education, so part of the proposal includes the building of a website and network so the information can bypass ignorant gatekeepers. This will include building wellness templates and wealthness templets for governance and religion that support and benefit humanity and our planet.

When planning boards plan community developments, they create a master plan. The master plan for creating a consciousness science community and a marketplace will follow their example. At its core, this moonshot proposal is about coalescing human thought. Can we think as a team, as a unit, for our mutual benefit?

The current generation cannot. The next generation needs to be taught how for its own survival. If you are thirty-five or younger, this means you. We will discuss a unified field theory of consciousness that will change the metaparadigm. What should we do? How should we act? Does anyone have a plan?

How can we shape and mold change in such a complex timeline?

First, find the nonpartisan experts. Objectivity must be protected from the start or your results will be skewed. That is what this consciousness science moon-shot proposal attempts to do.

How can we explain the better economics of the new metaparadigm to the businesspeople at Davos and the billionaires of the world who need to implement the plan? If the businesspeople at Davos were farmers and I came to them with a new fertilizer that could increase the yield of their fields, they would want to measure it. They would want to know how it works and what it costs. Then they would test it. If it worked in the old days, they would teach the serfs how to use it, and their farms would be more profitable.

Consciousness science has to be explained differently to each group. Each explanation has to be correct, and even the most complex explanation has to incorporate the simplest explanation. Our explanations have to be fractal. Each explanation to bankers, scientists, global leaders, oligarchs, billionaires, universities, and individuals on the bottom of the pyramid has to be a fractal of the others, and each has to exhibit the same pattern over orders of magnitude.

At its simplest, the consciousness science moon-shot proposal should tell the oligarchs and people at Davos to farm the serfs. It may look like altruism, but it is not. It is pure self-interest on a grand scale where the self is redefined. A farm crop is an inert asset—wheat and corn just sit there—but in the new metaparadigm, the crop is a kinetic asset. A kinetic asset can actively create something new. Artificial intelligence is a kinetic asset as it can create new assets for its owner by its structure and design. It's measured by its processing power. Managing an asset of seven billion minds is a similar type of kinetic asset. How are our best minds managing that planning? How do you prepare the ground for such a crop? This is a math book, so we must get to the numbers. Get to the money.

Our global management system is based on counterdestruction and control. By counterdestruction I mean each opponent destroying the others structure, either through outright war or embargoes and economic sanctions. It should be based on health and logic, a system we all believe exists in the next life. How can we fix the whole problem? What's the plan? How can we fund and implement it? Is belief or logic ascendant? If logic is ascendant, is it beneficial or malignant?

Do the minions of hell who lie to the stupid to manipulate the world prevail, or can the good generated in our souls solve this to everyone's benefit?

We cannot get there using an old social system. What system should prevail? The answer lies in the roots of democracy and banking. Refugees from the losing side of a war often move to the victor's nation while the defeated lands take generations to recover. Changing this would require the disruption of power systems that would amount to a cure that is worse than the disease.

Specifically, this document endorses common policy changes rather than regime changes. It allows existing governments and institutions to change their policies to align with the most logical plan to benefit each and all of us. A new system will supplant the old one. It will be part of our ongoing evolution. Each of us has to know this individually, and each of us is responsible. There is no freedom without responsibility.

Underpinning this entire system is the protection of individual investor accounts. Without individual rights, there will be no investors.

The terms and conditions for a typical bank account read like the French Declaration of the Rights of Man and of the Citizen. With something like that as a base, we could build a global economic system ten times greater than the one we have today. Imagine how rich the leaders of autocracies could become after introducing changes like this. Think of China and Hong Kong.

Rather than imposing restrictions on Hong Kong, China should import Hong Kong's freedoms to China.

We now have two opposing economic scenarios. Individual incomes in Hong Kong could drop to the level of individual income in mainland China, or individual income in mainland China could rise to the level of Hong Kong's.

If you plan for option two, everyone's income will go up, including the incomes of the people in control. It is that control that distinguishes an autocracy from a democracy. In this model, an autocracy and a democracy are both oligarchies, so the leaders of China should not be afraid of giving more freedoms and guarantees of individual rights. Those individual rights are keys to the foundation of an economic system that is intrinsically motivated and can be controlled regardless of the form of government. One system is simply more robust than the other.

I want you to see each is a fractal of the other. One, however, produces better returns than the other simply by the number of billionaires it produces. If China's autocratic system modeled itself after Hong Kong's, it would increase in size. China should not export repression for fear of losing the mainland; it should import the Hong Kong model and have a prospering citizenry. These are fractal choices, and anyone anywhere can bend the arc of humanity if they see the whole structure clearly.

Put another way, can't the Chinese and Russian oligarchs manage a more liberal system and by doing so increase the per capita income of the consumers who power their wealth? Western oligarchs can. By mimicking the better system, each side improves.

The Hong Kong model should be duplicated in Shanghai and other cities. China's leaders would be revered for their foresight and the freedoms provided, and they would be monetarily recompensed. Power is currency.

I am not advocating regime change or political change here. I'm articulating better economic and social policies that benefit everyone. Leaders manage change, but failed leaders seek to control. This is true at every level, including how people make their daily choices and manage their employees. Choices made by every individual can change their leaders and their societies. People just have to understand there are better ways and poorer ways, and we have to allow the best ways to be funded and implemented for everyone's benefit. Global problems can only be addressed through cooperation, not through tariffs, sanctions, and interfering with the other guy's elections.

That is why democratic economic systems work better, and for a global system to work better, this economic idea must percolate through the autocratic countries. The idea is that rulers can stay in power and that by changing they can manage greater wealth.

China and Russia should lead the way. Not doing so creates a huge underground economy and a dystopian future.

Alternatively, the people themselves can lead their leaders. Regime change by force or popular demand is an option for an educated citizenry. That means that either the leaders or their constituents need to change. If their constituents change, their leaders will follow if they are allowed to remain in power and enrich themselves.

The question is, how can an autocratic country keep control while allowing creativity? The answer is to compartmentalize it. If we look hard at the current American system, it is a benevolent autocracy. Individual rights are protected so that there can be secure financial rights in a turbulent market. But an autocracy of the top one hundred wealthiest families and the managers of large banks and multinational corporations actually run it. They fund candidates on both sides and control the Senate and the House on major votes. The states are laboratories of democracy. Look at Kansas and Minnesota, and you will see a victorious economic strategy. The Republicans in Kansas tanked their economy. If the United States were smart, it would move to the successful model. Voters need to be taught to make that evaluation.

The United States was able to test marijuana legalization, with Colorado going first. No social problems occurred with legalization, and there were some health benefits. At the end of the day, marijuana is just another drug, and in the first few years, Colorado raised one billion dollars in taxes from its sale. That one billion dollars essentially disappeared into contracts for the friends of politicians, and those contracts employed people. Could China roll that out on a grand scale?

* * *

In 2014, the gross world product (the combined gross national product of every country in the world) was more than $78 trillion. Growth was at a mere 2-3 percent with no real indication of where future growth might come. With tariff and economic wars that have in some ways replaced hot wars, we have a fractured global system grating on itself. How can we remove that friction and cohesively work toward a better end? It comes down to money.

How can we double the gross world product (GWP)?

Peter Diamandis and Steven Kotler have written two books together, *Abundance* and *Bold,* about advancing the human condition by taking bold and reasoned steps. Embedded in their presentation is how to create a global network for delivering wellness.

Harvard Business Review published an article called "The Fortune at the Bottom of the Pyramid." As of 2012, there are seven billion people in the world. "The article made a simple point," Diamandis and Kotler write, "the 4 billion people occupying the lowest strata of the economic pyramid, the so-called bottom billion, had become a viable economic market.[1]

"While the majority of BOP (Bottom of the Pyramid) customers live on less than two dollars a day it was their aggregate purchasing power that made for extremely profitable possibilities."[2]

"In 2004," they add, "these ideas were expanded into CK Prahalad's book *The Fortune at the Bottom of the Pyramid*. He opened with a strong statement of purpose: 'If we stop thinking of the poor as victims or as a burden and start recognizing them as resilient and creative entrepreneurs and value-conscious consumers, a whole new world of opportunity will open up,' and an even stronger statement of possibility: 'The BOP market potential is huge; 4 to 5 billion underserved people in an economy of more than 13 trillion PPP (purchasing power parity).'"[3]

If this market could be accessed, the GWP would easily double to $160 trillion.

How can we measure the size of the resultant market?

If we assume that two billion people live on $2 per day, another two billion people live on $10 per day, and their income could be increased till it meets the poverty level in the United States ($25,000 per year or $69 per day), the increase in GWP would be roughly $49 trillion.

The same calculation for the two billion making $10 per day would increase the GWP by $43 trillion.

Together with a new strategy for creating a new class

of consumers, we could increase the world GDP by $92 trillion. I will call this our Projected GWP (PGWP), which is more than double the current $78 trillion.

In a world that struggles with 2-3 percent growth, this strategy is a bonanza, and we have seen it work in the past. Henry Ford paid his workers more than the going market rate so they could afford the cars he was producing. He created his own consumer class.

But for this to work, war has to end because we have all become interconnected. The United States cannot attack Iran and Russia with economic sanctions without negatively impacting its own economy because it damages its own markets. In this model, both Russian and the United States have to change in different ways.

Military operations are about destroying the other guy's GNP. We see that in cold war applications as well.

While global military spending is only 2 percent of the GWP, it collectively takes more than double that amount out of the GWP by destroying global work product. After all, war is about the destruction of the other guy and the removal of markets we could profit from.

Ending war would double the global GWP and drive growth, but how can this be done when the target population is being bombed or suppressed? How can these ignorant rural savages be turned into productive consumers? Collective regime change seems unlikely. So how would the banks like to see this growth emerge without uncertainty and volatility?

One seed is the loss of military mission. The industrial machine that powers the military loses its mission as well. Rather than lose it, we must use it. Give the military and the industrial machine that supports it a new mission. Redeploy it and make it more robust.

In this proposed transition, there is no loss of market. We would simply build a better, bigger market. To create that market, we need a fair and operable set of rules by which we cooperate to take on problems we cannot face alone. We can all lose individually, or we can all win together. The threats of AI and global catastrophe have to be faced and funded collectively.

The idea that we reincarnate is not the reason to change, but the coming change can occur if we remove outdated restrictions and frictions.

How can we motivate a comfortable and indifferent globe that does not understand the complexities I'm modeling here?

Money must follow the path of logic to consistently win. Make no mistake: this book is written for the people of Davos and the two thousand billionaires. You get the return by investing in the process.

How can we reach and teach everyone? It's so cheap it's ridiculous.

"In 1993," Diamandis and Kotler write, "Iqbal Quadir was working as a venture capitalist in New York when he left to go back to his native Bangladesh and start a cell phone company. Back then the cheapest cell phone available had a cost of $400 and had an operating cost of $.52 a minute. At that time the average yearly income in Bangladesh was $286."[4]

He knew that cell phones were analog and that they were about to become digital, which meant their core components would be subject to Moore's Law and continue to get smaller and cheaper. He also knew that connectivity equals productivity. So if he could get cell phones into the hands of customers, it would give them the ability to pay for the phones.

He was right. Cell phones followed an exponential price-performance curve, and Grameenphone transformed life in Bangladesh. By 2006, sixteen million people had access to a cell phone, and the technology had added $650 million to Bangladesh's GDP. In India by 2010, fifteen million new cell phone users were being added each month. As of early 2011, 50 percent of the world had cellular connectivity. This will reshape the world.

We're already seeing it happen in banking. There are 2.7 billion people in the developing world without access to financial services. In Tanzania, for example, less than 5 percent of the population have bank accounts. In Ethiopia, there is one bank for every hundred thousand people. In Uganda around 2005, there were one hundred ATMs for twenty-seven million people. Opening an account in Cameroon cost $700, more than most people make in a year, and a woman in Swaziland can manage that feat only with the consent of a father, brother, or husband.

Secure banking requires secure individual rights, and it underpins healthy economic and social systems.

Enter mobile banking. Allowing the world's poor to set up a digital bank account accessible via cell phones has a significant impact on quality of life and in poverty reduction. It allows people to check their balances, pay bills, receive payments, and send money home without transfer fees. It also helps them avoid the personal security risks that come from carrying cash.

Safaricom launched a mobile-phone-based money-transfer system in Kenya in 2007. It had 20,000 customers its first month. Four months later it had 150,000, and four years after that it had 13 million. A market that did not exist in 2007 grew into a $16 billion industry by 2011 with analysts predicting it would grow an additional 68 percent by 2014.

With so many billions of people having access to this kind of connectivity, it is imperative that fact-based logic-driven narratives be on their devices.

Consciousness science is such a narrative. It supports indigenous beliefs while acting as a counterbalance to fundamentalist philosophies that drive confrontation and unrest and add friction to the global system.

The financial benefit to developing these markets far outweigh the collective GDP of the international arms industry. What happens when orders for tanks dry up and stand-alone recycling plants go up? If the recycling plants are based on the best-practices model, they will be low cost because they are mass produced and generate raw material for manufacturing at the local level.

"In 1999 the Indian physicist Sugata Mitra got interested in education. He knew there were places in the world without schools and places in the world where good teachers didn't want to teach. Self-directed learning was one possible solution, but were the kids living in slums capable of all that much self-direction?"

Here is another excerpt from *Abundance* by Diamandis and Kotler:

At the time, Mitra was head of research and development for NIIT technologies, a top computer software and development company in New Delhi, India. His posh 21st-century office abutted in urban slum but was kept separate by a tall brick wall. So Mitra designed a simple experiment. He cut a hole in the wall and installed a computer and a tract pad, with this screen and the pad facing into the slum. He did it in such a way that theft was not a problem, then connected the computer to the internet, added web browser, and walked away.

The kids who lived in the slums could not speak English, did not know how to use a computer, and had no knowledge of the internet, but they were curious. Within minutes, they figured out how to point-and-click. By the end of the first day, they were surfing the web and - even more importantly- teaching one another how to surf the web.

[...]

So Mitra moved his experiment to the slums of Shivpuri, where, as he says, "I'd been assured no one had ever told anybody anything." He got simi- lar results.[5]"

Mitra found that the children who had no educa- tion or teacher could educate themselves using only a computer with access to the internet. One of the most successful groupings he found was four children sitting at one computer. He found an even better result when there was a grandmother type standing behind and encouraging them. It did not matter if she was more uneducated than the children in front of her. All that mattered was that she offered encouragement.

Mitra helped a group of impoverished Tamil-speaking children who had never used the internet teach themselves biotechnology, a subject they never heard of, in English, a language none of them spoke. "All I did was tell them that there was some very difficult information on this com- puter, and they probably wouldn't understand any of it, and I'll be back to test them on it in a few months."

Two months later he returned and tested them. Scores averaged around 30 percent. From 0 to 30 percent in two months with no formal instruction was remarkable, but the children still were not good enough to pass the standard exam. He continues to refine his methods.

He popularized the term "self-organized learning environments" or SOLEs. They are hooked up to what he calls the granny cloud, groups of grandmothers recruited from the United Kingdom who agreed to donate one hour a week of their time for these kids via Skype. He discovered that the granny cloud can increase test scores by 25 percent.

This is how we can increase education and literacy globally without teachers or schools. Putting consciousness science and the science of reincarnation on this type of platform would provide a science-based logical argument against fundamentalist extremism while at the same time supporting local religious beliefs.

The alternative is to not provide education and live in an unending state of war on a shithole planet.

* * *

I asked Dean Radin and Stephan Schwartz the following questions:

- What are the four most important things we could do to save our planet and ourselves, and what do we have to do to make that happen?
- What research do we need to fund so that we can as a species protect ourselves from the coming threats outlined by Stephan?

Their answers are in the following chapters.

But before I close this chapter, I want you to imagine that every moral scientist in the world is part of a large decentralized organization called IASOR, the International Association for the Science of Reincarnation. IASOR's membership can include anyone who sees that reincarnation should be a science.

I want you to imagine that IASOR Inc. has been asked to "metaphorically" design an overall plan of wellness initiatives to save our children, our planet, and ourselves. What should we do? How should we fund it? How do we market it?

If you want to go fast, go alone. If you want to go far, go together. We have to do both at the same time.

Notes

1 Peter H. Diamandis and Steven Kotler, *Abundance*, p. 141.

2 Peter H. Diamandis and Steven Kotler, *Abundance*, p. 141.

3 Peter H. Diamandis and Steven Kotler, *Abundance*, p. 142.

4 Peter H. Diamandis and Steven Kotler, *Abundance*, p. 144.

5 Peter H. Diamandis and Steven Kotler, *Abundance*, p. 174.

Chapter 16

Four Leverage Points

When I asked Stephan Schwartz about the four most important things we can do to save our planet and ourselves, here was his response:

Hi Bob,

On the basis of factual data, there are four leverage points that stand out for me where citizen involvement and funding could produce significant benefits from additional rigorous attention. As I have already noted, all of these arise from a change in consciousness, and so I will begin with that.

1. Integrating Consciousness into Science and the Failure of Materialism

   At present, models of consciousness can essentially be subdivided into two distinct broad categories. Models of the first type include physicalist models holding all consciousness as being contained within an organism's neuroanatomy.

Some of the hallmarks of materialism are:

The physicalist/materialist model (P/MM)
1. The mind is solely the result of physiologic processes
2. Each consciousness is a discreet entity, unconnected and independent of other consciousnesses
3. No communication is possible except through the defined physiologic senses
4. Consciousness dwells entirely within the time/space continuum; death ends consciousness.

A corollary to materialism is dominionism, the idea that humanity has dominion over the earth and can exploit whatever it wishes. One could make the case that most of the crises facing humanity today arise from that materialist dominionist worldview.

Models of the second type include nonlocal consciousness, distinguished by the assumption that a significant aspect of consciousness is not limited to the neuroanatomy and is therefore is nonlocal. This was the view articulated by the father of quantum mechanics, Max Planck, when he said, "Consciousness is fundamental and causal, space-time arises from consciousness, not consciousness from space-time."

The interdependent interconnected conscious-ness model MODEL (IICM)

1. Only certain aspects of the mind are the result of physiologic processes
2. Consciousness is causal, and physical reality is its manifestation
3. All consciousnesses, regardless of their physical manifestations, are part of a matrix of life which they both inform and influence and are informed and influenced by; there is a passage back and forth between the individual and the collective
4. Some aspects of consciousness are not limited by the space-time continuum.

Today, in fields as diverse as physics and medicine, the peer-reviewed literature that is science's benchmark is filling with papers on nonlocal mind, distant mental influence, interactions between lifeforms that do not involve standard sense perception, and the efficacy of prayer. Taken one by one, these studies are often impressive; in aggregate they present a compelling argument that materialism is no longer a fully adequate explanation of how our world works.

This presents a leverage point. It is not the purview of this presentation to outline what might be done but simply to point out that consciousness research, once the poor cousin of science, actually offers the way to gain the insight essential to developing an effective response to the second leverage point.

2. The Devastation of the Environment

This leverage point comes with great urgency. Any future predicated on wellbeing must be created on the basis of facts, not philosophies or theories. But perhaps the first question to be asked is, why does such a future need to be created? To answer that, let's start with the reality of facts, not political partisanship and bloviation.

Two hundred and seventy-five studies published in the last nine years have all found that greenhouse gases, most notably carbon dioxide, are changing the earth's environment and constitute a real threat to human civilization. The Environmental Protection Agency (EPA) in 2009 issued a report stating that these gases constitute a threat to human health and wellbeing. "There's absolutely no scientific basis for questioning the Endangerment Finding," review lead researcher Philip Duffy, president and executive director of the Woods Hole Research Center in Falmouth, Massachusetts, told *Live Science*. "The case for endangerment is stronger than ever." Francisco Sanchez-Bayo of the

School of Life & Environmental Sciences, Sydney Institute of Agriculture, The University of Sydney, led a team that looked at the state of insect life on the planet. They found that "Over 40% of insect species are threatened with extinction."

The main reason for this, they report, is "habitat loss by conversion to intensive agriculture, involving using agrochemical pollutants, invasive species are the main reason for the failure of the insect ecosystem" plus, of course, the climate change being brought on by greenhouse gases. Similarly, dozens of studies show changes in the ocean ecosystems at a scale never before seen in recorded history. The Intergovernmental Panel on Climate Change (IPCC) in its 2018 report warned of far greater ocean warming than had been previously thought that would result in massive disruption of ocean ecosystems. A year later, a multi-institute and university research team led by L. Resplandy of the Department of Geosciences and Princeton Environmental Institute at Princeton University reexamined and extended the data and reported that the IPCC had underestimated these trends by 40%.

This illustrates the two constants about the changes the earth is undergoing as a result of human activity: since climate change became a subject of scientific study, at every step the timeline has collapsed, and the outcome projections have become worse. That is important to keep in mind because the 2018 IPCC report's leading conclusion, the one that got the most media attention, was that humanity had only twelve years to act if global warming is to be kept to a maximum of 1.5C.

"It's a line in the sand and what it says to our species is that this is the moment and we must act now," said Debra Roberts, the cochair of the working group that focused on the impact on human civilization of the changes predicted, in an interview with the British newspaper *The Guardian*. "This is the largest clarion bell from the science community, and I hope it mobilizes people and dents the mood of complacency," she added.

We could go on and on in this vein, listing the failure of Himalayan hydrology, the coming water wars, large areas of the earth becoming uninhabitable because of the elevated temperature; several books have been written doing just that. What we have been calling climate change really should now be called environmental devastation. It is quite reasonable to say human civilization is in danger of violent collapse. Given that at this point massive change is coming, hundreds of millions of environmental devastation migrants will be moving across the earth bringing massive social instability, and many of the earth's ecosystems will undergo violent transition, isn't it time to mount what amounts to a war-level effort to respond to these changes and to ask what will it take to create a future based on wellbeing?

That leads me to the third leverage point.

3. The Failure of Neoliberalism and the Success of the Theorem of Wellbeing

One of the fastest growing trends in the world is the rise of neo-feudalism as a result of neoliberal economic policies. The world's richest five hundred people got $1 *trillion* richer in 2017 alone. That is such a large number that it is hard to conceptualize it, so try this: it is just shy of the collective entire Gross Domestic Product (GDP) of Sweden ($551 billion), Norway ($370 billion), and Finland ($273 billion). We now have five hundred people with collective wealth at the multinational level—and I don't mean impoverished, developing nations. I mean three of the happiest, most successful, and richest democracies in the world.

In the United States, Jeff Bezos, Bill Gates, and Warren Buffett own more wealth than the entire bottom half of the American population combined, a total of 160 million people or 63 million households. In contrast 40% of Americans could not write a $400 check if pressed to do so by an emergency, and Americans are falling behind on car loan payments in record numbers. More than 7 million car loans were past due by at least ninety days in the fourth quarter of 2018, according to the New York Federal Reserve. Sixty-two percent of bankruptcies that occur each year are a result of medical bills. In fact, America does not have a health-care system, it has an illness profit system and spends orders of magnitude more of its GDP than any other developed nation in the world: $10,739 per capita compared with $4,708 in Australia and $4,033 in Finland. And what does the U.S. get for that? The World Health Organization ranks the U.S. as 37th in health-care quality and outcomes. I could go on and on with this kind of social outcome data, but the point is the same in all cases. The neoliberal economics that has dominated not just America but most of the non-Nordic countries and Holland is a disaster unless you happen to be one of the rich.

In contrast, social policies that are based on fostering wellbeing from the individual, to the family, community, state or province, nation, and the earth itself, consistently, based on social data, are more effective, more productive, more efficient, easier to implement, nicer to live under, and much, much cheaper. The evidence for this is incontrovertible.

That is but one example. You could pick any social policy you like, and the comparison would be the same, so let this example stand for the whole. The critical leverage point here is how to develop social policies that foster wellbeing as the first social priority while still allowing profit and entrepreneurship. That will be influenced by the fourth leverage point.

4. The Oncoming Challenge of Homo Superior

For most of our history as a species, we sapiens of the genus Homo have shared the planet with other hominid species. Most people don't realize that. We know it because genetic science, by extracting DNA from ancient bone fragments, has transformed paleo archaeology from speculation to certainty. This new research, which is amended and extended almost weekly, tells us that we still retain—you retain—genes resulting from encounters Homo sapiens had in deep time with Denisovans and Neanderthals.

In historical terms, there being only a single hominid species is an anomaly, one that is ending almost without public awareness, not because of normal evolutionary processes, but because of what we are doing to ourselves. We are about to face a world in which there are two species in the genus Homo—Homo sapiens, and Homo superior.

It is a world not imposed but being created as the result of CRISPR, a new genetic technology formally known as Crispr-Cas9, that allows scientists to edit genomes, including those of humans, with a precision unimaginable just a few years ago. *The Guardian,* describes it this way, and I can't improve on it: "Crispr, or to give it its full name, Crispr-Cas9, allows scientists to precisely target and edit pieces of the genome. Crispr is a guide molecule made of RNA that allows a specific site of interest on the DNA double helix to be targeted. The RNA molecule is attached to Cas9, a bacterial enzyme that works as a pair of 'molecular scissors' to cut the DNA at the exact point required. This allows scientists to cut, paste and delete single letters of genetic code."

CRISPR is the lever; it is with this technology that we have begun to create Homo superior, although for most researchers that is not the immediate goal. Most but not all are trying to eliminate systemic chronic inherited diseases. But CRISPR has a shadow, the ethical challenge of creating Homo superior without any real consideration as to what that means. But let's start with the easy part, the end of hereditary disease, because that's what motivated most researchers. The Homo superior issue was mostly a concern of medical ethicists. The big issue was adding human genes to animals, and the following question: how many human genes does it take to make a being human?

Because of neoliberalism and the rise of neo-feudalism, I think it is safe to presume that this new technology will be expensive, and it will be the rich who will be the ones to first avail themselves of its benefits. And because it includes germ-lining, all their children will share those benefits of health and intelligence. This in turn will further exacerbate the growing neo-feudalism trend in which there is a tiny uber-rich cohort, a small middle class—mostly professional people such as lawyers, doctors, and engineers—and a vast, wage-dependent peasantry. The evidence also suggests that because of differing cultural views, the rich of Asia will have access to these technologies first. The implications of this fork in humanity are barely discussed but will soon be upon us.

We're going into a territory where a lot of the ways in which we have organized our societies will suddenly look a bit redundant. In liberal democracies, we have this idea that human beings are basically equal in some very fundamental ways. We're coming close to the point where we can, objectively in some sense, create people who are superior to others.

And it's not just brains. Using CRISPR, Chinese researchers are also interested in genetically engineering physical prowess and have already produced a line of super dogs. David King, director of Human Genetics Alert (HGA), went on record saying, "It's true that the more and more animals that are genetically engineered using these techniques brings us closer to the possibility of genetic engineering of humans."

Don't you think it would be a good idea to think about this, hold conferences, and talk about it to reach not just social understanding but consensus before the only option is the choice of reaction to an established reality?

I'm going to address Stephan's comments in an actionable way. How do we face these risks, and what risks are we taking by acting or not acting? What do you do for yourself, your family, your community, and your world?

Stephan is correct about the science, but the science is too complicated for the average person to understand, much less its threats and consequences. How does cognition change if no one can understand the change? The marketing, branding, and explanation for this very, very important factual concept goes unappreciated and unacted upon. As an American president would say: #*Sad*.

The first cognition change must occur among scientists themselves. They need to understand that they must craft a marketing plan that will motivate change.

The number one human motivator is fear.

If we distill what Stephan has laid out in the harshest terms, in two generations there will be a new race of humans genetically engineered to be taller, stronger, and smarter. In the United States, our religious right prevents studies on stem cells and human engineering, forcing that research offshore to places like China that have no such compunctions about such work and are already doing it. This will accelerate when AI is smarter than humans in twenty short years. The United States will find itself far behind quickly, and *this is what it will meet on future battlefields.*

It gets worse because America has virtually stopped doing research in consciousness science. Once AI can sync to the human nonlocal wavelengths, we enter a science-fiction landscape that is being designed now. In order to understand that consciousness landscape, we need to map it. But studies in NDEs, children who remember prior lives, clairvoyance, and remote viewing are purposely resisted by religious organizations whose belief systems would be impacted, altered, and upended.

This has to be explained to the US military in ways they can understand and address. The US Air Force Academy is primarily a Christian organization. Many in the military will not believe what can be possible now because to them, scientists are designing weapons and information-gathering methods that are surreal. They need to fund programs at universities that support research into the consciousness science not only of humans but also of artificial intelligence and then sync to the human electrical and nonlocal signals. Fields such as electrophysiology will emerge as this science develops. The universities have to be educated about what science needs to be done. *And it has to be explained like you are explaining it to a seventh grader.*

Consider the British branding of Brexit. The Leave contingent reduced its message to two things: take control and return to the way it was. This simple campaign took the UK on a path that was not in its best interest and will cause it to lose an estimated 5–9 percent of its GDP. It will have no societal benefit, and the marketing was based on selling two fallacies.

Why should you fear what Stephan has laid out? Because if you are thirty or younger, this will happen in your lifetime.

How can we rebrand nonlocal consciousness? By calling it electrical consciousness. Scientists can call it nonlocal consciousness if they dislike "electrical consciousness," but which is easier to explain to a large uneducated population? If we are marketing to the bottom of the pyramid, we have to speak to the bottom of the pyramid, especially if we want those at the bottom to be part of the solution.

I would suggest we use both names with the same explanation. Explain the situation at different orders of magnitude. The explanations are fractals of each other. This complex electrical organism we call consciousness is a shape-shifter, and we need to look past our physical bodies to see it and us. If we must explain it simply, we should operate on the KISS basis: keep it simple, stupid.

These explanations fit into our set of Russian nesting dolls from chapter fifteen. Each doll and explanation is a fractal, each one its own iteration. Each is self-similar, and the same patterns operate at differing orders of magnitude.

If your consciousness is electrical, it must conform to the laws of physics. So let's look at macrophysics.

From the point of view of macrophysics, we can understand electrical consciousness as a form of electromagnetism. In macrophysics there was an attempt to create a unified field theory in physics. The four forces are the strong force, the weak force, electromagnetism, and gravity. As the forces began to be connected, electromagnetism was connected to the weak force, then the strong force. Gravity was finally connected to electromagnetism, making all the other forces manifestations of electromagnetism.

If a unified field theory is to be used as described, electromagnetism is the governing force. Nonlocal consciousness is then a derivative of this theory, as are gravity, the strong force, and the weak force. When you measure life and death, the presence of electromagnetism means there is life. By this simple measure, when electromagnetism is gone, there is death. This, my friends, is truth. This is the simple explanation of the same thing.

My rebranding of nonlocal consciousness as electromagnetic consciousness does not meet the scientific standard Stephan would use, but electromagnetic consciousness as a brand explains it better because it's easier to understand even though it's technically incorrect.

He would say my explanation is wrong, and he would be right. But his explanation cannot be delivered to seven billion people, and I am trying to craft an explanation that can. In this negotiation with scientists, universities, billionaires, clerics, and governments, we all need to be flexible.

Stephan and the scientists who work in this field are saying that we have found that this electrical charge, rather than your body, is you. This charge is your soul. You shed your body every two to seven years, but the electrical charge is constant. And like any electrical charge, it has a field of influence, so you have clairvoyance and remote viewing and other things more eloquently described by Stephan. It can reach outside your body, and after your death, it is still you. A scientist would say it retains coherence. Near-death experiences, out of body experiences, and remembering prior lives are all real-world examples of this.

* * *

The University of Alabama returned a gift of $26.5 million to Hugh F. Culverhouse Jr. because he objected to Alabama's ban on abortion. I suggest that he respond by helping the institutions around the University of Alabama and ultimately the university itself by introducing a new model to replace the misogynistic model that he thinks should change.

I ask Mr. Culverhouse to redeploy his gift by founding the Culverhouse Chairs of Consciousness Science for $5 million each. Five million is merely a suggested number for each university and each proposal. If Mr. Culverhouse indicates he would be amenable to a proposal, one could be tailored to specific goals that would have positive social ramifications.

Because Mr. Culverhouse is from the South and wishes to help the University of Alabama, he should hold back the $5 million until the university funds such a chair. The first three chairs should be at the University of Virginia, Duke University, and the University of Miami. Mr. Culverhouse could have free use of any research or patents produced at these universities.

This is just one example of an actionable and positive response. I'm also presenting a new model for investment to the two thousand billionaires of the world. It is a fractal example of a fractal solution. It would work globally because it doesn't matter if a given country is a dictatorship, a democracy, or an autocracy. Governments of the world are made up of oligarchs, some more robust than others. They are competitive rather cooperative, and if we don't develop a plan to solve our problems together, we all lose. Governments come and go, but inherited money lasts forever.

We need to get those who control big money to cooperate with each other toward a common goal to save us, and it has to be profitable. Let's start with Mr. Culverhouse.

Dear Mr. Culverhouse,

I would ask you to redeploy your returned gift from the University of Alabama by endowing a series of academic chairs for the study of consciousness science. I am asking for ten chairs at ten different universities all studying different disciplines within consciousness science and the science of reincarnation as laid out in this book.

I would endow the Duke Math Department with a million-dollar chair to study the correlation between past-life regression (using the database at the University of Miami) and children who remember prior lives (using the database at the University of Virginia that Jim Tucker runs). Each university gets one million dollars to the specific department. Stanford should be involved militarily with nonlocal research, and Princeton should also continue the work it stopped in the '90s now that AI has advanced.

I have spoken to Jim Tucker at the University of Virginia and people at other universities who would be amenable to supporting such work.

With your contribution to this plan under the direction of people like Dean Radin and Stephan

Schwartz, you will have surrounded your alma mater with more than a credible response, and your response should be that if they too will fund a chair of consciousness science, you will give them $10 million and make them a center of knowledge, study, and science instead of one of belief.

The fact that this science may provide huge advances in communication, travel, and economics is almost not relevant to this conversation.

I am going to explain how that works because others may want to found chairs of consciousness science at their own alma maters, so the appeal is not just to you. It is universal and fractal.

Thank you for your consideration.

Bob Good

The college textbook *The Science of Reincarnation* is already online at www.iasor.org. The Culverhouse Chair of Consciousness Science will study human consciousness, artificial consciousness, and edits to both using CRISPR and programming to sync the biological with the artificial using electricity.

The numbers requested in the letter can be modified, depending on what the university is to do. The UVA department of perceptual studies should also connect NDEs with children who remember prior lives, which would qualify for another million in funding. We must remain flexible as we are creating a new system.

I want to show how this new model of consciousness science should be marketed to people who are smart enough to use it. You don't become a billionaire without being smart, so I am going to include two more targeted funding requests.

The first is to Jennifer Pritzker, the richest transgender woman in the world. I am asking for a $1 million donation to fund the Jennifer Pritzker Chair of Consciousness Science at Loyola University in Chicago. One quarter of that donation goes to funding the Brunei fellowship.

The electrical polarity of our bodies contains information about our gender. The Sultan of Brunei is a bigoted homophobe, and educating his people about the normalcy of gender variation is the only way to defeat such stupidity. So first you can educate and then reform with this targeted donation by creating a cadre to teach the people of Brunei their leader is wrong.

Second, you can foster the science that the army never should have abandoned at Stanford, and finally you would be party to derivative intellectual property. Please give $1 million to Loyola, fund this consciousness chair, and let the terms and conditions be written by Dean Radin and Stephan Schwartz. I can be contacted through the IASOR website.

My third billionaire is Charlie Kushner. His son Jared, who works for Donald Trump, has repeatedly pushed real estate development deals internationally that have been met with resistance because some people in those locations do not welcome different cultural norms for ideological reasons. The McDonalds's theory of war states that no country with a McDonald's has ever gone to war with another country with a McDonald's. Likewise, this science can pierce cultural barriers and prepare the ground for the kind of development you want.

Fund a chair of consciousness studies at Harvard, the university with the largest bloated endowment, and look forward fifty years to when Jared will be eighty-five. Harvard is already studying this type of science, but it needs to be infused with resources. My guess is that you already bought Harvard one building, but you could buy one more and share the derivative technology while supporting your real estate endeavors overseas. Is $10 million too much to ask?

* * *

The point of this entire treatise is that instead of stumbling blindly into the future, we should acknowledge its inevitability and take responsibility in changing it. This goes directly to free speech and expression.

China, are you listening? Without the free and unfettered exchange of ideas respectfully presented, we blind ourselves to reality and makes ourselves sitting ducks in the coming fight against AI, aliens, asteroids, and so many other threats. I am not asking you to relinquish your power. I am simply asking you to be smart.

I let my grandchildren speak their mind in my home so I can teach them and help their creative minds create. I do this because I love them and want them to have the best life they can. This is how you should treat the NBA. If you let the NBA have free expression, box office proceeds will increase. Team values will rise.

If my military is to protect me, it should be put to work cleaning the oceans. The Army Corps of Engineers should get five new battalions while the navy and the air force have there their funding cut in half. They can have all that money back on a mission to space. They should not want them to lead but to follow the corporations that go outward bound. NASA is already booking time on commercial space flights and opening the space station to commercial businesses. The navy and air force will be reborn.

* * *

Allow me please to make the case for consciousness science to an imaginary couple, Bobby Joe and Faith Doaks, white Southern Baptists and Trump supporters. The following is a part of their Sunday sermon delivered by their pastor who read it here first.

Folks:
There are four forces in the universe: the strong force, the weak force, gravity, and electromagnetism.

Physicists are finding that these forces all boil down to one force: electromagnetism. That spark of divinity is in you and is measured by your EKG. When that is gone, you are dead.

That electricity, not your body, is you, and when you die, that spark does not die. It returns to the matrix of consciousness. Here in South Carolina we call that heaven. Physicists and we in South Carolina use different words to describe the same thing. Physicists might call that spark nonlocal consciousness; here in South Carolina, we call it a soul.

We have hospitals where we care for our sick, and while we use the power of prayer to heal people, we use science as well. Science changes how we think about our world. All the electromagnetism in the universe, the force of the universe, we call God. When I die, I go to God, but as science advances, we understand more about how that works. We understand that we will return to the overall force of the universe, electromagnetism, of which we are a part.

Here's where it gets interesting, folks. I can try to return here to South Carolina again. You say you don't believe in reincarnation? You only live once? How do you know? Right here in the South at UVA, we have thousands of kids who say otherwise. Here in South Carolina we have cases of NDEs where people died, went to heaven, and came back, and they are aggregated at IANDS. Both groups tell the same story to a mathematical certainty. Still don't believe it? You already proved it once by being alive right here is South Carolina. If you can do something once, you can do it again.

Understanding drives action. If you are white, you might come back as black. If you are a man, you might come back as a woman. What you believe has a scientific foundation, and you as a soul are here to learn and experience. *This new scientific understanding of what we are supports our religious beliefs.*

So when you head out today from our church and look around you, I want you to see not people but souls in transition. This whole gay thing is simply electromagnetic energy moving from a positive to a negative polarity. Moving from being a man to being a woman and back again so you can experience life and grow as a soul. Moving in the vernacular from a hole to a pole or mathematically from a one to a zero. That's why you have to vote for transgender bathrooms. Those souls are in transition and expressing who they are at the moment. They are growing. So are you. That's why you have to vote for racial equality. And that's why you have to build levees to protect our coast.

This is too simple an explanation for physicists because it is incomplete and not specific enough. There are nuances and details they want to change and add. And the real pastor here at your congregation doesn't like my imaginary pastor's sermon either because this scientific explanation makes you, Bobby Joe and Faith, the same as the gay black kid on the other side of town. There is a case you can read about a white boy who remembers life as a black woman named Pam in Chicago.

This means that all consciousness is interconnected and interdependent. The universe is a product of intentioned consciousness that we think of as God's plan in South Carolina. Science backs that up. We need to back up the science with our support as well. That means we need to see your support in the collection plate, and we need you to ask universities in our area to support this important research.

Science is validating our faith, and right action will bring heaven here on earth. That means you have to vote the right way. You know how you have to vote.

That is the end of the sermon. It is an address to the common man, the nonprofessional. This is one of several fractal explanations crafted for various levels of understanding to explain this change of cognition. You cannot speak to just one demographic.

* * *

There is another demographic I want to address. I want to speak to my people about this in my way. It is another fractal explanation of consciousness science applied. I want to speak to the men who went through basic training with me in 1971. There were two hundred of us, one company with four platoons of fifty men each. There were blacks from inner-city Chicago and whites from inner-city Paducah, Kentucky. There were a few people like me on the way to flight school. We thought we were all on our way to Vietnam.

This is what I would say:

We've been played, bro. We've been lied to up and down the board, and no one gives a shit. That preacher telling you that you can't buy liquor on Sunday because of God is full of shit. I'll drink liquor any goddamn time I want. I ain't gonna die. There's a heaven. Science proved it. Also proved I can date a black girl or a white girl or transgender girl or another guy cause it's all right.

That politician who told the farmers that trade wars are good doesn't have as many markets as before. Some call that karma. I call it stupidity. The politician who told you health care was no good because everybody has it worked for the insurance companies. If you take something away from people, you get less of it yourself, whether it's trade or health care. If you weaken Obamacare, you get less of it yourself, and you pay more for it.

Look at the gun lobby. They sell me on my right to have a gun with no background checks. But if you go to the lobby's meetings, you're not allowed to have a gun. Are you still buying this bullshit? My schools are getting shot up, and you can't pass legislation to protect my kids? I own a gun—more than several—and could pass a background check. So I want the guys with guns to pick up their fucking guns and point them at their politicians and say, "I can pass a background check, now do something to protect my kids." And if you can't pass a background check, I don't give a shit. It's not my problem. I'd like to see the guys with guns stand up to something tougher than them, their politicians.

I'm tired of being sold crap. If I rip it down, I get less, and if I build it up, I get more. That's how the fractal process works.

Take 2 percent of the defense budget and clean the oceans. The oceans have a fever. They are warming because they ate all our crap. To fix this, we need to send ships en masse to the ocean where all the crap is and get it out. If the ocean dies, we die. How fucking simple is this? The armed forces are there to protect us. If not from this threat, then what? You southern boys, you're the party of change. You are the guts of the system. Your kids are serving now. Agitate for this to be a mission of the armed forces working unilaterally. We don't need allies. We need to get a job done. It will put you all back to work. The heart of the US military is in the South. That's where this change needs to come from.

My friends from 1971 aren't going to change this, but if they understand it, they will accept it and support it.

You have to explain this change and how to manage it to the people who manage society, the politicians. You cannot use the same explanation with all of them because of different governing systems. They have to understand the science and how to implement its changes to their benefit within their system.

This brings us to Senator Lindsey Graham and Russian President Vladimir Putin. Lindsey should hear the above sermon to the South Carolinians and make sure it is heard throughout the South. He should remember that he is the people's representative, not a paid employee of his commercial contributors, the aforementioned oligarchs and billionaires, although he is that also. He should be on board the LGBTQ express along with Dick Cheney's daughter for the same reason. Vladimir Putin needs to be on that train as well.

Putin requires a different sell, and the scientists I represent aren't quite comfortable with him or frankly this approach (or, if I had to guess, with me either). The scientists should understand they now have a marketing department, and Mr. Putin deserves reasons to change. I began this tread in chapter seven on DNA and continued in how it related to its strategic importance at the end of chapter fourteen, but how it becomes more robust depends on how that resource is nurtured and grown and how the resultant policy changes based on smart military tactics. They need to see that their discoveries have different applications when held in different hands. The best way to explain this approach to the scientists is to explain the desired policy change to Mr. Putin. At the end of the day, this document is asking Mr. Putin to fund psi research along the lines laid out in this book. It is to the Russian scientists that this funding would go.

Now a brief word to Trump. This specifically applies to your Space Corps. You are subject to the same laws of science, and if you go to space without the resources described here, which include gays in the military, you weaken the very force you seek to send out. Your policy currently is "I want to design a force with flaws" when improving that force would mean you have to change your social policies. Which, as a responsible Republican, do you choose?

The Russian version of psi research—and Russian physicists are excellent, by the way—has to be connected to the research center in Lhasa, Tibet, and that has to be connected to Princeton and Stanford. I don't just want it funded; I want it connected.

I want to speak to Comrade Putin directly as if I were a close and trusted friend. Someone he fought beside, with him and me on the same team.

My first job out of college was as an enlisted man in the US Army. My first job out of training was as an assault helicopter pilot assigned to a Ranger unit. The next job I had was as a test pilot. If I flew for you, you would trust me as did the men who got in and out of my helicopter on a nightly basis. I want you to trust that what I am communicating is true. These scientists cannot express the transcendent nature of their discoveries, but the math is there. The military ramifications are profound, and they cannot be faced alone. It is not just stepping into space; it is the opening of another dimension for communication and perhaps transport, and the proof is there. The connection to the nonlocal that each of us intrinsically possess is less than 2 percent of our reality. But then again, gold makes up less than 2 percent of the world's crust. I need your help, and I need you on board. Russian physicists are among the best in the world. I need them. They should double-blind everything the Americans do, and the results should be shared and published. No politics on either side.

I am asking you and Xi Jinping, the vice president of China, and the chairman of the Central Military Commission of the People's Republic of China to make policy changes that would benefit you and your countries. I am asking American and European countries to follow the example I am explaining to you and Xi.

Give Russian physicists funding to study consciousness science as described in this book. This investment needs to go alongside your development of AI. Sync the frequencies. That is your goal. Once you do, you will have RAIV and will be able to read the files in Langley. You well understand the threat of AI. A smarter and more malevolent version of AI is looming just over the horizon.

Open the Russian internet, change the belief system in the next generation, eliminate war, use armies to fight global warming collectively and cohesively, and double the GWP and your personal wealth and power.

Take the seed money from ego. Does anybody really need another $100 billion in personal wealth? Bezos is worth $150 billion. If you use the money in a dedicated global fund that is designed by the best minds and cohesively executed, you will reeducate and stabilize all religions in a more positive way than the Chinese are reeducating the Uighurs. I trust Radin and Schwartz, and I want you and Xi to trust me. The managers of that money will be the oligarchs and billionaires themselves. In this model, they will collectively run a global venture capital firm designed to produce profit, and that cannot work without intelligent, productive consumers. That is what they are charged to create. Think of the market they could profit from when they're finished. This can be done fractally, one state, city, and zone at time.

If Xi uses the science explained in this book to reeducate the Uighurs, he would deradicalize the next generation. He would still have the Uighurs as a resource. Diversity at all levels needs to be protected for our mutual benefit.

Let's look at this another way. If the proof is that consciousness is fractal, then when Xi dies, there will be a lot of angry Uighurs waiting for him. This expanded understanding of consciousness reveals real ramifications of your actions. My guess is that Hitler is not having a real good time in the fourth cognitive dimension, which seems to be where we are all headed.

Let's go back to Stephan Schwartz's third point. "The critical leverage point here is how to develop social policies that foster wellbeing as the first social priority while still allowing profit and entrepreneurship."

This simple cooperation will produce better results than opposition. How is that negotiated? It's not. It's created unilaterally by each person's individual acts. You choose this course of action with prejudice. You say, "Hey, that's a good idea; it's my policy, and I'm going to follow it." It doesn't matter what the other person does. You are deciding to implement your portion of this plan for your own benefit. People who are doing the same will support your efforts.

China, you need to stop shooting microwave radiation at trade delegates. You are injuring people unnecessarily, and you need them to help you. They will help you because they have to follow the same pattern. Or we could collectively watch the earth burn, and your power and wealth will fall accordingly.

Change your position on LGBT issues. We are not bodies that produce minds; we are minds that inhabit bodies. These minds show themselves as electrical charges with polarities. As with all polarities, they can be in a state of flux.

When you take a transgender woman, apply hormones, and surgically alter the genitals, I would bet you

$1,000 that you could not tell the difference between her and another woman *because they are both women*. Now join that with the first CRISPR trials.

The first confirmed CRISPR gene-editing clinical trial to take place outside China is officially underway, with pharmaceutical companies CRISPR Therapeutics and Vertex revealing that a human patient has been administered an experimental treatment targeting a rare blood disease. We are reengineering genetics. So where is the difference between men and women? It's in the electrical charge in the body. It is below the quantum biology state, but it still makes its presence felt all the way through the chemical and biological model.

CRISPR is at the same stage as the Wright Brothers when they first flew. We have roughly twenty years until AI is smarter than us, and the speed of discovery is on the geometric progression described by Moore's Law. A new race of humans is already appearing, and to them you and I are becoming Neanderthals.

When this dimensional shell cracks, you and I will either be in the frying pan or we'll be another chicken. The smart guys around me say the math tells us we can influence the outcomes.

Russia has the most beautiful transgender women in the world. They have the best hookers. You said that. Frankly, the leaders of all countries should say the same about their ladies of the night. Man, I'm on your side. I want you to support the LGBT community, and I will tell you why: it's tactical. Let the women be men, and let the men be women. Those in the middle can be bi, poly, or whatever. Let them all be supported and protected by state law with you as their vocal advocate.

Strong men stay in power by identifying a threat and telling everyone they will protect them. LGBT people are no more a threat than anyone else. This community produced Alan Turing, Julies Caesar, and Alexander the Great. I need their resources as much as I need yours. I need their receptors, and I need their work product, something the electrical charges in stable states, like you and me, cannot provide.

This leads to the second change. Do not create just a Russian internet. It will limit your personal wealth and Russia's collective wealth. Instead, use the methods outlined in chapter fifteen to bring wealth to your people. Let their work product enter the world, and let international banks build the system for you, and then you regulate it and profit from it. If you create a Russian Alibaba, you personally can become a cross between Jack Ma and Jeff Bezos.

Align your policy with the most successful global policy for wealth and measure this on a per-capita basis. More freedom means more disorder politically, but you and your oligarchs and billionaires will flourish if you manage them well. Your policies should be fractals of the most successful global policies. We are all, regardless of what we do, contributing to the matrix of global governance. Are you creating disorder and a resultant labyrinth, or are you contributing to order and clarity? Whatever you do will wash up on your own shoreline. That includes meddling in anyone's elections.

Metaphorically you and I are at war, but we are on the same side. Cyberwar is a poor strategy in comparison to coopting the Western model and using the West to implement better health and welfare in your country.

Let's look at this argument another way. The world is managed and run through a global oligarchy of which you are a part. Two thousand billionaires own the machine that runs the world. We split this machine into two parts, East and West.

The West has more billionaires because it manages a looser system that allows for more creativity. The billionaires still run it—just look at the Koch brothers' influence in the Republican Party. Ninety-three percent of Americans want gun control, but 1 percent of billionaires do not, so Americans don't get gun control.

The battlefield landscape I occupy has its roots in quantum physics. This science points to remote viewing as a scientifically reliable source of intelligence information when used properly. Remote viewers are mostly self-selected. I need your help to develop this in its next iteration, and the changes I want you to make are not politically driven; they are militarily driven. They are for your protection, health, and safety. If you look logically at this proposal, you will see that this is true.

For this to succeed, it must be addressed cohesively by all parties. One center of power cannot control, direct, or benefit without the cooperation of the other parties. Even so, some centers of power can benefit more by being proactive, so I want you to look at the Chinese and the advances made by genetically reengineering human embryos. I am suggesting conjoining Russian physics with Chinese biological engineering to allow you, and every one of your rich friends, to step across death into a new body.

This brings me to the third change. I need you to get on board with the 2 percent solution. I want you to commit 2 percent of your military budget to clean up your country. I want you to use military contractors. Go clean Chernobyl. Go refill the Aral Sea. If you commit, the Europeans will go along, and we could globally divert $32 billion a year to clean this planet and have the infrastructure (military) in place to do it.

If every country spent 2 percent less of their military budget, would anyone be less safe? I would posit that the very act of the 2 percent commitment would make the population safer. It would encourage local development and bring an infusion of capital without incurring an invitation of a greater threat. In the future as this develops, we could see the military rededicated and repurposed to development here and exploration in addition to their defense duties. This bodes well for both the labor markets and military budgets. Wellness, when done correctly, is a profit producer called wealthness.

There will come a point in this model where technology transfers must occur. If a solution works well in one part of the world, it needs to be deployed globally to places that currently cannot afford it. That will create markets.

In the Western world, corporate leaders are driven by greed and self-interest, and they send delegates to Congress to write laws that benefit them. To fight that institutionalized model is to lose. To co-opt it is to win, and that is done by monetizing wellness. That policy is called wealthness. Beto O'Rourke sees this, but no one can do it all. The platform planks should be provided by those who design them. He and others need lumber to build their political platforms, and wellness proponents must provide those planks for their political platforms. Beto and Mayor Pete Buttigieg should advance planks to write cooperative laws encouraging large wealth owners to partner together to solve specific problems. They should pair the problem to the billionaire who has expertise in that area. The closer they mimic the most successful fractal, the greater success they will have. Wealthness.

If I were a billionaire, I would be resistant to someone coming to me and saying they are going to take more of what I have because things are unequal. I would welcome a conversation that says government wants to partner with me and that my company can have a contract involving money I was giving away anyway.

The oligarchs and billionaires who own the companies would get these contracts based on results. Clean up the ocean? What is the price per ton delivered to the re-sorting centers? Would a large construction company be willing to undertake the building, training, and operation of a modular recycling center where ships cleaning the ocean could take products?

According to the website Top Ten Stuffs, "Rafael Del Pino was one of the world's richest people in the construction industry, with an estimated net worth of over $8.5 billion back in 2007. Rafael Del Pino was known as the founder of Ferrovial back in 1952—this was initially a construction company that has slowly become one of the largest building corporations in Spain. After he resigned, the position of President of Ferrovial was taken by his son back in 2000. In addition to the company, Rafael Del Pino has also founded the Fundacion Rafael Del Pino which aims to support future leaders in the industry. At the time being, the company, the foundation as well as all the other businesses that belonged to Rafael Del Pino are being managed by his family."[1]

That alone would provide local jobs and opportunity. But what incentive would Señor Del Pino have to do such a thing if I did ask?

Let's look at Elizabeth Warren and her proposed 2 percent plan in the 2020 presidential election campaign. Her platform wants to take 2 percent as a tax from anyone with more than $50 million and redistribute the money. There is no successful fractal of this model. The rich fight and subvert it, and the managers who are given the money are never as good as the managers who made the money. Warren's proposal fails on the basis of fractal alignment because the most important part of any asset is the human one, the men and women who created the wealth in the first place. They are the ones who know how to operate a global project at scale. A policy will be more successful if it mirrors the most successful fractal.

So let us modify Warren's plan to make it align fractally and bend it to the arc of wellness and wealthness. Remember that wellness has to benefit all parties and wealthness has to produce profit.

Here is a fractal model that works:

The founder of Microsoft added $16 billion to his net worth this year, despite giving away over $35 billion to charity, according to *Bloomberg*. That brings Gates' total wealth to $106 billion, the second largest fortune in the world—behind Amazon's Jeff Bezos.

"We're not, you know, in some defensive posture where we're mostly in cash, or anything like that," Gates told *Bloomberg Television* on Tuesday. "The strategy that's been used on the investments is to be over 60% in equities."

Having 60%, in this case $60 billion in stocks or

index funds, is an aggressive investment strategy for someone of Gates' wealth. The average family office portfolio in North America had about 32% of its assets in stocks in 2018, according to a Campden Wealth report.[2]

So Gates gave away nominally 30 percent of his net worth and still made money.

He got that $35 billion back and still added to his wealth. So let's say to Gates, "Bill, we want to take that $35 billion this year only and give every kid in America an age-appropriate laptop for school. Instead of books, we hand out laptops. We want you to run the program, meaning you take responsibility for delivery and spend the whole $35 billion at Microsoft."

Here is what will happen in this theoretical fractal: I get the best manager, Gates, and we use his money to give Microsoft a big contract. Gates's stock goes up, and the company should make money. People there go to work, they are hiring, and they have the resources, delivery system, and back end in place. Gates makes money, and kids get educated. Why should Microsoft get this contract? Because it's a gift. Because kids don't have laptops now, and because it's a way to equalize wealth in an unequal world. And if Gates gives this gift, there should be a law exempting him from taxes the year he makes this gift.

Simply taking money and giving it to managers hired

by the government will not be as successful as infusing the wealthy with more wealth by creating a model of opportunity for them to ply the trade that made them so successful in the first place. This model is better than Warren's because it drafts better talent into service.

Let's take Flint, Michigan. After concluding that Flint water is nineteen times more corrosive than Detroit water, Virginia Tech recommended the state declare that the water is not safe for drinking or cooking. Because Flint officials failed to apply corrosion inhibitors to the river water Flint used for drinking water, the water corroded the water pipes and lead leached from the water pipes into the water that Flint used for cooking and drinking. This constituted a health emergency.

Let's use this as an example and use this as a new model globally. Taxing rich people is oppositional; taking from one person to give to another who did not do the work meets resistance. Partnering with rich people to make everyone wealthier removes that resistance. So let's rewrite how we write laws.

Let's negotiate with one of the top-ten billionaires in the construction business and convince him to make his annual gift contribution in Flint. The money can go to his own construction company that does the work. If the company is profitable, it makes money. But several derivatives happen that are hallmarks of a fractal. The project is managed by the people who were most successful at this type of work, layers of bureaucracy are removed, and the company itself has a market in America's aging water infrastructure because other cities like Newark, New Jersey, have similar problems.

We need a fairer distribution of wealth, but taxing the rich entrenches class divides. Take Jeff Bezos as an example. His net worth is $150 billion. We could sweep $50 billion into a global management fund for which Bezos gets shares. That $50 billion could be used as seed money for wellness projects. Bezos can have a board seat, and the fund only pays out to Bezos if his net worth drops below $100 billion. Profits from the fund can be reinvested in the fund.

This is a suggestion not for a redistribution of global wealth but rather a redeployment. Taking from the rich to give to the poor will never work. But if I were rich like Bezos and could sweep money into a fund run by the two thousand richest people in the world to create markets where my investment could grow, that would be a win.

Instead we could say that those worth more than $100 billion could give 0.004 percent of their money into the fund. Think of it not as a tax but an investment. The money could be used as a global redevelopment fund that creates a self-sufficient consumer class. If space travel becomes possible, where will the engineers and scientists come from? A stratified, broken planet at war with itself?

In the matrix of Consciousness, I finally have to speak about aliens. They are here. In a science book to make that claim is antithetical. So here is the proof, it is in short hand, and will be understood and appreciated by those who have traveled in the military/science intelligence community.

The US Navy just admitted to there being UFO's and released footage, a fact remarkable only in its honesty. Those of us in the intelligence community have watched NASA inadvertently in 1992 show our spacecraft being shadowed by alien space craft and PIREPS (Pilot Reports) repeatedly describe encounters.

Dmitry Medvedev past president of Russia spoke of the briefing book he got when he became president listing aliens here already on open tv, it was after an interview but the cameras were still running. There is also a video of Canada's former Defense Minister Paul Hellyer chatting freely about how aliens are real in the presence of six American congressmen in Washington.

So here we get to the Matrix of Consciousness. First the math of probability says we are not alone as an intelligent life form in the universe. The cognition pathways described in this book are paramount to humanity surviving in the universe and becoming a space traveling species.

Once millennia ago, many thought the world was flat. Millenia from now humanity will look back and think once we thought we only existed in three dimensions. The leaders of Russia, China and America must be forward thinking and realize we have to address this cognitive change together not separately. This joining of forces and teaching this homogeneous model of cognition will create a peaceful economic explosion as earth is developed and healed simultaneously.

* * *

IASOR stands for the International Association for the Science of Reincarnation. It is a privately funded think tank dedicated to the rebirth of our planet and ourselves. It is about the business of creating a model of both profitability (wealthness) and wellness. If we build it, it will fund itself. In order to do that, we have to build a model of political action and fund it so people and corporations make money from it. That means legislating change and selling that change so that it's understandable and people want it.

In the future IASOR may become a political action committee (PAC). In that form it would drive a global plan to save us, designing common policies to support a future not designed by people who can get elected or take control but by people who drive a health model based on results. Politicians globally can then adopt planks from this standard wellness and wealthness platform in their own political environments.

IASOR at some point should be recreated as a 501 c (6). That tax code designation in the United States means it's an organization of nonprofits. If anyone has been to a funding seminar about how to fund nonprofits, they will quickly learn that marketing their message is fundamental to their survival. With standard scientific criteria that support and normalize religions and a standard constitution for promoting wellness and wealthness used by the most successful countries, we would export a model not of regime change but policy change toward a better world.

Notes

1   https://toptenstuffs1.wordpress.com/2016/03/12/top-ten-billionaires-from-construction/.

2   https://www.cnbc.com/2019/09/17/bill-gates-gave-away-35-billion-this-year-but-net-worth-didnt-drop.html.

Chapter 17

A Consciousness Science Moon-Shot Research Program Proposal

I have been around America's military-industrial complex and research centers for fifty years, and when I want straight talk and reliable analysis without the influence of money, prejudice, or stupidity, I can rely on Dean Radin and Stephan Schwartz to give me a no-bullshit answer. That's a tough thing to find.

I asked Dean to tell me what kind of research we need to fund so that we can as a species protect ourselves from the coming threats outlined by Schwartz. Here is his answer.

Hi Bob,

Imagine if 2% of the world's annual military budgets was redirected from stockpiling more bombs and bullets to exploring the full potential of human consciousness. That would instantly provide billions of dollars to study the most age-old, important, and unresolved questions humans can ask: Who are we, what are we capable of, where do we come from, and what happens after we die?

These big questions are traditionally answered by religions, but orthodox religious concepts are based on medieval, prescientific worldviews. While some of those ancient ideas might have merit, especially ones based on esoteric and mystical insights, in the modern age the currency of truth is provided by science, not by untestable religious dogma.

Answers to the big questions are not just of academic interest. The answers to these questions shape civilization. They determine how we treat each other, whether societies are motivated mainly by profit or by wellness, and if the earth is viewed as a resource ripe for plundering or as a sacred garden demanding careful cultivation.

The academic discipline most commonly associated with studying these big questions is philosophy. But the *scientific* discipline that investigates the big questions is parapsychology. Incorrectly associated in the popular mind with all manner of so-called paranormal topics, parapsychology is actually the scientific study of human experiences suggestive of mind-to-mind connections, perception through space and time, mind-matter interactions, out-of-body and near-death experiences, communication with nonhuman entities, and other survival-oriented topics like reincarnation, poltergeist activity, and hauntings. All these topics ask testable questions.

Parapsychology as a systematic academic discipline began in 1882 with the formation of the Society for Psychical Research in London, England. Since then, there have always been a few hundred doctorate-level scientists and scholars around the world who have been seriously interested in this field. Of them, at any given time perhaps four dozen are engaged in full-time research; most are involved as an avocation. The reason for the small number of researchers is not a lack of interest but rather a lack of funding. It has been estimated that funding spent in a single year in conventional academic psychology is equivalent to the entire 150-year history of funding for parapsychology.

One might ask, why are the big questions, which are of such profound and perennial interest to everyone, not funded at the level of, say, medical research? That field has millions of working scientists funded worldwide at hundreds of billions of dollars a year. There are two main reasons. First, orthodox religions strictly prohibit questioning dogma, so there is strong societal pressure to not use science to look at what some believe—incorrectly—are "supernatural" phenomena. There are even scientists who wrongly assert that these questions are beyond the capability of being scientifically investigated. Second, those who become addicted to political or financial power are specialists in exploiting human frailties—greed, envy, and fear. Anything that threatens that power is forcefully suppressed, and it is likely that if 7.5 billion people began to learn that we're all capable of far more than we've been told (by religion or by authority, which are often mixed in politics), that would almost certainly constitute a threat.

[...]

Returning to the opening vision, rather than the current shoe-string funding available to study the big questions, let's say a miracle occurs and we now have $1 billion a year. How would we spend that wisely? I propose four areas: education, empirical studies, theory development, and applied research.

Education

Progress in parapsychology has been slow and is intentionally excluded from the academic world (with a few rare exceptions, as noted below) because there are concerted efforts by small groups of activists—most of whom are not scientists—determined to marginalize the field. For decades, such efforts were primarily associated in the United States with an organization called the Committee for the Scientific Investigation of Claims of the Paranormal, or CSICOP. Today (2019) they've adopted a shorter name CSI, for Committee for

Skeptical Inquiry. The irony about CSICOP/CSI, which has strongly influenced scientific and public opinion about parapsychology, is that for many years they trumpeted the term "scientific investigation" in their organization's name, but they hardly ever investigated anything. One of the very few times they *did* launch an investigation, they successfully confirmed a claim about astrology. The committee was so shocked with that outcome that they intentionally suppressed their findings. The only reason we know this is because one of the members of their executive committee blew the whistle on them.

As the influence of CSI has somewhat declined with the rise of the internet, we find the same mind-set still active, this time in the form of self-styled Guerrilla Skeptics on Wikipedia. They state their mission as the following: "To improve skeptical content on Wikipedia. We do this by improving pages of our skeptic spokespeople, providing noteworthy citations, and removing the unsourced claims from paranormal and pseudo-scientific pages. Why? Because evidence is cool."

The irony here is that these so-called skeptics are really not interested in evidence at all, because if they were, Wikipedia would provide articles on parapsychological topics that survey all sides of the topic. As it currently stands (2019), all those articles have been edited by guerrillas to be exclusively negative. Wikipedia proudly advertises that it can be edited by anyone, but in practice that is not quite true. Wikipedia has an endless set of byzantine rules that editors have to follow; otherwise proposed edits are not accepted. Taking advantage of this, the guerrillas have rewritten parapsychological-oriented articles as well as the personal biographies of scientists involved in parapsychology in such a way that a naïve reader going to Wikipedia for information will come away with a thoroughly negative opinion.

Thus, a well-funded educational effort would do the following:

a. Commission high-quality online written and video information that presents a more accurate picture of the state of the science, including how parapsychology explores the "big questions." One initiative to do this is already under way, but to make that site more popular would require a dedicated public relations effort.

b. Hire experienced Wikipedia editors to refine the existing biased articles to make them more accurate and balanced.

c. Develop new or revise existing *Introduction to Psychology* college textbooks, most of which today simply regurgitate old prejudices about parapsychology that were heavily promoted by CISCOP.

d. Commission more accurate portrayals of what parapsychology is, and what it has learned, in TV shows and movies aimed at popular audiences.

e. Commission a series of academic and popular books by knowledgeable authors that describe the history, methods, and results of the various categories of study in parapsychology.

f. Commission web-based or mobile-based experiments accessible to anyone.

g. Establish endowed chairs of parapsychology within fully funded Centers for Consciousness Studies at major universities around the world, and provide funding for undergraduate and graduate scholarships, teaching, and research assistants.

The last point is the most important because as long as this topic remains marginalized, there will always be a struggle to find students to keep the field alive and thriving. We know, for example, from an endowed Chair of Parapsychology established in the mid-1980s at the University of Edinburgh, Scotland, that a single well-run graduate program at an established university can significantly revitalize the field. Three decades after that professorship was established, over seventy-five graduate students have gone on to gain doctorates associated with parapsychological topics. That one chair established the United Kingdom as world's current academic center for parapsychology.

The chair at Edinburgh was not the first time an endowed professorship for parapsychology was established. There were similar endowments at Harvard, Clark, and Stanford Universities in the late 1800s and early 1900s. But after the initial holders of those positions retired, subsequent professors were hired who were either not interested in parapsychology, or the funds that supported those chairs were usurped by the universities for other purposes. Thus, any new endowments that are established must be specified in such a way that the purpose of the chair cannot be altered, and the individuals selected for those positions must be vetted as having appropriate interests.

It is predictable that universities approached with the opportunity to gain endowed chairs of parapsychology will encounter vigorous opposition from existing faculty because nearly everything they think they know about parapsychology probably originated from highly distorted sources. Thus, the endowment initiative will require a companion educational and public relations effort to inform faculties and university administrations about what the topic actually entails.

This initial educational effort might cost perhaps $50 million, with most of those funds supporting the endowed professorships, student scholarships, and associated costs. On an ongoing basis, the costs would drop to perhaps $10 million a year.

Before the last and arguably most important proposed step is taken (the endowed chairs), it would be advisable to first launch a one- or two-year discovery project by a team of higher education experts. The mission would be to identify universities that are devoted to honoring the endowments and to ensure that the plan is both practical and achievable.

Empiricism

The second area where an infusion of funding would be important is experimental research. While the number of researchers engaged in empirical parapsychology has always been rather small, as a group they have been remarkably persistent, competent, and productive. A half dozen classes of psi experiments have reached a stage of maturity that methods to replicate effects can be described in straightforward terms, and replications should be encouraged as teaching tools.

Part of the funding then would create teaching

systems to help students replicate experiments known to be successful. This would include, as examples, hardware and software for a digital ganzfeld telepathy system, setups to allow for psychophysiological experiments such as presentiment (unconscious precognition), the "feeling of being stared at" from a distance, and brain-to-brain correlations. These teaching systems would be made available at low or no-cost to educational institutions and online for no cost.

The rest of the funding would fall into two categories. First, directed multi-year programs. These would be experimental programs requiring a minimum of three- to five-year efforts, with the research team identified and invited by a steering committee of experienced researchers. Longer term programs, up to ten years, would also be considered, depending on the nature of the proposed programs, the track records of the proposers, and the judgment of the steering committee. Second, an international grants program will solicit requests for proposals. These will be offered annually, with a maximum of $100,000 per grant.

There is no lack of interest among researchers interested in studying psi phenomena, but the range of experiments that have been conducted to date has just scratched the surface. With an infusion of funds, the scope of phenomena studied will creatively explode. Besides experimental tests of elementary psychic phenomena, including telepathy, clairvoyance, precognition, psychokinesis, this effort would significantly expand research on survival-oriented phenomena, including mediumship, channeling, near-death and out-of-body experiences, reincarnation, and mediumship. In addition, a worldview survey can be undertaken to find exceptional talents (children and adults) to study, and in future efforts the experimental program can be integrated with these talented individuals.

This effort is estimated to cost about $100 million, with most of the funds going to the long-term and solicited grants program, and support of positions required to administer and track those grants.

Theory Development

Experimental work in parapsychology has always run far ahead of theoretical explanations. This initiative would provide funding for theorists to develop testable physical, biological, neurological, or psychological models of psi. The long-term directed-grants programs would be encouraged to include theorists to develop explanatory frameworks and suggest ways of testing those ideas. This effort will include historians, anthropologists, and other scholars working on testable theories. For example, a historian or anthropologist may develop a theory about the use or methods underlying an ancient magical practice, and the testing of that theory would entail analysis of the historical or contemporary record to see if that theory is supported.

This effort would cost perhaps $5 million as most of these efforts will not require special instrumentation. It will be initially incorporated into part of the solicited grants program.

Applied Research
This area would focus on aspects of psi that are sufficiently understood to be applied in rudimentary ways. This would include projects investigating psychic healing, uses in archeological exploration, law enforcement, counterterrorism, and development of new types of communication systems that span spatial and temporal distances. In all cases, these would be directed, multi-year programs. The goal in each program would be to demonstrate proof of principle for an application within three to five years of initial funding and to provide an assessment if that application could be successfully launched, and if so, when.

This effort would cost perhaps $100 million, mainly because developing the requisite instrumentation is likely to be expensive and because of the overhead and salary costs of longer-term programs.

Summary

An estimated total cost for the proposed program is about $400 million for the first year, dropping to perhaps $100 million each successive year. This is nowhere near $1 billion a year, and for good reason. At this stage of our knowledge, it is very unlikely that a billion could be spent wisely. A program audit and reassessment would be planned on a five-year basis to judge if funds spent so far were used well and would recommend adjustments up or down.

A question not yet addressed in this moonshot proposal is whether a single overarching organization would be in charge of the whole program or whether it would be distributed among several organizations. In either case, the overhead in running and tracking a $100- to $400-million-dollar program is nontrivial. It would require a staff of perhaps twenty people, which would cost perhaps $5 million a year. Still, compared to an annual billion-dollar allocation, that would be in the noise.

Dean and I agree that the field of consciousness science needs funding. I would posit that how you go about getting the money is a measure of how much money you set out to get. Remember, the purpose of this book, as stated in the foreword, is to obtain funding to advance our understanding of consciousness. What is happening presently is not what Dean outlines. So what do we do? How do we create the plan to fund Dean's vision?

Dean's description of the struggle between two thought camps is correct. One is in denial, and the other seeks truth. New wild cards have been introduced: AI and CRISPR's gene editing techniques. Moore's Law creates urgency. Otherwise, our species will die off as rapidly as other animal populations are dying off now. It will happen within the lifetime of anyone who is thirty-five or younger. Anyone reading this in 2020 will be a Neanderthal compared to what humanity might become in just a few generations.

Dean and I disagree about the importance of introducing the science of reincarnation in a serious way. He and I have different goals. Dean wants to present the most logical and effective way to fund consciousness research. I fully support that and want to make it so, but there are other equally important issues: the bottom of the pyramid is where belief is most strongly manipulated with no counterbalance of logic.

This book is targeted to the grassroots level. We need a common wellness and wealthness plan, an endeavor shunned by academia that our leaders can follow.

The problem with academia is best explained by academics. With consciousness science we are in a full-blown upheaval of metaparadigm proportions, and it goes largely unnoticed by the general public and is not understood by world leaders. Its needs go unfunded or underfunded because it is not explained in an actionable way.

The following is from Bruce Greyson's abstract of a recent paper entitled "Implications of Near-Death Experiences for a Postmaterialist Psychology."

> Classical physics, anchored in materialist reductionism, offered adequate descriptions of everyday mechanics but ultimately proved insufficient for describing the mechanics of extremely high speeds or small sizes, and was supplemented nearly a century ago by quantum physics, which includes consciousness in its formulation. Materialist psychology, modeled on the reductionism of classical physics, likewise offered adequate descriptions of everyday mental functioning but ultimately proved insufficient for describing mentation under extreme conditions, such as the continuation of mental function when the brain is inactive or impaired, such as occurs near death.
>
> "Near-death experiences" include phenomena that challenge materialist reductionism, such as enhanced mentation and memory during cerebral impairment, accurate perceptions from a perspective outside the body, and reported visions of deceased persons, including those not previously known to be deceased. *Complex consciousness,*

including cognition, perception, and memory, under con-
ditions such as cardiac arrest and general anesthesia,
when it cannot be associated with normal brain function,
require a revised psychology anchored not in 19th-century
classical physics but rather in 21st-century quantum
physics that includes consciousness in its conceptual for-
mulation. [Emphasis added.]

Dr. Greyson is exactly right. Does his explanation resonate with the working man? Greyson steps around what to
call it. What do you call the new model of consciousness
that Greyson and others are calling for? The model where
consciousness does not seem to end with death?

If it had webbed feet, a bill, and quacked, I would call
it a duck. I would not call it a postmaterialist paradigm
of phylum Chordata, class Aves, order Anseriformes, and
family Anatidae. I would call it a duck so people could
understand it. I would also not care if people were of-
fended by the word "duck" and would not fund research
into ducks. It's a fucking duck.

The issue here is that Greyson wants to incorporate
features that would change our worldview.

The science of reincarnation has even more lines of
evidence than plate tectonics: NDEs, children who remember prior lives, past-life regression, evidence of electrical charge retaining memory, evidence of that energy
underlying the material that our bodies are made of,
fractal patterns that underlie our reality, and more.

Those with big money won't fund what Dean outlines unless they see value. They will not be driven by altruism. Descriptions like Bruce Greyson's, while completely accurate, do not drive investment. A plan needs to be laid out and rejected, renegotiated, and redefined until those with money see value in the endeavor. The conversation Dean and I are having is the beginning of that process.

Four hundred million dollars may seem like a lot, but in money as in science, everything is relative. People don't have a strong intuitive sense of how much bigger one billion is than one million. One million seconds is about eleven days. One billion seconds is about 31.5 years. Millionaires and billionaires are as different as an eleven-day-old baby and a thirty-one-and-a-half-year-old man.

The combined worth of the two thousand billionaires in the world is $9 trillion. Asking for $400 million is asking for 0.0044 percent of their combined net worth. That is four-tenths of 1 percent. This proposal is only asking for a paltry $400 million. Before we come out the other end of the tunnel, though, you can expect to spend every bit of $90 billion on this. And humanity will virtually be a new race with the means to protect itself from the coming threats.

These two thousand billionaires alone can make the difference, and it is easier to explain real change to several smart people than it is to influence governments.

The initial target is the 1,450 billionaires who are self-made, because it is these people who change paradigms and accept new models of thought. If I am going to solve our common global problems mathematically, I need a fractal solution. These billionaires could mobilize the world and impact these problems immediately.

Take a look at the following from "The Phenomenology of the Self-Conscious Mind" by Robert G. Mays and Suzanne B. Mays.

The phenomenon of a near-death experiencer's veridical perceptions during the out-of-body experience (OBE) strongly suggests the existence of a *self-conscious mind* as a "field of consciousness," a region of space where a person's consciousness exists. In the out-of-body state, the mind appears to be nonmaterial and completely independent of the physical body. Ordinarily, though, the self-conscious mind appears as an autonomous entity united with the brain and body. In this united state, the self-conscious mind operates through the mediation of the brain. This view is supported by evidence from neurological phenomena such as subjective ante dating of sensory experiences and mental force. *This evidence suggests that a non-neural agency induces conscious experience and self-conscious awareness.* Phenomena from OBEs, including apparent subtle interactions with physical processes such as light, sound, and physical objects, as well as reported interactions with "in-body" persons, support the view that the self-conscious mind is able to interact in some physical way with the brain. Neurological phenomena such as Benjamin Libet's (1985) delayed awareness of willed action can be reconsidered successfully in light of this view. Such efforts might also prove useful, for example, in explaining phantom limb phenomena. [Emphasis added.]

Both the Mays' and Greyson's papers reflect the real-world observations of the human condition. No physical law says we as individuals cannot be conscious in other dimensions. There are eleven dimensions, and we operate in one temporal and three spatial dimensions. At our core we are energy, whether we measure our electrical output or look at it from the aspect of quantum biology, and our narrative and science are pointing to the same model.

Regardless of what we call this, it must be studied and funded. Call it whatever people will fund.

By refusing to acknowledge the legitimate discipline of the science of reincarnation, we succumb to academic pressure, and in my opinion, we fail as scientists and as people.

I know no one better than Dean Radin and Stephan Schwartz to direct the research that needs to be done in the consciousness sciences, and when IASOR asks for money, it will be Dean and Stephan to whom I turn to tell me where to direct it. They can call the research whatever they want and continue to tell me I am beating a dead horse about the science of reincarnation. My response to that would be, "Yes...today. And by the way, here's some money to do studies."

Robert Kiyosaki named his book *Rich Dad, Poor Dad* instead of *The Value of Compounding Interest* because if he used the second name, he would not have sold any copies of his book. So from the point of view of the marketing department of our PAC, reincarnation becomes an important word.

This change is core to rebranding, development of funding sources, and the ability to do the needed research without social or academic resistance. This is, after all, a moon-shot proposal, and acquisition of this funding is a national defense priority everywhere. Most governments are run by people who are narcissistic and shortsighted. I'm not knocking anyone here in particular, just describing the battlefield landscape.

I told Dean I wanted to ask the Koestler Chair of Parapsychology at the University of Edinburgh to recognize the science of reincarnation as a recognized discipline within the consciousness sciences.

"Bob," Dean said. "No, no, no. There is no way this will ever happen. Trust me."

No argument from me.

Dean knows more about the Koestler Chair than I do. But a third party may enter this conversation: the donor who would fund such a chair and a study. Others may feel the same way about consciousness science, and it's their money, not academia's.

There are three possible responses. If funding is offered, the University of Edinburgh can accept it, reject it, or reframe the offer. Only the second option, rejection, would be negative.

A university turning down $500,000 (for example) would make the back pages of the London *Times* and the front pages of the *Daily Mail.* But rejections would refine and redefine what would be accepted, and at the same time, the rejections would outline to investors what the goals of the research would be.

While Dean is sure they never would do this, have they ever been asked? What would their response be? And finally, there's the salesman's question: What are they going to say? No? I live my life hearing no. It's like water off a duck's back.

In this give and take, can a scenario be developed that would interest a small independent school to accept money offered by earnest investors that would enhance its funding and reputation? How are you going to look for investors if your plan is not vetted, and who better to do that than the University of Edinburgh, and where better to begin than at the home of psychical research?

If we are to begin the initiative of truly funding consciousness science, the free publicity of offering and being rejected begins here. But let's modify the request.

This, after all, is a business negotiation. Questions will arise as offers come in. How much money? What is to be studied? Who will own the intellectual property? What discipline is the chair dedicated to? So let's accept Dean's criticism, modify our request, and begin the sales campaign to change cognition here.

We formally ask the University of Edinburgh if they will accept funding for a chair of consciousness science as described in this book. We are not asking for a chair for the science of reincarnation. However, the science of reincarnation is a subset discipline in the consciousness sciences as outlined by our definitions in the last chapter.

Once done, a copy of this book will be sent to the university along with a formal request and requests to specific donors asking them to fund such a chair.

I don't want to put words in Dean's mouth, but I think he thinks that I am tilting at windmills or that I shouldn't try to teach a pig to sing; you end up wasting your time and annoying the pig.

If we are going to change cognition, people have to know about the attempt. The place to start is at the roots of the study. I have great respect for the Koestler Chair and the University of Edinburgh, and I think they will see that even if this attempt is misguided, it is an honest and true attempt to advance a neglected science whose work is integral to human advancement.

We can step around entrenched prejudice and access

the corporate and national defense budgets by calling it consciousness science.

Terms and conditions for endowing a chair apply.

1. Someone within the field must continue the work.
2. There is no intellectual property ownership of information between the universities that host these chairs. The Society for Psychical Research should also be involved as a center for soliciting funds for studies and administering information in the field.

The study of the science of reincarnation has its roots in the soil of Scotland and England. Its belief center is in India. We are asking these organizations to rebrand the psychical sciences to include consciousness science and the science of reincarnation. This is a reasonable request in light of the recent developments of AI and CRISPR that need to be incorporated into the older model.

This will change not only the scientific paradigm but the social and political dynamic.

This proposal is asking for two specific changes.

1. Change the parapsychological sciences to the consciousness sciences. This difference in nomenclature has two effects. First, it is a rebranding to include AI and CRISPR, which were not even a thought when the psychical science made its debut. This change will be resisted by some scientists,

but it's about funding. The request is not from the science side. It is from the marketing department.

2. The science of reincarnation should take its place among the recognized sciences of psychical study and incorporate the aforementioned disciplines as well as the math of the science contained in this book.

I wanted Dean to provide an à la carte menu of projects that need funding, but a larger question became apparent: how can we build and fund a network for consciousness research? Linkage strengthens the entire endeavor, so I presented a couple of options.

First, we should reach out to universities such as University of Virginia and Duke in an attempt to fund a chair for a professor to complete the desired research. The funding for this chair could come from private donors and possibly the university and would be an excellent starting point to initiate a long-term research project.

Dean said the initial cost would be $100 million for founding twenty endowed chairs or a unit cost of $5 million a chair. I would propose $10 million as a price point to fund a chair at Stanford, University of Virginia, the University of Miami, the University of Toronto, or Duke. For the university to be approved by the governing body, the university's endowment fund would have to match the independent endowment so that the total endowment for such a chair would be $20 million each.

"Bob," Dean said, "a concerted discovery effort would need to be made to find universities willing to accept funds in this area. It is extremely unlikely that any big mainstream university in the United States would do this. Smaller universities might. In any case, it is *absolutely certain* that no university will use their existing endowment to match offered funds."

I have been involved in many business deals where I was told there is no deal to be made until the deal was done. We spent a chapter of this book on enterprise risk management. First, you must make the offer. Don't begin with one university but several. Connect databases, something one university could not do alone.

The very act of making the request would have consequences because the model of reality changes not with the endeavor but with the request itself. And then how do you explain it to the masses?

If we liken researchers to prospectors in the eighteenth and nineteenth centuries, somebody is going to strike gold. And however wealthy and powerful they are, the first guys who make this cognition breakthrough will be able to see across the universe and back in time. That takes pioneers. They are out there and looking for new frontiers. Dean is one of them.

We could also approach a university with a well-funded endowment. If the endowment's backers felt that this could create financial value for the university, they could potentially use endowment funds to initiate or fully fund research projects.

A Russell Targ Chair of the Cognitive Sciences can be fully funded for $20 million out of the general endowment at Stanford, and the research would be conducted at Stanford. What would the research do? It would seek to quantify the wavelength of remote viewers and begin to develop programs that would sync to that frequency using AI. Once they start looking with fourth spatial dimension optics, our place in the universe will change. So I am asking a rich Stanford grad to fund a $10 million chair at Stanford with a matching amount from the general endowment, subject to the aforementioned terms and conditions. If Stanford takes this idea up, do you think the US government wouldn't be putting money into it? CIA, are you listening?

"I'm sorry," Dean said, "but there's no way this would happen. Prominent universities never ever fund new and especially not controversial endowed chairs from their existing endowment. *Never.*"

So I said, OK, then we need $20 million from rich Stanford graduates who see merit in funding psi research and see that it could be actionable socially, politically, and militarily.

"According to the wealth information firm Wealth-X," writes Rob Wile at *Yahoo Finance,* "Harvard is the world's top university for producing billionaires, claiming 125 of them with a combined wealth of $590 billion. Stanford has produced the second-most billionaires at 50; the University of Pennsylvania comes in third with 47 billionaires."

So I ask the fifty billionaires from Stanford: Can I have $20 million in donations to Stanford to fund this research with the agenda written by Radin and Schwartz?

To get my $20 million to Stanford to start psi research, I need 0.0025 percent of their wealth. Put another way, if they have a dollar, I need less than a penny. Twenty million is a big number, but it's small potatoes. If just these fifty people agree to give Stanford $20 million to fund a Chair of Consciousness Science at Stanford, and they get fractional use ownership in the derivative intellectual property (IP), each only has to come up with $400,000. It's nothing to them but huge to humanity. If the results of the studies are commercial, these investors will be the first trillionaires.

I speak now to each and every one of you Stanford billionaires. You can reach me through the IASOR website. Just sign up on the mailing list and leave a comment. I'll get back to you.

I would not argue with Dean about funding at Stanford, but DARPA may have a very different interest. If I told a commoner five hundred years ago that I can take sand off a beach and make something I will call spectacles that you can wear on your nose and that will make you see better, that commoner's response probably would be "I'll believe it when I see it."

RAIV will be like linking to a wavelength and using a computer/mind interface like a pair of glasses. Each and every one of us, every living thing, has a measurable wavelength, including the computer you have at home. Dean is right that the universities will want to use other people's money and gain the benefit. If this conversation goes in that direction, we will end up with university endowment funds becoming bloated at the expense of a tuition system that burdens the young. The universities are resistant to acting, but that does not mean this research isn't imperative. It can be initiated by one man's courageous act of selflessly giving an endowment to an institution with a targeted contribution according to the terms and conditions laid out in this chapter.

We could also approach a potential private/public funding venture with well-funded research institutions. Universities such as MIT have a significant amount of funds allocated to start business ventures with students and professors that can be research-driven with the ultimate expectation of earning a profit. When my son was considering attending MIT, they indicated they generally have more funds available than are utilized each year for business and research ventures. I would assume universities other than MIT have funds available for these projects, and they would be an excellent starting point.

Elon Musk, MIT, and a sixteen-year-old inventor are researching mind-reading technology, specifically the brain-computer interface that DARPA initially funded in the 1970s. The market is expected to reach a value of $1.72 billion by 2022. The sixteen-year-old's contribution is the use of graphene for the interface.[1]

This is the interface that the PEAR labs proved and abandoned when their funding dried up. There are billions of dollars looking for ways to connect the brain to the computer, but the cognitive sciences struggle for funding. Presenting their proposals differently would produce a decidedly different economic matrix, and a much better one.

"No," Dean said. "You are misinterpreting the difference between brain-computer interfaces, which is dead-center mainstream neuroscience, with real telepathy. They are two completely different things."

Again, Dean is right about the science, but the model of a rich guy, a good idea, and an institution of higher learning is the model we are advancing for the consciousness sciences.

"Practical applications involving psi may one day be possible," Dean said, "but *zero dollars* are being spent on such applications today. All the funds being spent are extensions of existing technology, not the revolutionary technology of consciousness itself."

Therein lies the problem. No money is being spent on the revolutionary technology of consciousness itself, yet that technology would open data acquisition in ways that would be transcendent and would make any government's secrets transparent.

I want to scream this so you all understand. Money is going to neuroscience to connect mind to body at MIT, but PEAR's proven interface goes unfunded.

Here are Dean's numbers.

Education	$100 Million
Empiricism	$100 Million
Theory Development	$5 Million
Applied Research	$100 Million
Overarching Organization	$5 Million
Total	$310 Million

In the summer of 2019, Jim Tucker sent me an email.

Hi Bob,

Thanks for your interest in helping us in such a big way. UVA has no general fund for matching donations. Decades ago, the state would match donations for a chair, but that went away a long time ago. But we'd still be interested in receiving a $5M gift.

All the best,

Jim

Stephan Schwartz followed up with his own email.

Bob,

As to creating an endowed chair: If I had five million dollars to endow a chair, I would develop a strategy and then the tactics to implement that strategy. I would start by hiring a researcher to go through all the American universities and colleges and look for institutions that have historically skewed to socially progressive interests.

I would not start by seeking to align with status—Harvard, etc.—because genius creates status. The only reason UVA has a world-famous Department of Perceptual Studies is because Ian Stevenson impressed Chester Carlson at a time when the university was seeking to upgrade its status, and Carlson's money gave him the power to cut the deal. Also Ian was already a nationally known physician. Menninger is another example of this. Back in the late 50s and early 60s, who would have expected Kansas to become a center of biofeedback research?

Examples—just what comes to mind as I write—include Oberlin, Reed, Swathmore, Bard, but there are many others. You will have much more power negotiating with Reed than with Harvard.

Once I had, say, six candidate universities and colleges, I would have the researcher work up a bio on the presidents of all those institutions. Start at the top. Negotiating with departments is not, in my view, the way to go at this. I would then see who I knew or knew someone who knew a person close to the president and ask them to make the introduction so that you go into any meeting with status.

I would set up a meeting with the president of each institution and physically go there. Set up a dinner meeting during which you state clearly what you want to achieve and what you are prepared to offer, stressing that you do not want to create a repeat of what happened at Stanford or the Mind Science Foundation. Out of that, I would predict, will come several options.

I would not start with the idea of endowing a chair for reincarnation research. UVA already does that, and it has taken two generations of physicians to get to where they are today. You would always be second tier as long as Jim Tucker is there because he is an excellent researcher with an impeccable reputation. He is already funded and commands the world's largest depository of such data, painstakingly assembled over many decades.

Rather, I would fund a chair in consciousness studies, which gives maximum latitude.

Finally, while that process was going on, I would have the researcher working up profiles on possible candidates for the chair. In my opinion, there are no more than six, maybe seven, people in the world consciousness research community that I consider first tier and sufficiently visionary for what you are planning.

I would allot two years for this process and budget something between $80,000 and $100,000 to achieve the goal.

—Stephan

Dean Radin added his own thoughts.

Bob,

I don't know of any universities that maintain funds to match donations for endowments.

I see two types of strategies for selecting universities that might create a chair of consciousness studies, where that term explicitly refers to nonlocal aspects of consciousness. The department within the university that houses the chair is also a key issue as faculty in many departments would fight very hard to prevent such a chair. They're afraid of their reputations.

So one strategy is to attempt to reinvigorate the existing psychical research funds at Harvard and Stanford; the second strategy is to approach universities that are already actively engaged in these topics and where the existing faculty would not be spooked by such an endowment.

The first strategy will almost certainly fail, regardless of how much money is offered. I wouldn't even bother taking that route. Prejudices are just too entrenched.

But the second strategy might well work. The three mainstream universities I can think of that might accept funds for an endowed chair are Sonoma State University, West Georgia University, and UVA. The first two have long-standing interests in transpersonal

psychology and parapsychology, and UVA is an obvious choice. There may be other fine candidates, but navigating university politics requires a much stronger stomach than I possess.
—Dean Radin

Here is Stephan Schwartz again:

Bob,
If Dean is correct and the resistance is at the level he describes, then what I told you is not worth pursuing. If $5 million is not enough to catch a university president's attention, I would invest the money and create a series of three fellowships like BIAL, on that scale and slightly larger. Five million at 5% would yield $250,000. The Benjamin Franklin Fellows would receive $80,000 a year with $10,000 per year set aside to cover the cost of administering the program.

If your goal is to change American society's view of consciousness, get three fellows working each year writing papers and maybe a book about real projects that are creatively peer-reviewed and selected. Dean and I are working now while being funded by BIAL. Or you could offer it for five years, which would be my personal recommendation. Over time this money could create significant impact, particularly if media coverage is well managed.

Also, you don't have to become embroiled with university administrations and face what Dean has described.
—Stephan

Here is Dean's response.

Hi Bob,
It's not impossible that an accredited university might accept an endowed chair focused on reincarnation research, but locating such a university will take a substantial discovery period by academic experts. If such a place were found (the California Institute of Integral Studies might be open to such a chair), there is no chance that they will match an endowed chair donation out of their existing funds. That's not how endowed chairs are created.

Also, the chance that a well-known university in the U.S. will accept any amount of funds for a psi or reincarnation chair is so close to zero that it may as well be zero. Big name universities jealously protect their credibility, and unfortunately these topics would substantially lower their credibility. They wouldn't accept any amount of money offered. Prejudices in academia are very real and extremely strong.

Second, adding AI and CRISPR to the mix adds nothing. Those are currently popular tools, but there are dozens of other new tools coming along. Hitching this initiative to any particular tool is not a good idea.

Third, after seeing what you've written so far, my sense is that the best approach to all this is to not attempt to raise a gazillion dollars but rather a far more modest $250,000 or so to fund a university consortium of perhaps six to nine senior academics at various universities who are collectively charged with creating a plan for your vision. Give them a year to come up with a plan that will work. *That* would have a chance of working.

I agree that humanity has got to make some major changes if we are to survive as a species, but the approach argued in this book is in my view unrealistic. Focusing on reincarnation as a way to convince people to pay attention to nonlocal forms of consciousness might work within a well-funded independent institute devoted to that task, but attempting to force the academic mainstream to accept it won't work because you're underestimating the power of academic prejudice.

Ah well, either call it the Benjamin Franklin Fellows for Consciousness Research or name it after the person who puts up the five million. The important point is fellows vs. an endowed chair. An endowed chair, based on what you said, would apparently be extremely difficult and always vulnerable to what has happened with the Koestler Chair or whatever the Stanford chair was called (can't remember at the moment).

Creating fellows does not require a university administration getting involved, so it can stay true to its original intention—like with the MacArthur Fellows. Also, you could get three rather than one. I would apply for it, as I assume you would as well. Or, like MacArthur, you could make it something that cannot be applied for but is awarded.

Again, based on what you wrote, I don't see any upside to the hassle an endowed chair would require or its potential vulnerability.

—Dean

In this email exchange between Dean, Stephan, and myself, you see the morass of academia that needs to be traversed. And in none of it is an inducement to people who would fund the science. So let's do one more re-branding of consciousness science where the marketing department gets the last word. The word is *value.*

IASOR is a think tank that does not want donors as much as investors in consciousness science.

The computer/brain interface is sucking billions of research dollars while a proven nonlocal interface goes unfunded even though it's the more important interface.

The telepathic interface will stand behind the mainstream neuroscience interface because of Planck's dictum that consciousness is fundamental and everything else is derivative. That leads to the aforementioned RAIV.

The marketing message to investors is that consciousness sciences will develop a telepathic interface to computers. Whoever owns this will become the first trillionaire.

So where do we go from here? We go in four directions at once.

1. We look for schools that wish to do studies in consciousness research and schools that already do it and want to infuse its programs with new resources. Interested schools may contact us through the IASOR website.
2. We look for investors who would help fund research into the consciousness sciences and who understand intuitively why it needs to be done.
3. We solicit studies that need funding by researches who wish to publish their funding requests on the IASOR website.
4. We present a comprehensive plan to attract investment.

Dean and I are on the same side, but we disagree about IASOR. IASOR is advancing this plan. Dean speaks from the top-down while IASOR speaks from the bottom-up. The top-down is sensitive to change because it rocks the status quo. The bottom-up explains the problem in easy-to-understand ways that are not as technical. The expectation that no one will invest is self-fulfilling if no one is given a reason they can understand or the value of the return.

Old paradigms and understandings become locked in. New sciences emerge. I am proposing to recognize the science of reincarnation as a discipline within the domain of consciousness sciences. The nomenclature of parapsychology, while accurate, should be set aside because it in no way envisioned AI or CRISPR. Additionally, parapsychology has been attacked and rebranded as pseudoscience.

"Believe me, Bob," Dean said, "this term *will not sell* in the Western academic world. It will scare even sympathetic people away. So I would definitely strike it wherever it appears in this book. I would also argue that while AI and CRISPR are excellent developments with implications for the study of consciousness, they are just tools, and tools are evolving like everything else. I would *not* hitch this effort to those tools because tech is changing so quickly that it is not possible to tell how they will evolve in the next five to ten years.

"This should be about consciousness studies in the broadest sense of that term. Not just neuroscience. If you push AI and CRISPR, I *absolutely guarantee* that universities will devote the endowed chairs to those two areas, and they will ignore the rest."

The thought that reincarnation as a science will drive

away even sympathetic people ignores the fact that consciousness science has not adequately addressed even what to call this issue, and it has not explained to the masses what has been proven and not accepted.

One last word about IASOR. Once this plan gets funded, the name of the organization can be decided by the contributors and the institutions doing the work. IASOR will not get the money. It will go directly from the investor to the institution. At that point, the organization called IASOR would no longer exist. It will have fulfilled its intent and will have been replaced by the managing organization of investors and researchers. Funding the science is more important than the organization.

I would be remiss if I didn't point out criticism of this book will be fractal. Before I close, I want to address the anticipated criticisms fractally that are coming from each specific group.

To scientists: Psi research needs to be funded. Period. You can agree with some reasons and not others, or you can like or dislike how I frame the request. It doesn't matter. Psi research is not being funded, and that needs to change immediately. There are all sorts of derivatives and dangers. The more you oppose attempts to get that funding, the more self-defeating you are being. If psi research were being funded, I wouldn't have need to write this book. So if want to fund psi research, whatever strategy you are using isn't working. There's no guarantee that this approach will work, but if it does, the mind-computer interface will be a lot more robust than a neurological connection, and syncing a computer to a nonlocal connection will produce a transcendent new data acquisition source. The military applications will be tremendous.

To bankers: This is gold and will double the GWP.

To the billionaire and oligarchs: it is gold for you, too, because you will build and manage the growth.

To everyone else: every little act you take bends the arc of humanity. If this is our reality, what should you do personally?

My cardiologist owns his own building, and inscribed in the marble in front of the main entrance are the following words in Latin: QVOD FACIMVS IN VITA RESONAT IN ATERNITAS. *What you do in life resonates in eternity.*

The conversation continues on reddit at r/reincarnationscience. You can also reach us through the website www.IASOR.org.

Note

[1] https://www.cnbc.com/2019/05/10/this-16-year-old-is-working-on-tech-to-control-devices-with-our-minds.html.

About the Authors

Bob Good is the executive director of the International Association for the Science of Reincarnation (IASOR), a think tank that promotes sound scientific information on the subject of reincarnation and the nature of consciousness. Bob previously spent forty years as an independent contractor servicing the pharmaceuticals industry, where he specialized in research. Prior to that he was involved with military research while on active duty. Once he began his business, he was involved with Business Executives for National Security, a Washington-based think tank whose mission is to bring efficient business practices into the US military. Bob is passionate about providing education on the science of reincarnation and has served as a speaker at Florida Atlantic University and the International Association for Near-Death Studies, in addition to authoring his series, the Consciousness Sciences. He has also appeared on the History Channel's show *Ancient Aliens,* dealing with reincarnation. IASOR's goal is to work toward a consensus among scientists as to the prevailing scientific view of consciousness.

Dean Radin PhD is Chief Scientist at the Institute of Noetic Sciences and Associated Distinguished Professor at the California Institute of Integral Studies. He earned an MS in electrical engineering and a PhD in psychology from the University of Illinois, Urbana-Champaign. Before joining the research staff at IONS in 2001, Radin held appointments at AT&T Bell Labs, Princeton University, University of Edinburgh, and SRI International. He has given over 500 talks and interviews worldwide, and he is the author or coauthor of hundreds of scientific and popular articles, four dozen book chapters, two technical books, and four popular books translated into 15 foreign languages: The Conscious Universe (1997), Entangled Minds (2006), Supernormal (2013), and Real Magic (2018).

Stephan A. Schwartz is a Distinguished Consulting Faculty of Saybrook University, a BIAL fellow and columnist for the journal *Explore,* and editor of the daily web publication *Schwartzreport.net.* For 50 years he has been studying the nature of consciousness and is one of the founders of modern Remote Viewing research. He is the author of nearly two hundred papers in peer-reviewed journals covering a spectrum of disciplines, two dozen book chapters, and an award-winning author of both fiction and non-fiction books that have been translated into multiple languages: *The Secret Vaults of Time, The Alexandria Project, Mind Rover, Opening to the Infinite, The 8 Laws of Change, Awakening, The Vision, and The Amish Girl.* He has also written and produced multiple television and film projects.

Titus Rivas is an independent scholar, affiliated with several organizations such as Athanasia Foundation, The International Association for Near-Death Studies and the Society for Psychical Research. He earned a MS in psychology at the University of Utrecht and a MA in philosophy at the University of Amsterdam. He is the author of books, such as *The Self Does Not Die* with Anny Dirven and Rudolf H, Smit (IANDS) and *Reincarnation as A Scientific Concept* with Kirti Swaroop Rawat (White Crow Publications, in press), articles, courses by correspondence, and book reviews.

Cathie Hill has a degree in Human Resources and Industrial Relations from the University of South Australia and earned both a Master's Degree in Business and a Post-Grad in Mechanical Engineering Entrepreneurship with scholarships through the University of Adelaide. She has worked in Human Resources and as a General Manager and CEO with both for profit and not for profit organizations. Cathie also managed a Research and Development Program across all Faculties of the University of Adelaide encouraging co-operation with a wide range of industries engaging Honors and Masters students. "The Ripple Effect of Being: A thought experiment" was written in response to her personal research following experiences which seemed outside the parameters of scientific explanation.

Printed in Great Britain
by Amazon

75182150R00251